CHRISTIANITY AND POLITICAL PHILOSOPHY

FREDERICK D. WILHELMSEN

CHRISTIANITY AND POLITICAL PHILOSOPHY

THE UNIVERSITY OF GEORGIA PRESS
ATHENS

Copyright © 1978 by the University of Georgia Press
Athens 30602

All rights reserved

Set in 10 on 13 point Mergenthaler Electra type
Printed in the United States of America

Library of Congress Cataloging in Publication Data

Wilhelmsen, Frederick D
  Christianity and political philosophy.
  Includes bibliographical references and index.
    1. Political science.   2. Christianity and politics.
  I. Title.
JA74.W53   261.7   77-22754
            ISBN 0-8203-0431-X

To My Daughter
ALEXANDRA
"Heart speaks to Heart"

Testimonium Animae,
Naturaliter Christianae

Tertullian, *De Testimoniae Animae*

CONTENTS

ACKNOWLEDGMENTS

The author wishes to thank the editors of the following journals for permission to reprint material: *Modern Age*, "The King: Sir John Fortescue and the English Tradition," 19 (Summer 1975); *Triumph*, "The New Voegelin," (Jan. 1975), substantially altered in this text; *The Occasional Review*, "The Natural Law and the American Political Experience," (Feb. 1974); *The Intercollegiate Review*, "Cicero and the Politics of the Public Orthodoxy" (with Willmoore Kendall), (Nov. 1967) and "Donoso Cortés and the Meaning of Political Power," 1968; *National Review*, "The Death of American Optimism," 1960 (for some concluding paragraphs to chapter 5 of this study). Very special thanks are due Mrs. Willmoore Kendall for her permission to allow the republication of an essay originally written by the author in collaboration with the late Dr. Kendall. Thanks are proferred as well to Mrs. Del Hall for generous help in typing the manuscript. That the author's assistants, Mr. Terry Rogers and Mr. Robert Bauman, helped him wrap it all together at the very end speaks well for their patience and friendship. A note of gratitude is due to Mr. William C. Koneazny, Polish metaphysician, for his kind suggestions in reference to Saint Augustine's theory of politics. That the book was written at all is due to Dr. Melvin Bradford: let all who take umbrage blame it on him.

CHRISTIANITY AND POLITICAL
PHILOSOPHY

INTRODUCTION

⊷§ The advent of political philosophy in a society usually augurs ill for the society itself. Political wisdom drifts into the public forum as do leaves in early autumn portending the coming of winter. Almost always a meditation by men who remember past glories, fancied or real, political philosophy grips the souls of men who are stiffening themselves for the ice and the gales and the snows of an inclement and soon-to-be-suffered season of hardship and even danger. No political philosopher worth his salt ever thought that he could restore a golden past threatened in the autumn of an aging civilization too tired to take up its burden of responsibility or too numbed to understand the splendor of its inheritance. The very irreducibility of history as it is lived not only by societies but by every man in each fleeting hour of the day prohibits calling back into being what has sunk into nothingness. The past can be expiated by penance and it can be propitiated by piety but the past cannot be perpetuated by the present. Mythic return to the timelessness of things as they were "in the beginning" is an illusory door through which the philosopher must not enter at the peril of betraying his vocation. Philosophers do not construct utopias, be they reactionary or futuristic. Wisdom is not an ideologue who justifies his desires by masking them under pseudosciences. Political philosophy as understood by the author in these pages has nothing in common with the rationalism of the Enlightenment or the resentment of the Marxes and Hegels who truly do believe with Leibniz that at bottom the only tragedy is not to be God.

There does exist, nonetheless, an affinity between political philosophy and a preoccupation with the past. As the sick man thinks about health as it slips out of his body, the philosopher tends to think about the health of the body politic when it seems to be sliding out of history. This commonplace was lifted to the level of theory by Vico who insisted that a civilization can be articulated and fashioned into ideals only when it has ceased to be exercised as a necessity of life. The *polis* became the acme of political excellence for both Plato and Aristotle at the moment when it had ceased to be a viable instrument for Greek political life. Everything summed up by the symbols of the Roman Republic became dear to Cato and Cicero when the Republic found its substance if not its form threatened by the promise of the Eagles of Empire. The medieval political world order, Christendom, expressed and lived in a bewildering host of actions and symbols that reached into the very household comings and goings of every European peasant and knight and churchman for centuries was only articulated in theory long after that world had been destroyed as fact.

But sympathetic reactions to the past do not make theory, and it is precisely here where head joins heart in looking back on what men have done in history. The Western tradition of thinking about things political insisted, until Marcilius of Padua, that among the tasks confronting theory was the construction of models or paradigms by which men could test existing political societies and even guide them in future action. There are no political acts in the past, and every political act made by statesman or politician was made in the present with the hope of effecting something in the future. But the future is faceless until it becomes a past. Therefore political results are never predictable with apodictic certainty. They are the effects of prudential decisions and prudence is irreducibly personal and existential—hence not teachable at all. What is prudent for this society may not be prudent for the next and what is prudent for me today may be rash or cowardly tomorrow. The teaching is standard Aristotle. Politics is risk but risk rationally undertaken. In order that men might face political decisions wisely, decisions whose very being will constitute a tomorrow, philosophical models are given statesmen by philosophers. These models are necessarily constructed out of past experiences. The knowledge of how men have acted is the only field I can plow in order to harvest a teaching on how they might best act tomorrow. Possibly Aristotle was getting at this point or at something very similar to it when he pointed out in the *Rhetoric* (1363b–1364b) that moral action sanctioned by ethical philosophy can only be presented to the people through examples taken from heroes who have incarnated these virtues in history. In a very literal sense we cannot admire the future but only the past. Even a putatively admired future is artefacted as is a house out of preexistent lumber: the synthesis is new but what goes into it is old. Models for political action tomorrow are the conclusions of men who march forward with their eyes glued to the backs of their heads. The Heideggerians are right when they tell us that the future fashions the past, but the future does so only because the past has already yielded to man the materials with which he can make a future.[1] The causality is mutual.

Moved by the fading away of things cherished and loved; quickened by a sense of approaching danger to things consubstantial with man's good life in society, his *bene esse,* political philosophers craft into models typical human situations and draw moral conclusions from them. They ask questions as to how good men and bad men would act in this or that kind of society as Plato in the *Republic* (8.562–564, 571–580) traced for us the typical behaviour of tyrants in power. If they be wise, these philosophers know all along that the best they can do is sketch rough roads that are always in fact traversed by men in ways which are as unpredictable as is the will of God.

Political philosophy in America today is following the

curve of political philosophy elsewhere in its past: as things get worse for the nation, they get better for the political philosopher! The country has emerged from a series of wars and traumas, badly shaken both psychologically and physically. The boast of never having lost a war is a living memory only to the middle aged and older. The United States has retreated from undisputed leadership in the world to embattled and quite lonely defender of an inheritance it can hardly articulate to itself. The nation in these last years of a declining century is wracked from within by doubts concerning its own identity, by widespread spiritual treason to venerable confessions of faith in its own meaning and destiny, and by a clerisy that makes a fetish of materialism and relativism. The snows of skepticism have made of the land a winter of dead expectations. And now once again scholars and others begin to ask the old questions about man and society, the soul and God, good and evil. The new flowering of political theory is largely a rebirth within the hothouse incubator of a few colleges and universities. There is little evidence that answers concerning these questions, even if there be any today, are being heeded by those in power. But all Americans, even the most sanguine, agree that a deep malaise lies over the land. The nation, most especially in its response to the Soviet Union and to the Communist world at large, drifts rather than sails. This is a zone of danger because it is not of the essence of the West that it drift.

The genius of the West constantly questions its own presuppositions but in questioning them the West renews them. The Eastern world has never been able to come to terms with history.[2] History lies like a gigantic corpse, uninterred, whose huge paws strike from out of death and strangle into death any new living body that would disturb the slumbers of those vast lands that lie to the east of Hungary and the Germanies and all things familiar to us. The East stifles any questioning about its past or—in a kind of dialectical frenzy—the East turns on its past and savagely throttles it into oblivion. There is no tension in Asia, no balance, no paradox. The East either lets the past suffocate the present or the East murders its own dead and scatters their members to the scavengers of history: we need think only of Mao and of the Red Guard. And when the East takes this second course it finds its executioners in the West. Thus was Marx imported to the East, encased in the cadaverous skull of Lenin as he brooded murder on that long trip eastwards in a German freight train in 1917.

The West has constantly renewed itself because the West has always nervously put to itself new questions. But to ask a new question is to have transcended history as a past by projecting history into the future. And this projection is not a return to a mythic past but a veritable transfiguration: the past enters whole and entire into the future but it enters wholly and entirely changed. Past is no longer past as past but past as future. Was it not Aristotle who insisted that philosophy begins in wonder which is a kind of ignorance which is new and fresh precisely because it was caused by an ancient ignorance that knew itself to be ignorance? Both past and future, as indicated, cause each other. The Christian, for example, can sense as a pain the despair of pagan antiquity and only the Christian can—and did—retrieve antiquity's treasures for itself. Only the Christian can go to confession for sins committed yesterday by his fathers. I for one would have placed the McDonalds on the right wing of the Jacobite army before the Battle of Culloden Moor in 1745. I for one would have urged Patton in 1945 to have hurried his tanks to the east in order to prevent the Russian occupation of the east of our own West. The examples have emotional over-tones because they are engendered by deep personal convictions which are not germane to the issue. They do illustrate, however, how Western men react to their own past: they absorb it into their futures. I can deduce with more than a fair degree of accuracy the politics of tomorrow of journalists and intellectuals in this country by their attitude to the Spanish Civil War of 1936–1939. Past resonates as future in our civilization. If the West should lose its past because it laughs at its own heroism—and there are signs that the West is indeed losing its past even as it mocks it (who is a hero to our youth from the war in Vietnam?)—then the West will cease to exist. The future would then be shaped in some different way by those barbarian faces that peer at us from out of the wastes, as Belloc once put it. And upon those faces there is no smile.

But what the West does when it reflects on a past to be put to use for a future reiterates the structuring of any question asked by any man about anything at all. In turn, the same noetic situation is encountered at that peak of reflection which is philosophical questioning. This includes, of course, philosophical questioning about the political order, questioning which is impossible, as suggested, except in the light of history. Once again Aristotle can be our teacher. In searching for a description of wisdom, he did not begin with an abstract definition but with what men in general associate with wise men when they encounter them (*Metaphysics* 1.1,980–1,983a). Some knowledge of wisdom is already presupposed before we ask questions about what is wisdom. Knowledge is the ground of ignorance, not the other way around. A totally debased man could never study ethics because he would not even have a nominal understanding of what the word *good* means as applied to human action. No philosophical and hence no political questions are formulated in a vacuum. There is nothing particularly wrong with a so-called presuppositionless philosophy except the claims of its practitioners that philosophy must begin without presuppositions—which last, of course, is itself a presupposition. Putting the issue in strictly logical terms we must conclude that the proposition "Philosophy ought to have no presuppositions" is no more analytically self-evident than the proposition "Philosophy ought to have presuppositions." The business cannot be settled on the supposed self-evident character of either proposition. Wisdom here lies in another direction: in attending to what we do in fact when we ask questions about anything at all and, in this context, about things political. We ask these questions within the context of history. There simply is no other context within which they could be asked. Although our philosophical questioning can emerge from personal history as Unamuno's life-long meditation on death was prompted by his own anxiety about his own death, most philosophical questioning is prompted by cultural experience. Experiences are not philosophy but without them no paradigmatic models can be artifacted by political theoreticians and no speculative conclusions can be drawn as to how men ought to act morally in this or that hypothetical situation.

All of this is by way of a preface to the studies making up this book. Each one of these chapters addresses itself to a philosophical problem generated by history, and most of these chapters locate that problem within its conception by some man of wisdom who passionately wanted to know where he stood within his own world. Cicero, in the declining glory of Republican Rome, counterpointed his own obligations to philosophy with his obligations to Rome and opted for the latter on philosophical grounds. Constantine, Eusebius, and Lactantius tried to bend the Cross of Christ to the Eagles of the Roman legions, and Augustine gainsaid them and thus transcended the pagan failure to come to terms with the tragic dimensions of existence. Sir John Fortescue in the full sap of English medieval Christendom attempted to solve the perennial mystery of power's relation to authority by bending both to the laws of England, and thus he justified his patriotism by his philosophy and his philosophy by his patriotism. Juan Donoso Cortés in total reaction against the triumphant liberalism of the nineteenth century looked back to medieval Christendom and found in it, to his satisfaction, the very exercise in historical existence of the same power-authority structure explored five hundred years earlier by Fortescue. Each man philosophized within historical materials that enabled him to craft into cognitive existence paradigms or models illustrative of permanent truths about man's life as a political animal. And this marriage of philosophical universality and concrete historical irreducibility, a paradox in being, worked itself out in time in a peculiarly dramatic fashion in the marriage and then divorce of natural law philosophy from political institutions and from religious authority. This book is about politics and history, and I have composed it around vignettes that put history to work in the service of wisdom.

The author philosophizes within Christian history because that history is his own; he has no other. The questions would come out of that past even if he had lost his faith. Who today can get excited about not believing in Thor, as Chesterton once put it? The "public orthodoxy" of the West is deeper than philosophy: philosophical traditions must be located within the world of revelation as either positive or negative reactions thereto. Whatever there be of polemics in what follows—and I have limited that genre largely to the last two chapters—is functional within the vision of a man who is convinced that either the principled suppression of the Christian experience by philosophy (Strauss and the Chicago school) or the reduction of Christianity to mythic or mystic experience whose only authority is itself (Voegelin) drains both Christianity and philosophy of their intrinsic interest. When Tertullian thundered his famous "What has Jerusalem to do with Athens?," he uttered for all time the fundamentalist's rejection of reason in the name of faith. But his own position by no means exhausts the range of possible relations that men can find between both of them.[3] Saint Thomas Aquinas's insistence that grace perfects nature and that man's rational nature has thereby been perfected is a theological conclusion which the author of this book cannot demonstrate to a nonbeliever. But the proposition that Christianity opened up to philosophical speculation an entirely new range of questions that issued into answers that today are part and parcel of the intellectual tradition of the West is a proposition itself demonstrated by history. We cannot go back to Greece. We can only do for our time what our fathers did for their own: incorporate Greece into Christendom.

If our nation today is drifting and if the West at large is drifting; if our beliefs are being shaken to the foundations, to borrow a figure from Paul Tillich; if we are emptying our public life of our spiritual substance, it is largely due to our having divorced politics from religion. To bring Christianity back to the forum of history we could well first bring Christianity back to political speculation whose business is the rational elucidation of the forum. The philosopher has no power as Plato lamented in the *Republic* (5.473-474). All the philosopher can do is proffer what portion of wisdom there be in him, his authority, to public power. As shall be argued in these pages, the response is power's alone. This work is offered to its readers by a man who suggests that we begin to think politics again in terms of questions prompted by (or, as in the case of Cicero, answered by) Christian history and experience. Our answers, if we have any, must be reasoned answers and hence philosophical conclusions. They are advanced in the hope that they might aid, if but modestly, a new flowering of Christian political wisdom in this nation in the service of man's well-being in the postmodern world of tomorrow.

THE LIMITS OF NATURAL LAW

◄§ The decay in the vigor of the natural law tradition in our times of trouble—a decay I take as evident and without need of any special documenting—involves a shift in the status of man himself within the universe, or at least it involves a shift in what men think about man. Natural law convictions take root and flourish only within moments of time when man becomes aware of himself as that curious being who both belongs and does not belong to the world, as that being who has a share in his own perfection and who can say either "yes" or "no" to his own being. The content of natural law, its specific commands and prohibitions, emerges as the result of a series of deepening insights about man made by man himself within the crucible of history. The codification of natural law is not the law itself, which is simply man's nature understood as the wheel of the bark of humanity. We become keenly aware of this when we remember that the remote origins of natural law were not juridical as such but rather ontological. Natural law, before its articulation at the hands of the Stoics, was thought to be the perfection or full flowering of human nature which thus followed upon a law written into the symphony of being, the law dictating that things grow up, that they throw off the trappings of infancy, that they perfect the latent dynamisms consubstantial with all natures, and that they become themselves. The metaphysical roots of what was to become the natural law tradition were bound up intrinsically with a view of the universe that was both dynamic and constant.

The universe is composed of an indefinite number of constant natures, each one of which is capable of actualizing itself through the individuals sharing that nature. Nature for the Greeks was a principle of birth and growth, *dynamis*, an unfolding of treasures which are written initially like promises within the scroll of being. Natural law as something specifically human involved the recognition of the human spirit by itself and hence the recognition that man alone in the universe can affirm or deny his own nature. This awesome freedom, often frustrated by fate and fortune and by the inscrutability of chance, in a terrible sense involves the whole order of nature: man, when he affirms himself, affirms the whole and when he denies himself he denies the whole. Thus it was that Saint Thomas Aquinas could hold that suicide is a sin against the community of existence; that Chesterton could write that were the trees capable of knowledge they would shed their leaves and wither into hideous stumps when insulted by the same cosmic blasphemy. Nor must we forget that if justice plays a central role within natural law it is because justice does mean more than simply to give a man his due. This last is an impoverishment of the classical understanding of justice. Justice harmonizes into unity what otherwise would be chaos, so Plato teaches us in the *Republic*. It follows that natural justice is a condition not only of justice everywhere but of the very order of the cosmos. We can sum up by saying that natural law, as it slowly developed within the Greek tradition, implied three things: (1) natural law was both an extension of, and a crowning of, a dynamic propensity within all nature to develop and become fully itself; (2) natural law was the specific perfection proper to a man who was aware in an adult fashion of the imperatives of his own humanity; (3) natural law was a principle of harmony and of order within society and within the cosmos.

The classical Christian statement of the structure of natural law is found in the first part of the second part of the *Summa Theologiae* of Saint Thomas Aquinas. This treatise has been hailed justly for its chisled and lapidary perfection, although specialists in the thought of Aquinas know that the teachings found in the *Summa Theologiae* must be fleshed out by being read in the context of cross references to other treatises in which Aquinas takes up issues in greater detail and leisure.[1] Saint Thomas never said everything he had to say about any one point in any one book. Nonetheless, there is a kind of terse completion to his natural law treatise in the *Summa* that has made of it a text to which all natural law philosophers return as to a classical statement.

The natural law doctrine of the Common Doctor as it is carved in those pages emerges as a sculpted tribute to man's ability to scrutinize with reason his own nature and to think through to conclusions certain truths that follow from that nature. Avoid evil and seek the good is the first principle of the moral order.[2] But why seek the good? There is literally no answer to this question because there is nothing more profound upon which such an answer could be justified. Seeking the good yields happiness and all men desire to be happy. Aquinas has been accused by some of having developed a quasi-hedonistic ethics in that his emphasis everywhere is on man's happiness. But happiness for Saint Thomas is not that one extra drink for the road that the word suggests to men who are suspicious of happiness on the grounds that an ethic built around it might become a kind of Christianized Epicureanism. Happiness for Thomas is a drive built into the structure of man as he finds himself in existence. There is nothing much men can do about being as they are. To complain that the human desire for felicity is selfish is to confuse some specific response to the desire for happiness with the desire itself. This kind of reasoning is equivalent to scolding a one-armed man for wishing he had two. The one-armed man can reconcile himself to being deprived of a second upper limb in the name of the will of God or patriotism (he lost the arm in battle) but the one-armed man is not going to be talked into agreeing with the proposition that men, given their four-limbed nature, simply are being selfish if they desire to be as their natures constructed them to be. If the Mongolian idiot brings tears to the eyes of his parents who love him, the tears are not the result of any hedonistic aberrations but the effect of parents who mourn that their child cannot be what children ought to be.

Aquinas cannot be understood in the light of "value philosophy," itself the consequence of German idealism. It is interesting to note that the entire Western world got along without that very word *value* until sometime well into the middle of the nineteenth century. Value theory is an antithesis of natural law theory. *Values* imply that something is interjected between man and reality to which he must respond intuitively. It is probable that value philosophy is an invasion of aesthetics into ethics and politics. In any event, natural law is deeper than our response to moral situations because natural law understands this response as growing out of the law, not the other way around. Given that the law is nature, man's nature, the realism of the doctrine is almost frightening to an intelligence weighted by over four hundred years of rationalism.

Probably the biggest disadvantage to natural law philosophy is the rhetoric associated with the word *law*. No matter how much effort we make in attempting to refine the word, *law* continues to suggest, even if but subtly, something imposed on us through legislation passed "on high." Saint Thomas, in commenting on the Roman jurisprudential dictum that "the will of the prince has the force of law" (*ST* 1–2, q. 90, a. 1), answers that the princely will does indeed have the force of law, positive law, if his law be reasonable: "otherwise, it is more iniquity than law." Although positive law, the law of political societies, is a law that is passed by some legitimate authority acting reasonably for the common good, natural law is not passed in any profound sense at all. We can argue, with justice, that natural law was "passed" by God when he made man, but it was "passed" not in the sense of being a corpus of legislation imposed upon him. In making trees, God made them to act in a certain way. In making men, he made them to act in a certain way. Law is always a measure or a rule of action, and the measure here is nothing more than man's very own nature. Man as a living being shares drives with vegetables and brute animals and, as rational, has drives peculiar to himself. He cannot not be in the way in which he is built. Violations of his nature may bring, indeed often bring, temporary satisfaction but ultimately they work harm to the very fabric of his being; and nature for Saint Thomas is the fabric of being, the *modus essendi*, the way in which things exist.[3]

As stones fall when dropped and as big fish eat little fish and as little fish try not to be eaten by big fish, men, thanks to the nature in which they subsist in the entire order of being, have finalities which are one with themselves. Men do not "think these finalities up": they are already there and simply need to be discovered by rational inquiry into the structure of human nature. The closer human reason approaches these primordial goals, the less risk it runs in misinterpreting natural law. The farther it moves away from these sources as sources, the more dubious become its conclusions and the more man needs to lean on the learning of experts in the matter. "Murder is evil and is not to be done" is a judgment that only the most depraved of men would deny, but whether or not executing a spy or capital punishment is or is not murder are issues not immediately deducible analytically from the universal proposition condemning murder. That war ought to be fought only with just cause is a conclusion come by without great difficulty (absolute pacifism is condemned by natural law theory) but what precise conditions must be fulfilled in order that a war effectively be just are not intuitively cognized by men of good will simply because they are men. Natural law, in a word, requires that its conclusions be known by men who think them through from more fundamental and better known propositions. Natural law demands elucidation and that elucidation traditionally has been considered to be the work of philosophers.

But philosophers are notorious for disagreeing with one another, and nobody can explain away the scandal that philosophical disagreement has brought to the West, producing skepticism and even cynicism concerning the capacity of man to know the truth through the exercise of his own reason. We cannot explain away the scandal but we can explain it. Obviously, only reason itself can arbitrate between competing opinions which themselves are advanced as being reasonable. But the time and the skill and the education and the good will needed in order merely to follow a philosophical argument and grasp the implications of its meaning, to say nothing of assenting to its purported truth, is simply beyond the scope of the man uneducated in philosophical thinking. We confront the paradox that although men, left to themselves, follow the road of their own natures spontaneously because that is the way men are, a reading of the road map itself is not all that spontaneous. Saint Thomas attempted to come to terms with this discrepancy between what is natural and our knowledge of what is natural in the light of his distinction between a twofold aspect of God's Revelation to man: (1) God has revealed truths about himself which totally surpass human reason; (2) but God has also revealed truths about himself and man theoretically knowable by philosophical science. But what is theoretically knowable is usually never known at all to the majority of mankind because men, taken in the large and by the handful, are either too busy or too uneducated, simply not bright enough or perverted by their passions, to achieve this knowledge, a kind of knowledge all men need in order that they might be saved (*Summa contra gentiles* 1.3–7). And even the wise men so exalted by the Greek philosophical tradition come to these truths only in bits and pieces and then only after long years of meditation. But these men of wisdom need to know the law of their nature long before the advent of decrepitude: they need to live the law of their being even before they have had the time—or the luck—to discover it by themselves. Therefore God revealed the content of natural law to all men.

The position of Saint Thomas is intelligible and philosophically justifiable on the grounds advanced in the introduction; every philosophy is guided by presuppositions historically anterior to itself. Christian revelation concerning the nature of man, already adhered to in faith, can prompt a kind of rational probing about man totally missed in another civilization that knows nothing of Christian faith. There is probably only one way to evaluate two such philosophies; if the insights of reason without faith fail to come to terms with problems, philosophical problems, that emerged only within a context of faith, then the context of faith for philosophy is superior to its contrary. Man's natural desire for transcendence and therefore his desire to transcend political existence is a key instance in question. Stumbled upon by Aristotle in his awareness that friendship, while of use to politics, cannot be reduced to politics, man's transpolitical elan towards a felicity beyond the city is natural, hence rational. However, this truth was discovered only after man had been redeemed by Christ or—to placate the nonbeliever—after he at least thought he had been redeemed by Christ. Questions concerning man's spirituality and the immortality of his soul and the dignity of the person exemplify as well the point being made. Practically all metaphysical questions concerning existence are Christian questions whether they be answered with the optimism of an Aquinas or the despair of a Sartre.[4] Greeks never thought about such things.

But Saint Thomas's frank admission that the very elucidation of the natural law in its fullness requires revelation involves a double limitation. Philosophy is limited by an authority deeper than itself and politics is limited by philosophy. The issue demands exploration because it is central to the subjects which engage the attention of the author in this book.

Every concrete political order is limited in its claims unless, of course, it promises to incarnate the law of history as does World Communism. Setting aside this last and most dangerous of all political movements in history, we might well note a phenomenon in the text of Aristotle commented on by Eric Voegelin.[5] Whereas the Stagirite enumerates *natures* in his work on the "Parts of Animals" and whereas he differentiates natures according to a multifold specification of a number of genera, he simply cannot so operate when he turns his attention to political life. In his own words, constitutions do not grow like trees. Although man's political nature is natural, his political life is artifacted, constructed by himself. Because the order that man makes is other than the order that he discovers, (*Nicomachean Ethics* 1.1094a–1095a) there is a kind of metaphysical "strangeness" between nature and art. They are not estranged from one another but are strange because the one is simply given and the other is crafted by man, one of the givens in the universe. Now natural law has a claim on all men that politics cannot make. In civilized societies men are always free to change their nationalities and hence the positive laws under which they live, but no man is free to change his human nature. A law transcending political boundaries and concrete allegiances, a law pretending to cut across all of them in the sense of applying to all of them

[17]

indiscriminately, is a potential threat to the pretentions of all politics. A law so natural that the positive law of the state must be built on it—or at least not built in opposition to it—is a competitor given man as we find him. Such a law must bridle the pride of legislators and the presumed sovereignty of states. If natural law is limited by revelation, then natural law in turn limits politics. Within this double limitation Western man has lived for some two thousand years and the evidence is everywhere around us that naked politics, the will of the prince, reinforced by bayonet and bailiff, judge and jail, will not be so limited. The exploration of these limitations in a model situation is not a task of natural law theory; it is a work of political philosophy.

Legal positivism and historicism wear different garb: the former is bleak and dull; the latter is often rich and lavishly burnished with the glitter of tradition. Both, however, teach at bottom the same thing: legal positivism would have it that law is what the prince says it is and whether that prince be the authority of a legislature or a judiciary or an executive is irrelevent; historicism would have it that man is so bound to the phenomenologically given that he simply cannot transcend his circumstances of time and place and his law is simply the expression of history. Both of them deny that the laws men make must be measured by that deeper measure which is man himself, not man bent to this or that concrete order of things, not man white or black or brown, not man medieval or modern or contemporary, but man. When this last is denied, then the political philosopher truly can learn nothing from history nor can he watch the drama of philosophy expressing wisdom under the pressure of questions thrown up by history. If we are nothing other than our histories then we could never use them or learn from them. The difference between a Burke and a Cicero, both conservatives in the current understanding of that word, is that Burke thought that laws were good because they were old whereas Cicero thought that if they were old, they were probably good (*De Republica*). Natural law suggests a presumption in favor of age in our evaluation of the decency of a political order, but this presumption must be tested. After all, being tends to be as a good oak table tends to perdure. Things do not collapse because of what is good in them and the more they endure, the greater presumption there is that they endure thanks to their being, not their propensity towards nonbeing. And the only rational tool mankind has for making the test is political wisdom, political philosophy. Saint Thomas teaches that the very first precepts of the natural law can never be eradicated from man but that secondary and tertiary precepts of that law can be lost if man is dulled by vice or vitiated by the powers of evil (*ST* 1–2, q. 95, a. 1). A climate must be created, an atmosphere nourished; a world cherished, within which sound political philosophy might escape the smell of decadence that usually attends its arrival in history.

It is very difficult to get men debased by the modern state to ask the right questions concerning the good life because their questions today come out of a world in which natural law is not only denied in theory but exercised in practice in only the most obvious and pitiful of ways: even Marxist college professors do not defraud their garage mechanics or cheat on their grocery bills, but from such elementary and even banal decency we are not going to get very far in attempting to remedy the ills of the age; even positivist professors who insist on television that the "quality of being human" must be earned and is not to be presumed to be something given with birth do not poison or shoot their neighbors' subnormal child. Even Senator Kennedy who is opposed to antiabortion laws would never have one done on his own wife. The natural law is still operative everywhere because it is natural in its spontaneous affirmation of the good, but that spontaneous affirmation is being put down by doctrines that either think that man is much less than he really is or that he ought to be some kind of superman dominating all creation.

We have argued that man's felicity, the achievement of which is the content of natural law, cannot be grasped in isolation from questions that emerge out of history even though this felicity is a constant within the dynamism of history. The emphasis is needed in order to avoid confusing natural law with the "Rights of Man" propounded by the French Revolutionary school of the Enlightenment. These "rights" were presumed to be abstractions divorced from prescription and custom and hence liberated from the supposed shackles of history. The results would be amusing had they not worked so much blood and tragedy into the body politic of the West and even the world itself. All that pompous rhetoric about abstract rights divorced totally from time and place today has about it the ring of its brittle eighteenth-century origins and the brass and tin of the philosophes in their Parisian saloons. Their laughter brought down around their heads the ruins of their own excessively tolerant world of the ancien régime. Every pretense to escape history is so burdened by history itself that it never outlives its own guillotine.

If custom has the force of law, as Saint Thomas insisted (ST 1–2, q. 47, a. 3); if custom can be presumed to incarnate natural law unless proven otherwise; if even bad laws which are not manifestly tyrannical ought to be left alone unless a recognizably greater good can be achieved through removing them,[6] then it follows that the natural law tradition is no enemy of the friends of prescription and tradition. But if this law also transcends both tradition and prescription, even as it urges on all of us piety towards one's own land and one's own as a natural virtue, then it follows as well that natural law can never become the captive of this or that political order. Natural law is a check on every polity: therefore, an irritant. Natural law remains a potential enemy of every tyrant, and we ought never to forget that tyranny is a sliding scale often measured by inches as the "tyrannical soul," in Plato's words, edges himself into the body politic in the name of blind passion or ideological insanity (*Republic* 8, 562a–565d). To the degree to which men have surrendered their manliness and their decency, their minds have been corrupted; to the degree to which a man's mind is corrupted, he cannot understand the reasonableness of ethical considerations grounded in the natural law. No methodology can ever preceed its actual exercise. The being of honorable and virtuous activity must antedate its meaning. The venerable dictate which insists that man must live before he philosophizes means literally what it says, but it also means something also present in the literal statement but not usually adverted to: philosophical conclusions are only as good as their premises, and in matters moral these premises are the experiences of a man, of a family, of a tribe, of a nation. In his *Posterior Analytics* (1.24a–25a) Aristotle called this the *experimentum*, that experience built up by repeated experiences without which no universal statements are possible.

Political philosophy differs from ethics as does the more general from the less general. There is an old-fashioned textbook example, often used by natural law teachers, of the submarine captain's dilemma: his ship is being bombed by enemy aircraft and he must submerge to save it but there is a crewman on the maindeck and he will be drowned if the ship submerges. What should the captain do? He may not will the death of his own crewman directly but he consents to his death in order to save his ship and thus gives the order to submerge. The captain only consents to the death: he does not will it. The famous double-effect argument according to which I may permit evil (the death of my crewman) for the sake of the common good (the safety of my vessel) but that I may not directly do evil in order that good may issue therefrom (abort, hence murder, an unborn baby in order that I may finish my education), is a natural law argument. Uncorrupted men will respond in such situations according to the natural law but most men when corrupted are corrupted by going political orders. The broader ethics of the submarine—the ship of state, to use the classical Hellenic metaphor quite proper to a sea-going people—is applicable to the exploration of political philosophy.

Nobody has examined with greater brilliance the tension between political philosophy and ethics than Doctor Willmoore Kendall.[7] Socrates faced the Assembly and told the truth as he saw it: the authority of philosophy (never mind that this authority was smuggled in through the back door by the Delphic Oracle: that would spoil the story and load the dice in favor of the writer). The Assembly, representing the authority of Athens, deliberated and then executed Socrates. But Socrates, through the mouth of Plato, had already pleaded the case for the Assembly on purely philosophical grounds. Socrates has become the hero of pure reason facing the "irrational" power of the political order, but Socrates versus the Assembly is utterly too distant and simplistic for those who have lived during the last two thousand years. A return to Socrates is simply not possible to anybody who takes history seriously—and that history, altogether without apologies, has been Christian history.

Political philosophy in constructing paradigms seeks heroes because heroes incarnate dramas which are universally true as they resonate within the consciences of each one of us. Our Christian hero cannot be the pagan Socrates. He only uttered a number of questions the answers to which have been known by every youngster educated in Christendom for decades of centuries. Socrates was a good man but the saints are our own. A hero to natural decency for our time will incarnate the dependence of politics upon natural law and natural law upon revelation.

There was a German officer in World War II, Count Klaus von Stauffenberg, who came from a very illustrious family. He loved his nation and its traditions. He was a man of piety. He gave one eye and one arm and two fingers from his remaining hand for his country. His family's origins reached back into the mists of the early Middle Ages. He was no ideological fanatic who resented Adolf Hitler on the grounds that the Fuehrer violated the dictates of the French Revolution and of European liberalism and democracy. Von Stauffenberg and his friends agonized for years over what they ought to do. They knew—and this they knew after thinking and praying long on the issue—that the National Socialist regime was taking their beloved country down the road towards a Götterdämmerung from which it could never recover. Von Stauffenberg was a "natural law" man. He was not a Kantian and therefore did not hold that duty was totally without moral content, a categorical imperative that sealed morally without recourse his sworn allegiance to the flag which formed part of the ceremony making him an officer of the German army. Von Stauffenberg in agony came to the decision that Hitler had to be killed. But the appalling prospect of killing the head of state of his own country, a man to whom he had sworn an especial oath, was a cross Von Stauffenberg did not wish to take up on his own. Let the Church give him that crown of thorns! He asked the ultimate authority on matters moral to sanctify his act. He pleaded for counsel under the seal of the confession and thus confessed natural law's dependence on Christ's revelation. And, so goes the story, the priest, a lofty prelate, threw the obligation back in Stauffenberg's face and thus abdicated the Church's authority in matters moral: follow your conscience! Thus it came to pass that a good man whose reason told him that Hitler must die, whose sensibilities—themselves not divorced from reason—recoiled against the deed, whose priest told him that were he to so act he had to act on his own authority, did so. In placing the bomb under the table at the Wolf's Nest in East Prussia and in then dying in Berlin, machine-gunned to death under the glare of the lights of Remer's armed cars, Count Klaus von Stauffenberg died a martyr to Christian political wisdom and courage. That he might have died a martyr to something deeper I leave in the hands of those competent to judge. Within our kind of paradigm, drawn not from pagan myth but from Christian history, the political philosophy of tomorrow must be sketched. It will be sketched in blood. The crimson crayon will be as harsh as the glare of those lights before the Bendlerstrasse and as agonizing as was the decision of the man whose body went down under the bullets of the tyrant. From the living flesh of Christian history, political philosophy will justify its existence tomorrow or it will have no existence whatsoever. Nobody tomorrow is going to die for philosophy as did Socrates, even granted that Socrates did die for philosophy. Our world is too serious for such baubles. After Von Stauffenberg, Solzhenitsyn, and thus the world to come.

CICERO AND THE POLITICS
OF THE PUBLIC ORTHODOXY

(with Willmoore Kendall)

◆§ An incandescent irony has burnished natural law theory from its very inception. Representing, as it does, the testimony of reason on what is reasonable conduct for men, the authority of natural law has always been counterpointed by the authority of society which necessarily preaches its own convictions on what is proper behaviour and ultimate truth in matters political and ethical. As suggested, natural law would ultimately sink or swim thanks to some public authority capable of interpreting its command. In medieval Latin Europe the authority was to become the Church. Today we have long passed that moment in history, and our own drama bears within itself lineaments already traced in pagan and republican Rome. The central figure was Cicero because he lived within a tension he discovered between the dictates of philosophy and the dictates of Roman *pietas*. Public faith might very well enshrine natural law theory but then again it might not. Socrates against the Assembly and Plato's Republic that was too pure to be lived in by men suggest at the very least tension and at the most opposition between what a society believes to be true and what a philosopher discovers or thinks he discovers concerning truth. The issue cannot be resolved theoretically by merely opting for one or the other authority. Their relationships must be explored and this exploration belongs properly to political philosophy, but

[25]

to a political philosophy that takes seriously the role of religion and piety and prescription in man's corporate life. Such a political doctrine was shaped under the pressure of history by the genius of Cicero.

My immediate topic: the meaning of what we shall call "public orthodoxy" in the political philosophy of Marcus Tullius Cicero. Our objective: to throw light on the meaning of public orthodoxy in political philosophy in general. We shall investigate Cicero's position on the issue, that is to say, with an eye primarily to its possible usefulness in the resurrection and reconstruction of politics as *scientia*, which is rendered necessary today by the theoretical decay into which that science has fallen under insistent pressures from positivism.

Positivism denies to the concept of public orthodoxy, in effect, any theoretical meaning at all. It reduces public orthodoxy to a factual datum; one, morever, which cannot be penetrated scientifically because it is based upon an irrational charisma—the study of which, we are told, belongs properly to the sociology of religion or to the psychology of the collective unconscious.

Clarification and defense of the concept of public orthodoxy as a concept pertaining integrally to politics as science, we shall contend, is crucial both to an understanding of Cicero's teaching and to an understanding of the very meaning of political science.

Let us provisionally define the public orthodoxy as that tissue of judgments, defining the good life and indicating the meaning of human existence, which is held commonly by the members of any given society, who see in it the charter of their way of life and the ultimate justification of their society.

This provisional definition, it might be objected, raises more problems than it solves. Our reply must be that this is the classical role of a provisional definition within Western logic: to name a reality simply by pointing at it, in order that

that reality may be brought within the scope of the human intelligence for the sake of scrutiny and ultimate clarification. By pointing at a thing, we make that thing a subject of a future judgment, a judgment potentially scientific in nature. And the present essay proposes, *inter alia*, to give to the subject *public orthodoxy* a predicate—a predicate distilled by the Roman experience as understood and thought through by Cicero. That predicate will by no means exhaust the issue at hand; but it will, we think, make it more intelligible to the student of political philosophy.

Let us notice, to begin with, that there can be a purely legal "orthodoxy," in terms of which the members of a community merely agree upon the political instruments that are to govern them—for example, the formal orthodoxy that unites most members of the Conservative and Labor parties in Great Britain today, which is a set of common convictions concerning the "goodness" of a bicameral parliamentary system under a ceremonial and symbolic monarch. Such a legal orthodoxy is certainly a constituent part of the way of life of most societies; but it cannot be simply identified with that way of life, and it is, therefore, a more restricted topic than ours. As Professor Leo Strauss puts it, "way of life" is a rough translation of the Greek *politeia*, which means the character or tone of a community, and is itself dependent upon "what the society regards as most respectable or most worthy of admiration."[1] In classical political philosophy an aristocratic republic, tempered by monarchical and democratic elements, was considered the best form of government because the urban gentleman, whose wealth rested on the land, was considered, for purposes of government, the highest type of human being. The excellence of the urban gentleman, in turn, was both measured and created by his allegiance to the institutions of the City, the highest of which were the religious rites that propitiated the gods and thus guaranteed their

[27]

continued providence over the politeia. The aristocratic values enshrined in this class were regarded, accordingly, as the ideals of the politeia at large, and acceptance of these values and the commitments they involved constituted the public orthodoxy of the classical society.

Hilaire Belloc detailed a similar public orthodoxy for the England that emerged from the Whig triumph over the Stuart kings and that endured well into the present century—that is, the public acceptance of the gentleman as the standard of excellence and as the embodiment of what Britain stood for.[2] As Belloc argued, with his characteristic irony, a cad might in the long run stand a better chance for salvation than a gentleman, but to suggest that this theological consideration ought to alter the fabric of English society would be unthinkable. Writing far earlier than Belloc, in a vein that might shock those who find Machiavellianism in every blunt statement of political ends, Lord Bolingbroke, in his famous letter to Sir William Wyndham justifying his political role in the months preceding and following the death of Queen Anne, candidly stated that he and his men, representing as they did the landed party of the country gentry, the still powerful yeomanry, the older aristocracy, and the Church of England, considered it only "natural" that they should seize power and exercise it for their own ends against the new financial and commercial aristocracy represented by the Bank of England.[3] When Bolingbroke wrote, the English politeia was still rural and aristocratic, rather than urban and aristocratic, still agrarian and Christian, rather than commercial and latitudinarian; and the defense of the existent politeia seemed to Bolingbroke as absolute and unavoidable a duty as the defense of England itself: England and its politeia or way of life, were, for him, one and the same thing. That Bolingbroke himself was neither Christian nor rural illuminates rather than obscures his grasp of the meaning of the public orthodoxy as defined here, of a standard of goods maintained publicly as ideals even if often sinned against in practice.

The politeia, then, is something more fundamental than laws. Cicero locates the study of laws in a hierarchy of science which first answers the question as to the best regime—as Cicero does by identifying it concretely with the Roman Republic. The law must fit the politeia, not the politeia the law: what is just in the best society might be highly unjust in a less perfect society; what is just for a free man might well be crying injustice if done to a slave. Because it is the source of all laws, though capable of being articulated in law and governmental institutions, the politeia raises issues that are prior to those of law and governmental institutions. To what we, following Professor Strauss,[4] call "regime," T. S. Eliot applies the term *culture*—as when he writes that if bishops and darts do not belong equally to British culture, they nonetheless equally belong![5] What we point to, in a word, is that matrix of convictions, usually enshrined in custom and folkways, often articulated formally and solemnly in charter and constitution, occasionally summed up in the creed of a church or the testament of a philosopher, that makes a society the thing it is and that divides it from other societies as, in human thought, one thing is divided always from another.

That is why we may (and do) speak intelligibly of a Greek, a Roman, or an American way of life. The nominalism that would deny meaning to these phrases might conceivably be defensible, to be sure, if it restricted itself to borderline cases, such as, say, the Bavarian and the Austrian way of life. But it renders itself absurd when it attempts to deny any essential distinction between, for example, societies like the Chinese and the British, because the denial then becomes a denial of what is evidently true. The serious political philosopher sim-

[29]

ply cannot converse with the nominalist on this primitive level; all the less because there is no way in which we can prove the evident, no way in which we can demonstrate strictly that what is evident is evident. What replaces argument on this level is the ability, pure and simple, to see what is there to be seen. We must, therefore, draw a distinction between the scientific elaboration of the social disciplines and that intuitive grasp of a cultural complexity which itself precedes all science and, in truth, makes science possible. In fine, the denial of meaning, of intelligibility, to the terms *regime, politeia, way of life, culture,* cannot be refuted rationally because the source of the denial is an intelligence and a sensibility blunted to the historically and socially given; and if the principle of contradiction is the unquestioned point of departure for metaphysics, then the existence of the politeia is the unquestioned point of departure for political philosophy.

Should it be objected here that we are labouring the obvious we reply that it is necessary because the denial of the obvious regarding these points has been and is laboured constantly elsewhere, in the political literature inspired by positivism, which refuses to touch the question of the politeia because the politeia enshrines an orthodoxy, and because an orthodoxy is composed of what the positivists call "value judgments," which are precisely what the positivists tell us that political science is not about.

The issue may be elucidated further as follows: the politeia, in the terminology of Eric Voegelin, is a *cosmion* of meaning illuminated from within by and for the members of a society. Enshrining as it does convictions concerning the existence of God or of the gods, the good life, and the destiny of man and of society, the politeia can ultimately be defined only in ontological terms, be they strictly religious, strictly metaphysical, or a combination of the two. These convictions can be understood, therefore, only on their own terms, terms that are by definition theological and metaphysical. Thus positivism's refusal to admit within the temple of political science judgments of a philosophical and theological nature prevents it from coming to grips with any politeia whatsoever. In order to understand a politeia, we must think through its ultimate philosophical presuppositions; and the thinking must be thinking, not mere reporting. If, therefore, we are denied the right to exercise our philosophical and theological intelligence when functioning as political scientists, the unavoidable result is that while we can understand a politeia in our capacity as philosophers or theologians, we can never do so in our capacity as political scientists. In short, a *polis* can never be understood by the science of politics!

The positivist tries to escape from the horns of this dilemma, but his maneuver only succeeds in goring him the more. I can, he insists, understand a public orthodoxy as fact, but I cannot criticize it as "value"; to attempt the latter would be to fall into subjectivism. What he fails to see is that if the phenomenon in question be a judgment about the good, a judgment that bears integrally upon the meaning and destiny of human life, then the understanding (for every critique presupposes understanding of the criticized) of that judgment as it objectively is involves understanding it as a judgment about the good. And the so-called refusal to fall into subjectivism is itself subjectivism because it converts what is in fact a good into disemboweled fact, and so blocks on principle that which it originally sets out to do—namely, to understand the judgment as objectively *there*, as *fact*. There is something radically wrong with the use currently being made of the distinction between judgments of *fact* and judgments of *value*, an epistemological blunder which has prevented contemporary political science from coming to terms with the first indisputable principle of its own discipline—that is, the existence of the politeia as a cosmion of meaning ultimately metaphysical and theological in structure—the existence, in short, of the public orthodoxy. If, then, Cicero can help us understand the meaning of a public orthodoxy, he can do so only if we are prepared to philosophize with him. Which we can do only if we exorcise the notion that value judgments are never scientific.

In classical and medieval philosophy the *subject* is nothing more than merely the thing presented to the intelligence; the *object* is the intelligible light under which the subject is understood—that is, the subject as objectified in this or that fashion. There is, in other words, no split between subject and object: what we have, rather, is an intelligible relation between (in Aristotelian terms) a *potency* and its *act*: the subject is *potentially* objectifiable in any given number of ways; it is *actually* objectified in single judgments, in each of which the intellect predicates meaning or intelligibility of the subject—that is, asserts that what it understands of the subject actually exists in the subject.[6] The contemporary use of the terms *subject* and *object* is, in consequence, far removed from the classical usage and the doctrine that underlies it—so far, that we can fairly speak of the meanings as having been reversed. The objective, in the classical and medieval sense, is not only subjective in the modern sense, but more subjective in the modern sense than the subject itself in the classical and medieval sense. The objective belongs properly to the mind; it is the subject as thought in this or that way. Similarly, the subject in the classical and medieval sense is more "objective" in the modern sense than is the objective in the classical and medieval sense. For the subject is the thing "extramentally existing,"—that is, in independence of the mind.

Now, the separation of subject and object, which begins as early as the fourteenth century, reaches its apotheosis in

German idealism. For it, the human spirit is the sole subject in a world of objects, and brings out of its own depths values, proper to itself, that are duly imprinted upon the world like seals upon wax. But the decay of idealism did not restore the *status quo ante*; rather, it left intact the subject-object dichotomy, and so prepared the way for what we know today as the positivist banishment of values to an interior and irrational world, the Freudian cave of the psyche, a reservoir of demonic and charismatic forces that has nothing to do with the daylight world of facts—a world that belongs properly to science, which enumerates the facts and classifies them.

In classical and medieval philosophy, the political depends on the metaphysical, as we may see most clearly in Aquinas. For Aquinas, the *ought* is consubstantial with the fullness of the *is*; it is the Good proper to man. The Good, viewed most broadly, is that which can perfect; that which can perfect, however, can do so only to the degree to which it is perfect in itself; things are perfect in themselves to the degree to which they are in act, and things are in act to the degree to which they are, because existence (*esse*) is the act of all acts and the perfection of all perfections.[7] It follows that the Good is rooted in being itself, and is, in truth, the fullness of being, of existence. Thus, Aquinas can go on and say that the *ratio boni* belongs to the *ratio esse*: not only is there no discrepancy between the Good and the Is; the Good is, we repeat, the fullness of the Is, its flowering into perfection—into an actuality fully perfective and desirable, lovable. Obligation, be it personal or social, is not the command of a deus ex machina, but is the in-built dynamic push towards perfection which is man's act of existing and within which is inscribed his humanity. And his humanity is itself the structural limit and therefore the determination of his existential act.

We recapitulate: the root of all intelligibility is being; the act of being is existence; the Good is the fullness of existence.

Therefore, the Good is eminently knowable, and from knowledge of the Good there can flow, given a will rectified in the good proper to a man, the life of virtue itself.[8] That is the beginning of wisdom in the order of politics, and it has been lost to positivism because the latter has not given itself the pains to master the inheritance that it presumes, out of its ignorance, to supplant.

We have, up to now, fixed attention on the positivist objection to scientific penetration of the public orthodoxy. We could equally well have discussed the issue, however, from the standpoint of either historicism or existentialism. With respect to the public orthodoxy the three doctrines coincide materially, for all that they move from distinct theoretical positions. The denial of a properly theoretical dimension to the public orthodoxy—this is the point towards which we have been moving—reduces itself, on the one hand, to a positivism that must accept any old orthodoxy on the grounds that it is politically viable, that it is simply given. But that denial may reduce itself, similarly, to a system that identifies transcendent meaning with historical factuality, even if this factuality be only an irrational charisma. And it may reduce itself, finally, to a position that justifies the public orthodoxy on the grounds of its brute factuality. Theoretically speaking, positivism, historicism, and existentialism come here to one and the same thing, and if we tend to ignore this it is because the three are the existential representatives of three distinct dynamisms within history: positivism, today the ally of liberal democracy in America and yesterday, through the pen of Maurras, the ally of absolutism; historicism, the ally of the marriage of idealism and nationalism within the Germanies and of its progeny; and existentialism, the ally of the counterrevolution against the bankruptcy of nineteenth-century rationalism and liberalism in all its forms.

In sum, the denial that propositions concerning the good

life and the end of man have a trans-immanent validity leads to the identification of the content of those propositions with a factual datum, a given, whose meaning and justification does not transcend its factuality. And this is equally true whether the factuality be termed "the useful" (as in pragmatism), "the historic" (as in historicism), or "the national inheritance" (as in German existentialism's flirtation with National Socialism); in each case justice and law are conjured away in the name of the relevant factuality, and the ontological must be subordinated, theoretically, to the political—with, in all three cases, the same existential consequences: subordination of both religious and intellectual freedom to the state; reduction of transcendent truth to existential truth; the pressing of God into the service of man.

Now, this three-headed refusal to face the issue of a public orthodoxy on properly theoretical grounds, however interesting historically, would lack a properly philosophical interest but for this: the three positions—positions that dominate in varying degrees the academic world within the West—do possess a theoretical dimension, do represent an attempt to come to grips philosophically with a genuine political problem. The no-longer-tacit assertion that the public orthodoxy is the central fact around which a society's greatness and even existence must be organized, be that fact the American myth of democracy (which is capable of being exploited rationally and scientifically, as in Dewey) or be it the French myth of the ancien régime (which can be exploited rationally and scientifically by a Maurras), points to a profound truth, as disturbing as it is unavoidable: the public orthodoxy is, after all, useful. Not only can society not avoid having a public orthodoxy; even when it rejects an old orthodoxy in the name of "enlightenment," "progress," "the pluralist society," "the open society," and the like, it invents, however subtly, a new orthodoxy with which to replace the old one. As

Aristotle is always at hand to remind us, only gods and beasts can live alone; man, by nature, is a political animal whose very political life demands a politeia that involves an at least implicit code of manners and a tacit agreement on the meaning of the good life and, therefore, on the meaning of man within the total economy of existence. Without this political orthodoxy—itself involving both a metaphysics (and we must never forget that the denial of the metaphysical is itself a metaphysical proposition) and a theology sketched at least in broad outline—respect for the state withers; contracts lose their efficacy; the moral bond between citizens is loosened; the state opens itself to enemies from abroad; and the politeia sheds the sacral character without which it cannot long endure. The public orthodoxy implies, that is to say, a commitment to metaphysical propositions whose claim to acceptance cannot be mere political utility or historical sanction, but the very structure of things as they are in themselves. And this poses a genuine problem: to accept those propositions on existentially political grounds is not really to accept them at all; while if they are not accepted, the political order decays. And we run up hard against the paradox: the political order can be served politically only if its ultimate foundations are *not* accepted on political grounds! Is this perhaps the apparently insoluble dilemma between whose horns man has always been trying to escape?

Such a dilemma certainly faces any man who is aware both of the demands of the transcendent and of society, any man whose soul is turned out towards the truth of things as they are (that is, apart from political considerations), but also faces his responsibilities as a member within a society that incarnates a way of life involving a certain (at least apparent) commitment to the Absolute. Such a man, unable or unwilling to reduce ultimate meaning to utility or to historical factuality, must either find ultimate meaning within his society's orthodoxy, or face up to two alternatives: to seek meaning beyond that orthodoxy, and preach this new truth to the citizenry—thus corrupting the bonds that have hitherto kept his society in being; or to seek meaning beyond the public orthodoxy but keep the new truth to himself, thus living a public lie. He must choose between rebelling against his society and sinning against the light. His dilemma is terrible, since either choice is evil: to destroy an essentially decent society is wrong, even if that society repose upon theoretically erroneous foundations; but to fail to speak the truth when the truth demands that it be spoken is wrong, too. Whatever our hypothetical citizen-philosopher does or fails to do is, on the face of it, evil—at least within the context we have proposed, within the circle we have drawn. If political theory can break this circle it can do so only by exploring it carefully, for the circle captures the insights alike of positivism, historicism, and existentialism, along with those of the classical tradition that modernity in all its forms would jettison.

Now, the citizen-philosopher we have sketched above is one of the giants of the Western tradition, Cicero; and we believe that after following him as he walks around the circle we have drawn we may be able to do what we have proposed, namely, to give a predicate, a meaning, an intelligibility, to the subject of the public orthodoxy, a light that may lead us beyond the hideous dilemma with which we are confronted: betrayal of the light or betrayal of the community.

Let us speak first of the setting in which Cicero places the opening passages of his *De legibus*: a long summer day in Cicero's estate at Arpinum, that Arpinum which he considered his second fatherland, where grew the Marian Oak, planted not by the hand of man but by the voice of poetry (1.1). The reader will remember the grave and eloquent discourse in which Cicero sets forth the doctrine that the whole universe is "one commonwealth of which both gods and men are members" (Loeb Library, tr. C. W. Keys, 1.7). That which binds men to the gods, especially to the "supreme god," is reason itself, the most divine attribute "in all heaven and earth" (1.7). And reason, Cicero goes on, implies right reason: "Since right reason is Law, we must believe that men have Law also in common with the gods." Further, "those who share Law must also share Justice; and those who share these are to be regarded as members of the same commonwealth" (1.7). For Cicero the commonwealth is not a cosmological but an ontological reflection of the universe. The universe itself is an order of reason and law and therefore a commonwealth in its own right (1.7). Seeking the roots of law and justice deep within virtue itself (1.8), Cicero asserts that virtue "is nothing else than Nature perfected and developed to its highest point" (1.8). Penetrating further, he lays it down as a first principle that although penalties in fact often do keep men from injustice, that which ought to make them just should be nature itself. He thus attempts to disengage the concept of justice from brute factuality and to root it in the structure of nature (1.14). He comes to grips, so to speak, with positivist and historicist contentions (as we know them) when he affirms that "the most foolish notion of all is the belief that everything is just which is found in the customs or law of nations" (1.15). That is, he separates the concept of justice from its historical incarnations, and holds that "Justice is one; it binds all human society, and is based on one Law, which is right reason applied to command and prohibition. Whoever knows not this Law, whether it has been recorded in writing or not, is without Justice" (1.15).

Let us be quite clear as to what Cicero is doing here: he is defending the naturalness of justice against the historicists and utilitarians and positivists of his own day. According to Cicero, the doctrines that he is attacking coincide in insisting that the sanction of history gives to the law its usefulness; that history has tested the laws and found them good, and good because useful to the preservation of the state. He is even willing to use the argument from utility against the utilitarians, and, by extension, against the historicists: "But if Justice is conformity to written laws and national customs, and if, as the same persons claim, everything is to be tested by the standards of utility, then anyone who thinks it will be profitable to him will, if he is able, disregard and violate the Laws. It follows that Justice does not exist at all, if it does not exist in Nature, and if that form of it which is based on utility can be overthrown by that very utility itself."

As far as Cicero is concerned, we see clearly, the historicists and the pragmatists are one and the same crowd, at least as regards the central issue. If the former maintain that written and national custom gives the law its sanction and imposes upon us the obligation to observe the law, the latter maintain that the very existence of the law, linked with our existence under the law, makes it expedient that we obey the law. The unexpressed premise is obvious: to disobey the law would be useless to us since, willy-nilly, we find ourselves subject to the law. Exposing the fallacy of this argument, Cicero points to the clear and cynical truth that a man can disobey a law not profitable to him if he thinks that disobeying would be useful to him. Were utility itself the very ground of law, it would follow that laws not useful (read: useful to him) could be overthrown by the very principle that establishes them. And Cicero's conclusion is lucidly expressed: "Justice does not exist at all, if it does not exist in Nature" (1.15).

Now, on the surface, this argument against utilitarianism itself does seem to be utilitarian and pragmatic in structure. Justice will go down if justice is based on utility alone. Why not, then, accept the conclusion and let justice go down?

Why *not* accept a political jungle? Cicero apparently considers the answer self-evident, though he never tells us, in so many words, why he does. But however that may be, his apparently utilitarian treatment of the issue indicates sufficiently the ontological springs of his thought. Without justice, "where will there be a place for generosity, or love of country, or loyalty, or the inclination to be of service to others or to show gratitude for favours received? For these virtues originate in our natural inclination to love our fellow-men, and this is the foundation of Justice" (1.15). The key word, of course, is *natural*. The ground of justice is the ultimate character of nature, and a challenge to nature is a challenge to the very structure of reality. The Ciceronian call to virtue, though fundamentally Platonic, is one with the Stoic insistence that virtue is nothing other than nature itself perfected through right reason.[9]

But these same philosophical considerations, on which Cicero bases the natural foundations of justice, catch up also the religious foundations of the state. If justice is not founded in nature, "not merely considerations of men but also rites and pious observances in honour of the gods are done away with." And he hastens to state the reason: "For I think that these ought to be maintained, not through fear, but on account of the close relationship which exists between man and God" (1.15). The reasoning, in other words, harks back to Cicero's opening observations on the grand community of nature, which links man and the gods together in a commonweal as broad as the universe itself. Were justice not one with that nature in which both man and the gods share, then the laws and the customs of society would not join man to the divine in the intimate bond that is suggested by the very word *religion*.

The argument thus advanced is simply a corollary of Cicero's main discourse, but this corollary leads us into the heart of the problem: it is not only that the laws receive their sanction from nature; the religious rites of the state receive their sanction from nature as well. The theoretical issue could not be drawn more clearly: the religious rites, as also the public orthodoxy they enshrine, are sanctioned by the naturalness of justice; justice is necessary for the preservation of the state; whence it follows that the public orthodoxy can be maintained on utilitarian grounds: the law of nature demands the maintenance of the religious rites and observances for the good of the state. Cicero, we perceive, refuses to use the argument from utility to establish the naturalness of justice, but does not hesitate to use it to establish the naturalness of the rites. The philosophical precedence of nature and its law over religious convictions and the observances demanded by them forces us to base the latter on the former.

But why, we might and indeed must ask, are the rites of Rome so necessary to the well-being of the state? Here we reach one of those absolutes in evidence upon which all political philosophy is based. We reach here the meaning of the Roman politeia. The answer is one with the whole Roman tradition: belief in the gods and pious observance of the rites dedicated to them have bred in the Roman people that austerity and rectitude, that *gravitas*,[10] which has made Rome possible and which alone can assure her continued existence. But the Roman forefathers believed in the gods in the sense that they were convinced that the gods really exist, really guide the destiny of the city of Rome. Their belief was not a matter of calculated policy, seeking to instrumentalize a religion for the sake of the greatness or even the continued existence of a state based on justice. Rather, the gods dispense justice and providence to those who tend their rites. It is indeed useful to propitiate the gods; but the belief in their existence, which created the public cult of propitiation, is just that: a belief not a policy. Cicero, in deducing the utility

[41]

of the rites from the harmony of nature, indicates a philosophical sophistication within Roman thought that has moved far beyond the simplicity of belief that marked the attitude of the old Republic.

When Cicero speaks directly to the state in relation to the public orthodoxy, he does not hesitate, then, to give precedence to the political rather than the metaphysical or religious. In "the very beginning," he argues, we must "persuade our citizens that the gods are the lords and rulers of all things"; "what is done, is done by their will and authority" (2.6). The gods are "great benefactors of men" and, make no mistake about it, they "take account of the pious and the impious," watching each individual: the wrongs he does, the intentions and the degree of piety with which he fulfills his religious duties (2.6). If we do persuade the citizens' minds in this sense, they "will not fail to form true and useful opinions"; and let no one be so "foolishly proud" as to suppose that "reason and intellect exist in himself, [but] . . . do not exist in the heavens and the universe" (2.6). This would be tantamount to saying that no reason guides "those things which can hardly be reached by the highest reasoning powers of the human intellect," and that a man can remain a man and "not [be] driven to gratitude by the orderly courses of the stars, the regular alteration of day and night, the gentle progress of the seasons, and the produce of the earth brought forth for our sustenance" (2.6). The truth is that "all things that possess reason stand above those things which are without reason," and that "reason is inherent in nature" (2.6)—so that to say that anything stands above nature is "sacrilege" (2.6). Then the utilitarian note again: "Who will deny that such beliefs are useful when he remembers how often oaths are used to confirm agreements, how important to our wellbeing is the sanctity of treaties, how many persons are deterred from crime by the fear of divine punishment, and how sacred an association of citizens becomes when the immortal gods are made members of it, either as judges or as witnesses" (2.6).

Cicero's reasoning here is more subtle than a cursory reading of the text would suggest. The context is a discussion concerning Plato's contention that laws ought not merely to coerce, but should win some measure of consent on the part of the citizenry (2.6). Cicero attempts to locate the ground of such consent in a belief in the existence of the gods, and to this end asserts the following things: we must persuade the citizenry that the gods are the lords and guardians of all things and that they exercise a benevolent providence over all who propitiate them, because, to repeat, "minds which are imbued with such ideas will not fail to form true and useful opinions." A belief in the existence of the gods, therefore, is good because it is conducive to the formation of true and useful opinions. Cicero then discusses, one by one, the true and useful opinions that grow from such a belief, above all this one: he who piously fulfills his duties to the gods will be moved to consider the very structure of the universe in all its orderliness and thus come to assent to the proposition that reason exists, not alone in man, but in the universe as well. In short, Cicero puts religious piety to work for the sake of philosophy, "true opinions": a religious attitude in a man, itself bred by a pious observance of the rites and by a belief in the existence of the gods, is good because it will move him to meditate carefully upon the reasoned course of the universe. True opinions here serve the common good of the polity and true philosophy serves virtue. Although Cicero formally divides his argument into reasons for the forming of both true and useful opinions, his true opinions are themselves at bottom based on political utility. It is not merely that he argues openly that belief in the gods is useful because it casts a sacred character over all society, which in turn deters evildoers, sanctifies treaties, and guarantees oaths; his previous argument is equally utilitarian: faith breeds the virtue needed to consent to the laws and consent to the laws breeds a sound politeia. And what we want, at least as political philosophers, is a sound polity!

The political expediency of the public orthodoxy, of belief in the gods, is even more nakedly expressed further on in *De legibus*, when Cicero comments on the ancient Twelve Tables and Sacred Laws, those *sacratae leges* which were thought to have been formulated in the earliest days of the Republic and which gave inviolability to the plebeian tribunes (2.6). They read: "No one shall have gods to himself, either new gods or alien gods, unless recognized by the state. Privately they shall worship those gods whose worship they have duly received from their ancestors. In cities they shall have shrines; they shall have groves in the country" (2.8). And Cicero takes up the contention—astonishingly modern it must seem to us—that the divine can be worshipped not merely in temples and in shrines at designated times, but in any old place and at any old time that suits the whim of the worshipper, as witness his reference to the "Persian Magi, in accordance with whose advice Xerxes is said to have burned the temples of Greece on the ground that the Greeks shut up the gods within walls, seeing that this whole universe is their temple and home" (2.10). Cicero's reply is a precious text, not only because it reveals magnificently the piety and reverence of that Roman spirit of which we are all the heirs,[11] but also because it introduces us further into the heart of Roman religion and of Cicero's teaching concerning the public orthodoxy:

> The Greeks and Romans have done a better thing: for it has been our wish, to the end that we may promote piety towards the gods, that they should dwell in the cities with us. For this idea encourages a religious attitude that is useful to States, if there is truth in the

saying of Pythagoras, a most learned man, that piety and religion are most prominent in our minds when we are performing religious rites, and in the saying of Thales, the wisest of the Seven, that men ought to believe that everything they see is filled with the gods, for all would then be purer, just as they feel the power of religion most deeply when they are in temples. (2.11)

The psychological argument is evident: a sense of piety and reverence is more easily invoked in the atmosphere of a shrine, a place set aside for worship and for worship alone, than in the open air. Even the very conviction that the divine is everywhere is better bred in a man who meditates the divine in some predilected spot that bears in upon him the meaning of divinity in an especial manner. The religious argument is evident: Romans and Greeks set aside shrines and groves in order to produce a greater devotion to the gods. But the political argument is also evident and is, once again, evidently utilitarian down to its very wording: "For this idea encourages a religious attitude that is useful to States." (Adfert enim haec opinio religionem utilem civitatibus.)

The text would merely support our earlier conclusions did it not also, as indicated, finger the very meaning of the Roman religious experience and thereby lead us to the center of Cicero's dilemma concerning the politics of the public orthodoxy. "It has been our wish . . . that [the gods] should dwell in our cities with us." A Christian must read this text twice in order to believe what is before his eyes, which he can do only when he understands that what we confront here is the difference between transcendence and immanence. The gods come to dwell in the city—at the wish of Rome! Which is to say: the gods can be commanded by man to dwell where man would have them. To the Christian, who believes in a God who commands and is in no sense commanded, the very notion is shocking; but not so in a society that has not yet broken through to transcendence; there, nothing could seem

[45]

more natural. For the Roman world would have looked and in fact did look upon the Christian claim to a God beyond the cosmos as blasphemy. As Cicero puts it, the contention that "anything stands above universal nature" is "sacrilege" (2.6) and his "sacrilege" is precisely the Christian claim, the claim to know a God who forms no part of the world but who infinitely transcends it. The classical universe was a closed universe and the gods dwelt within it as ultimate principles of order, themselves immanent to the order they established.[12] There is hence a certain equality between gods and men, an equality that emerges at its clearest in Cicero because of the Stoic overtones in his thought: gods and men themselves share a reason more fundamental than either of them. Although man must propitiate the gods, man can in a sense call upon them to dwell in the city in order that he may the better worship them and, we must add, in order that the gods can better assure the common good of the commonwealth (which itself participates in a universal harmony that includes gods and men alike).

We can turn for assistance to Eric Voegelin: Augustine, he notes, could not understand Varro when he argued that "as the painter is prior to the painting, and the architect prior to the building, so are the cities prior to the institutions of the cities" (*City of God* 6.4). And Voegelin comments: "What St. Augustine could not understand was the compactness of Roman experience, the inseparable community of gods and men in the historically concrete *civitas*, the simultaneousness of human and divine institutions of a social order."[13] Cicero, when he argues that the Twelve Tables are in accord with the law of nature, would seem to avoid the blunt and more clearly formulated Varronic conception of the Roman experience. But if we examine Cicero's text we find that nature is made to justify divination, the ritual games, and the institution of soothsayers (2.13); and to the objection that the

House of Augurs was "invented to be of practical use to the State," Cicero can only answer vaguely that "there is no doubt that this art and science of the augurs has by now faded out of existence on account of the passage of time and men's neglect" (2.13–14). Moreover, after discussing the religious functions of the pontiffs in connection with the laws of burial and the consecration of land, Cicero tips his hand, and we see his real interest in the Roman religious observances, in the candid assertion that "we make so much of these matters" in order that "these rites shall be preserved and continuously handed down in families, and, as I said in my Law, that they *must be continued forever (perpetua sint sacra)*" (2.19 italics mine). Here again we are in the presence of the panegyrist of the Roman state. The *civitas* demands the rites for its preservation and grandeur. For this reason, regardless of the religious truth that the rites may or may not contain, they must be perpetuated and observed down to the last flourish of ritual so long as time shall be.

Eric Voegelin points up sharply the significance of the *De natura deorum* in the Ciceronian corpus.[14] The work of a man profoundly affected by Greek philosophy, especially in its Platonic and Stoic forms, the *De natura deorum* remains the exercise of a Roman who cannot really take philosophy seriously, who cannot permit philosophical conclusions concerning the meaning of things as they are and the structure of the soul to alter his inherited commitments to the Roman order. The key figures in the drama are Cotta and Balbus. The latter represents the claims of philosophy—claims that transcend the rites of the city and the institutions of the state; the former, a *pontifex maximus*, stands for the civil sacredness of the old Roman orthodoxy. He insists throughout the discourse on the differing sources of authority in any discussion concerning the gods.

There are, he says, those who rest their claims upon au-

[47]

thority, an authority inherited from the state. He, Cotta, as a pontiff, is bound by his very office to accept the authority of the state concerning the existence and nature of the gods and the rites required for their propitiation. Cotta admits the authority of Balbus ("the authority of reason, of philosophy"), as also, however, the justice of Balbus's plea that he (Cotta) remember that he is a pontiff:

This is no doubt meant that I ought to uphold the beliefs about the immortal gods which have come down to us from our ancestors and the rites and ceremonies and duties of religion. For my part I shall always uphold them and always have done so, and no eloquence of anybody, learned or unlearned, shall ever dislodge me from the belief as to the worship of the immortal gods which I have inherited from our forefathers. But on any questions of religion I am guided by the high pontiffs, Titus Coruncanius, Publius Scipion and Publius Scaevola, not by Zeno or Cleanthus or Chrysippus; and I have Gaius Laelius, who was both an augur and a philosopher, to whose discourse upon religion, in his famous oration, I would rather listen than to any leader of the Stoics. The religion of the Roman people comprises ritual, auspices, and the third additional division consisting of all such prophetic warnings as the intepretations of the Sybil or the soothsayers have derived from portents and prodigies. Well, I have always thought that none of these departments of religion was to be despised, and I have held the conviction that Romulus by his auspices and Numa by his establishment of our ritual laid the foundations of our state, which assuredly could never have been as great as it is had not the fullest measure of divine favour been obtained for it. There, Balbus, is the opinion of a Cotta and of a pontiff; now oblige me by letting me know yours. You are a philosopher, and I ought to receive from you a proof of your religion, whereas I must believe the word of our ancestors even without proof. (3.2–3)

Cotta represents the Cicero, if not always of the Platonic and Stoic meditations, at least the Cicero of *De legibus*, who lays it down as a first principle that the public orthodoxy must be preserved forever in order that Rome remain the Eternal City. Confronting the philosopher Balbus, Cotta is content to say that a "single argument would have sufficed" to convince him of the existence and nature of the gods, namely: "that it has been handed down to us by our ancestors." "But," he goes on, "you despise authority, and fight your battles with the weapon of reason" (3.3–4). On the surface, the issue seems to be quite simple: a Roman priest, representing the full authority of the civic theology of the Fathers of Rome, confronts a representative of that Greek philosophy that would meddle with matters long ago settled and agreed upon, who would meddle in the name of reason, of some authority superior to that of the politeia. Did not the Assembly so stand up to Socrates? And did not the eventual victory of Socrates, a victory achieved beyond his grave, mark the dissolution of the archaic Greek city state in the name of speculation and the impieties that spawn therefrom?

The issue, however, is not simple, though the critic is forced to read twice in order to understand what has really been said. Balbus, representing philosophy and her claims—claims that transcend allegiance to the state and to the public orthodoxy that supports it—takes his stand with the Stoics, throughout the *De natura deorum*, in favour of the whole pantheon of the gods, insisting that our very dreams were sent to us by Jupiter (3.11). Balbus rejects authority as a safe ground for believing in the gods, asserting that their reality can be established by reason itself. Cotta, the Roman priest and avowed representative of the gods, however, advances every argument in the arsenal of the classical world against the existence of the gods. He heaps scorn upon the philosophical arguments marshalled by Balbus. He stoutly maintains that a meditation on the heavens can lead to disbelief as readily as to belief (3.3–4); that awe before nature can lead to atheism (3.5–6); that divination even if it occurs, is beside the point (3.6–7); that the arguments of Zeno would force us to accept such absurdities as that "the world will also be an orator, and even a mathematician, a musician, and in fact an expert in every branch of learning, in fine a philosopher" (3.8–9); that the Stoic contention that a universal reason gave birth to all the arts in which man is skilled would necessitate our holding that the world was itself "a harper and a fluteplayer" (3.8–9). Admitting the irrationality of the pantheon of the gods, Cotta insists that when he reflects "upon the utterance of the Stoics," he "cannot despise the stupidity of the vulgar and the ignorant" (3.15–16). If the Stoic arguments hold that the world is god, "then why do we add a number of other gods as well? And what a crowd of them there are!" Admitting that intelligence is forced to combat superstition, the pontiff renews his attack by damning Stoicism for absorbing every god dreamed by the fevered mind of man within its system, which is itself little more than the personification of allegorized virtue (3.23–24). Moving to the core of the classical religion, Cotta points to the belief in providence and in a reward for the just and a punishment for the wicked: our experience, he maintains, simply fails to show us this hoped for providence because the evil are exalted and the good are often despised and trod upon by the powers of this supposedly rational and benevolent world (3.30–36).

Balbus, shocked by this defense of atheism, appeals to Cotta's character as a pontiff, declaring that the "habit of arguing in support of atheism, whether from conviction or in pretense, is wicked and impious" (3.27). Cotta replies modestly, perhaps coyly, that he only "desires to be refuted," and assures his philosopher opponent that he is "confident" that he can "easily refute" him (3.36–40). "No doubt," sarcastically answers Velleius, the partisan of Cotta, "why, he [Balbus] thinks that even our dreams are sent to us by Jupiter— though dreams themselves are not so unsubstantial as a Stoic disquisition on the nature of the gods" (3.40). The book ends with Cicero's doubtful affirmation that Balbus "approximated more nearly to a semblance of the truth" than Cotta (3.40).

We can marshall Cotta's arguments under five points, which follow one another in logical sequence:

1) He distinguishes between Stoicism, as such, and the authority advanced by Stoicism for the doctrines it maintains: an authority transcending that of society and of the state—that is, the authority of reason. Against this authority for belief in the gods Cotta—as a Roman pontiff—pits the authority of the fathers, of society, of the state. His attack must not, therefore, be read as though it were a philosopher's controversy with another philosopher. Representing as he does the authority of the state, Cotta sets himself squarely against the supposed authority of a reason that pretends to bypass the exigencies and demands of society. Cotta is the Assembly against Socrates.

2) Cotta grants that reason might lead us to belief in, and adherence to, the gods, to the public orthodoxy; however, reason might equally fail to lead us to such belief and adherence. Reason might lead us into impiety and unbelief. A priori, before I begin to philosophize, I confront two possibilities: a confirmation of or a destruction of the public orthodoxy. Philosophy is a risk, and nobody knows where its siren call may lead him.

3) In fact, philosophy might well take a man into atheism (Cotta's whole discourse is an exercise in metaphysics aimed at revealing that very possibility).

4) Should reason lead a man into atheism—and we must remember that Cotta never says that it must lead a man in that direction—belief in the gods will collapse and will bring with it the eventual ruin of the state. Religion is not only eminently useful to the state; it is the very cornerstone of the politeia.

5) The conclusion is inexorable: the authority of the politeia and the public orthodoxy it enshrines must have

precedence over that of reason. Should a man engage in the business of philosophizing about the origins of the universe and the ultimate truth of things, he must not do so seriously but only as though he were playing a game. And his conclusions, should they violate the public beliefs of society, must be set aside like toys.

Up until this point, Cicero speaks through Cotta, the high priest. But we must remember that Cicero is more than Cotta, that Cicero is not only a Roman statesman but a philosopher in his own right, a philosopher deeply grounded in Plato, and by no means the popularizer and rhetorician of Stoic doctrine that some commentators have made him out to be. Underneath the doctrines of Cotta, and forming a dimension of Cicero's thought, there are three Ciceronian positions, already adverted to, that buttress Cotta on philosophical grounds:

1) If the state collapses, justice collapses; and justice is rooted in the very fabric of universal nature. This is the central meaning of *De legibus*, which has as its heart—as we have seen earlier—the demonstration of the naturalness of justice.

2) It follows that reason itself, philosophy, dictates that we give precedence to the authority of society, to the authority of the public orthodoxy over that of private philosophical speculation. Philosophy must doff its cap to the public faith; it must even humble itself before the claims of religion, even to the extent of declaring irrational its own rationality, should that ultimate sacrifice be demanded. There is a fragment from the lost passages of the third book of the *De natura deorum* (3.40) in which Cicero, stating the case for the censor, makes the point in the most naked manner possible: Lactantius, filling in the lost text, writes of it: "Cicero was aware that the objects of man's worship were false. For after saying a number of things tending to subvert religion, he

adds nevertheless that"—and now we are given Cicero's own words—"'these matters ought not to be discussed in public, lest much discussion destroy the established religion of the nation.'" (Non esse illa vulgo disputanda, ne susceptas publice religiones disputatio talis exstinguat).[15]

Cicero was, clearly, confronted with a frightening contradiction between his natural law doctrine and his public worship of the gods—a worship that his own philosophical convictions rejected on theoretical grounds, but that he freely accepted in the name of his Roman citizenship. As a philosopher committed to justice and to the naturalness of justice, as a philosopher aware of the impossibility of maintaining the state (and therefore justice) without a public adherence to a commonly accepted religious orthodoxy, Cicero was forced into what we may fairly call a public lie for the sake of a properly philosophical truth. The Ciceronian position absorbs within itself the insights of positivism and pragmatism, of historicism, and of existentialism concerning the political order; but the Ciceronian position transcends them all in that Cicero was philosopher enough to know that all three positions are theoretically fallacious.

The positivist and pragmatist epistemology, as indicated, reduces truth to empirical factuality and usefulness. We find the doctrine in its most articulate form in John Dewey, who held that the predicate of every judgment is nothing other than a cerebral instrument for the solution of a problem presented by the subject. Predicates belong in subjects, are "true," only when they resolve the problem of the subject, only when they are useful; and Dewey tries to resolve the problem of American society in terms of the highly elaborated predicate, "the democratic society and adjustment thereto." This predicate, when applied in government, in education, and in life, "works." Democracy is the ideal solution to the complexities of the American experience. The predicate "adjustment to a democratic society" (the myth has been expressed in any number of ways) becomes therefore the sole content of the American public orthodoxy, and this orthodoxy is justified exclusively in terms of its utility. John Dewey is an admirable Cotta, a high priest of an orthodoxy, of a public faith. What Dewey and his disciples call "Absolutism" could not be made to work in America, and—asserts Dewey—given the American experience and temperament, ought not to be made to work. It follows that the utility of the democratic process (whether it be expressed mythologically or conceptually is irrelevant in this context) is its own justification to the title of public orthodoxy within twentieth-century America. From this American Maurrasianism have come forth "adjustment to the community," "education for life," "the open society," "the pluralist society," and many similar myths. Nor does it matter here that pragmatists, failing to distinguish between the existential and theoretical meanings of the term, avoid the word *orthodoxy*. Existentially, the orthodoxy they reject is the Western Christian experience as permeated by the classical inheritance. Existentially the term *orthodoxy* attaches in letters and in history to that doctrine; in rejecting that doctrine, positivism and pragmatism indeed reject orthodoxy. But theoretically *orthodoxy* refers to any public doctrine accepted unconditionally by a community, even if the orthodoxy in question is somebody else's heresy; and the emotional reaction of positivists to the word *orthodoxy* is only one aspect of their orthodoxy. From a theoretical point of view the positivist and liberal myth, that is to say, is as much an orthodoxy as any other that ever has existed on this globe: an ultimate frame of reference, a court of doctrine and dogma before which all other doctrines and opinions must present themselves for judgment. The fact that many Christians (Catholics and Protestants alike) in America feel obliged, at least publicly and academically, if not in their hearts, to justify their Christianity in terms of its supposed affinities with democracy and liberal myths indicates, moreover, that positivism and liberalism are well on the road, in certain quarters at least, to establishing their orthodoxy as the public one. The main point, however, is that the positivist insight is englobed within the Ciceronian experience: the utility of the existent (or nascent) orthodoxy justifies its preservation and commands for it the assent of the citizenry. In Cicero's time that orthodoxy was the public Roman cult of the gods. Without that cult, the state would collapse. Therefore its very utility was its laissez passer to the theatre of existence and meaning.

The notion (associated with the name of Dilthey) that man is his history, Cicero rejected when he spoke as a philosopher. But when he spoke as a Roman, when he spoke through the mouth of Cotta the high priest, he spoke good Dilthey. The House of Augurs may not be much good at divination nowadays, but the House of Augurs is the product of history, and history justifies its own products. The City of Rome is given us as a concrete cosmion, incarnating its own meaning in terms of its own historical experience. It stands up against nature as it stands against the forests and the mute skies above: every ultimate source of meaning must be found within the walls of the city itself. The city establishes its institutions, its own gods, insisted Varro; the city calls upon the gods to live within shrines and groves that they may better be seen and thus may better fill the hearts of the people with piety and awe, insisted Cicero. This is but a blunt way of stating the historicist thesis, of identifying meaning with its generation.

The existentialist contention that meaning is one with the brute existent, that theoretical formulation cannot look out towards a possible actualization that transcends the existent in this given moment of time, is due to the existentialist identification of existence and possibility, of actuality and potentiality. If man is nothing other than his own possibility, then possibility cannot look beyond man but is man, in the terrible drama of perpetual crisis. It follows that every theoretical formulation must be justified in terms of man as we find him here and now. There can be no appeal to a possibility beyond the present, itself promising a future and better actuality. All meaning is reducible to what is given because the annoying Aristotelian distinction between the possible and the actual has been rubbed away, thus leaving man a naked existence thrown into the world, an existence identical with its own possibility and therefore not the standard for a politics that transcends the immanence of the historical moment. In the political order the given is the state as we find it, society as we encounter it. Theory must be validated in terms of this given, and politics becomes a justification for a nationalist charisma or a gnostic dream simply because these happen to be the historical given. Thus with one hand Cicero rejects the existentialist thesis, but with the other accepts it. Commenting on *De Republica* (2.3), Voegelin writes, "In the debate about the best political order (*Status civitatis*) . . . Scipio takes his stand against Socrates. Scipio refuses to discuss the best order in the name of the Platonic Socrates; he will not build up a 'fictitious' order before his audience, but will rather give an account of the origins of Rome."[16] What we here find thrown up against a problematic universe is Rome herself: splendid; erect; the City Eternal. Let all political and philosophical meaning square itself with this thing, the *res publica*. The gods have this advantage over their enemies, that they exist as instituted by our fathers. This institutional existence of the gods is the ground of their theoretical reality, and let every theory—says Cicero through Cotta—be squared with the fact that these gods, our own, live with us, and that if we carried the house-

[56]

hold deities from burning Troy, they in turn blessed the enterprise that is Rome.

Cicero, we repeat, truly gathers the positivist, historicist, and existentialist insights into his philosophy. But unlike the proponents of these theories, Cicero—as philosopher—cannot really reduce meaning either to utility, or to history, or to factuality. He is forced, as we have pointed out, to invent two truths, two orders of meaning that cross and clash and that therefore find themselves related one to another: the meaning of theoretical truth, of philosophy, is not that of society; but the former demands that the latter be upheld, no matter how false it may be theoretically. Centuries later Thomas Aquinas, a philosopher who had absorbed the experience of the Christian West, met a similar doctrine, that of Siger de Brabant and the Parisian Averroists, according to which one and the same thing can be true theologically and false philosophically, can be and ought to be believed on faith while rejected by reason, and in his *De unitate intellectu contra Averroistas* pronounced it damnable. (We do not suggest that the Ciceronian and Brabantian positions coincide, but rather that the same theoretical principle is involved in the two cases.)

In order to live such a doctrine, a man needs an heroic cynicism that can face intellectual suicide in the name of the intelligence and the will at the service of society—an attitude that can be maintained only by a few, and by them not for long. Psychologically, man's drive towards unity pushes him to seek a third doctrine, a higher truth, that somehow reconciles the theoretical and existential contradiction. Cicero, writing in an age when ancient Roman patriotism was disintegrating but had not yet disintegrated under the impact of the Greek philosophical breakthrough to the truths of the soul, invented a strategy that soon collapsed in the tolerant theology of the late empire, itself destined to give way soon enough to the Christian empire of Constantine that incarnated a new orthodoxy (what we have since named *orthodoxy*), a faith that could be and was believed by Western society at large.

We have come close to fulfilling the purpose of this essay, the giving of a theoretical predicate to the subject, *public orthodoxy*. The public orthodoxy, let us recall, involves propositions assent to which must be made not on political, but on ontological and religious grounds. It asserts something, let us recall, too, about the structure of things as they are, about man's relation to the divine and about the destiny of the human soul; and assent to that something on purely political grounds is not really assent at all, since—let us emphasize, even at the risk of laboring the point—the assent required is theoretical, ontological. Cicero teaches, let us recall finally, that the public orthodoxy is necessary for the preservation of the state: that although philosophical inquiry into the public orthodoxy might well support it, it also might well destroy it; and that the destruction of the public orthodoxy is the destruction of the state and therefore of justice, itself an imperative of nature. Now, as we confront this circle of meanings and this vicious contradiction we might well conclude that there is no way out. There may, however, be a way in. Should transcendence cross over into immanence, should God speak to man and thus reveal His truth and His will, the public orthodoxy—enshrining that truth and will—would have a guarantee beyond itself, beyond the immanent demands and requirements of society: the will of God. Were this so, man could reverently and intelligently probe the rationality of this orthodoxy, knowing in advance that whatsoever he might discover would conform itself with what has been taught, since what has been taught has as its teacher God himself, whose grace guarantees the faith with which we receive His word. Such a man might well ask himself whether he has an immortal soul, whether justice is more than a word, and whether God exists. These questions would be the *videtur quod non* of the Middle Ages—not a doubt exercised on the origins of a civilized and Christian polity, but a weighing of possible objections to these origins, objections whose resolution man would confidently expect to discover by his own reason because God himself had guaranteed their resolution.

Our conclusion, our predicate, belongs properly to political theory, but to a political theory dependent on a metaphysics open to revelation. Where the public orthodoxy is not guaranteed by transcendence, it is always open to the charge that it is opposed to philosophical truth and is the enemy of man. Conversely, the friend of the soul (a soul well-ordered in accord with the structure of reality as it is) might well find himself the enemy of the state, a state not necessarily completely evil in itself; he might find himself, therefore, the enemy of justice itself. His choice will be awful: the guaranteed well-being of society versus the demands that wisdom may lay upon him, even if these demands mean the end of society as he has known it. Should he choose to philosophize, and should society then silence him or even kill him for his pains, let him know that society is acting in its own self-defense, a self-defense demanded on philosophical grounds. Let him, therefore, rejoice at the moment of his execution that society has fulfilled its duty, a duty that he as philosopher is sworn to uphold in the name of philosophy itself.

But when the public orthodoxy is guaranteed by transcendence, by the word of God, then the truths of the soul and of society, the first principles of the politeia and of metaphysics (that is, the very being of both), are theoretically guaranteed. Beyond this guarantee, which can be had only as a gift and as a blessing, there is no other for any human society born upon this earth.

[3]

THE PROBLEM OF
POLITICAL POWER AND THE
FORCES OF DARKNESS

◄§ Classical political philosophy has been understood historically to be that discipline which studies the finalities of political life in the light of the common good of society and of a
virtuous people. These are not different ends but merely
distinct ways of formulating one unique goal: a virtuous life
lived by men who set the tone for any community acts as a
yeast which leavens the social order into harmony and thus
brings forth a genuine public good. This equivalence covers a
cluster of problems whose resolutions require political wisdom. Nonetheless, any refinement of the identity between
common good and good people would deepen their ultimate
union rather than weaken it. In turn, these issues cannot be
abstracted totally from metaphysical considerations. The political philosophy in question was thought by its authors to be
an introduction to wisdom. Any common good in any political community synthesized with civil virtue reflects and par-
tially enshrines the structure of being. The philosophy of
being is the heart of philosophical wisdom. This common
Western doctrine began with Parmenides; it was continued
by Plato; it culminated in the pagan world with Aristotle; it
was transfigured by Christianity in Aquinas. The ancients
discovered a kind of stability and consistency in reality which
is menaced by its dialectical and existential opposite, nothing, chaos, corruption, death. Pagan antiquity had a number
of ways to symbolize what Christians grasp as the problem of

the Nothing. Just as all goodness lies on the side of being; just as all evil and negations are consequences of nonbeing, so too stability in matters political demands not demonstration but monstration, exploration. The good which is common in politics and the desirability of a life stiffened in virtue are as axiomatic for a decent social order as is the judgment of sinderesis in the moral order and the judgment of being in the metaphysical order. We discover an identity, granting certain refinements, between the triad, Being: Goodness: Virtue. The weakening of any one of the members of this traid weakens the other two.

Certain deductions follow and they pertain to the public orthodoxy. Public orthodoxy, as suggested throughout this entire book, is the constellation of convictions concerning the final meaning of existence as reflected in the political order. The public order knits a body of men into a community, renders conversation possible between its members, sanctions and confers the weight of the sacred to oaths and contracts, and guarantees both rights and duties. The common orthodoxy is a center of intelligibility or meaning which is venerated by the citizenry as incarnating a number of unquestionable truths.

The scandal of history throws up a bewildering number of public orthodoxies and each one of them contradicts all the others. A common faith may enshrine the conviction that political society is an analogue to celestial society as in ancient Egypt; the common faith can solemnly place the sword of the state in the hands of the church as in the Rome of Theodosius; it can divinize politics as in the France of the Revolution or it can divinize race as in the Germany of Hitler; the common faith can invest society with the imperative dictate of the laws of progress as in Communist Russia; it can entertain convictions concerning a presumed parallelism between politics and religion as in Christian democracy; it can honor its lords and protect its vassals as in the knightly code of feudalism; or—to round off the list—the common faith can read politics in terms of the family as does tribalism and paternalism. These instances and hundreds like them are civic religions conformed to publicly by governors and governed alike. Even the so-called pluralist society which admits a large measure of discussion and disagreement about the final things fences its polemicists within a field whose admittedly ample spaces are nonetheless walled by a thicket of affirmations commonly entertained by all. Should one of the debators question these affirmations, he excommunicates himself from the pluralist society.

The collapse of a public orthodoxy always entails the collapse of the society that once entertained it. A loss of faith in itself by any community is *eo ipso* a loss of faith in the future. An orthodoxy, in turn, can disintegrate from within through a failure of nerve, but an orthodoxy can also be simply destroyed by the sword of an outside invader.

Deducible from these initial observations is the truth that any honorable man who desires the best for his country will aspire to conserve and love the convictions which form its public faith. To the earlier triad, Being: Goodness: Virtue, we can add the pair, Common Good: Public Orthodoxy. All five sink or swim together. Any thoughtful man who would do well by his own polity wants its public faith to be a harmonious reflection of the laws of political reality. Nobody wants to be in error! Nonetheless, historical societies have conceived their orthodoxies in a bewildering number of conflicting faiths. Conflicting political convictions reflect conflicting views concerning the meaning of political life and the meaning of being itself. Political philosophy of itself cannot solve these conflicts. Ultimately they pertain to religion and metaphysics and that synthesis of both which is theology. But political philosophy can formulate a paradigm according to which a model society lived in accordance with *the* public orthodoxy in order to draw the consequences for political theory that would flow therefrom. Expressed in another way, the political philosopher can simply assume the existence of society annealed in a public faith assumed to be true, assumed to be conformed to the laws of reality. Under that hypothesis, the philosopher can then draw a number of conclusions. Neither his hypothesis nor his conclusion belong to the existential order, but they can subsequently be used as measures for judgment in the evaluation of existing polities. The procedure suggested here is as old as Plato and Aristotle and Cicero.

In the light of the above the following hypothesis can be formulated: if we grant that reality is knowable and is not sheer nonsense and if we postulate a polity that attuned itself to reality, then we could draw the following consequences. Politics, within the model, would reflect the truth of being; the essence of this hypothetical political order would be harmonized with the laws of being; this harmony, in turn, would constitute a public orthodoxy par excellence. Any imperfect or erroneous orthodoxy—all existing public orthodoxies because man is fallible—would produce a crippled society to the degree of its imperfect understandings of the real. These societies would lack being to the extent of their failure to conform to being. We take it here as evident that any violation of the laws of being fall on the side of nonbeing. In a word: we are operating here within the Augustinian and Thomistic conviction that evil lies on the side of a privation of being.

If the objection be raised that in fact there do exist many not merely imperfect but positively evil political societies and that they flourish despite their flaunting of the laws of being, the objection can only be conceded. But the issue does not bear on the mere factual existence of a polity but on

[63]

its well-being, its *bene esse*. We are talking about a theoretical best. A theoretical best regime would be wedded to the laws of reality, to truth.

The argument, as indicated, is based on the supposition that there does exist a relation between public order and the total order of reality. The supposition is buttressed by a reductio ad absurdum of its denial. A total skepticism concerning the capacity of man's reason to know the truth demands the acceptance of any old public orthodoxy at hand provided merely that it work, provided that it knit together a people into political unity. But, as indicated earlier in our study of Cicero, this posture cannot be lived for any length of time by men who are conscious that they publicly incarnate a lie. Charles Maurras and the philosophy of his *Action Française* attempted to do precisely that very thing but Maurras himself died believing in the Catholic faith that he had defended all of his life on the grounds of political expediency. Either the lie saps the will of the men who use it, or they finally decide that the lie is not a lie after all but the truth. A functioning orthodoxy must be believed in and not simply imposed by self-conscious deceivers. The fire goes out of Fourth-of-July speeches when the politician no longer believes in the country. If the public orthodoxy is to be efficacious then it must be believed as doctrine anterior to its being embraced pragmatically because it works. Ultimately the absolute skeptic is gored on the horns of a dilemma: either he abandons his skepticism or he opens himself to any and every public doctrine that might be at hand, be it Nazism or Communism or the public worship of Moloch. Without some common convictions there simply exists no society at all, not even a chess club to say nothing of an empire or a kingdom or a republic. Political community implies the prior metaphysical affirmation that man can know and can know with apodictic certitude at least something about the order of being and its laws.

But life is not as simple as theory. There is a fine old nightclub song that begins as follows: "Born to lose, I live my life in vain." And it is precisely in the context of the absurdity fingered by the song where the shoe of public orthodoxy pinches the foot of politics. Is every regime born to lose? A priori, a solid orthodoxy ought to guarantee a sound polity because the latter would be harmonized with the laws of reality. A posteriori, every historical society has believed that its own orthodoxy was sound. But search as long as we will, we can find no political order which has lasted perpetually. As Hegel pointed out, at first glance history looks like a pile of ruins. The problem for the political philosopher who is not disheartened by this vast junk yard of empires and republics, can be defined as follows: there simply must be some third factor that interposes itself between the laws of being and an honorable society, some *tertium quid* capable of frustrating the highest dedication of the human spirit to the common good. There must exist something irrational in the marrow of existence which breaks the heart of decent men and brings to nought the heroism of the best of regimes. The classical world found this zone of absurdity in the presence of contingency, luck, fortune. Cosmic caprice can destroy the pious and lift up the impious. The divinity called destiny can turn to dust the glittering hopes of any polity despite the fact that the polity in question reposes on the conviction that a private and corporate life constructed according to the laws of reality ought to be crowned by success. Was it good luck for the Allies that kept four German Panzer divisions off the Normandy beaches because Hitler had left orders that they should not be moved unless he expressly said so and he was in a drugged sleep on D-Day? Was it bad luck for Colonel

[65]

Von Stauffenberg that somebody inadvertently kicked the briefcase with its time bomb those few inches away from Hitler and thus saved his life and possibly altered the history of Germany for all time? Was the last Christian king of Jerusalem, Baldwin IV, simply a born loser because he was cut down in death by leprosy when a very young man and this despite the fact that he was the best of his line and could have saved the kingdom had he lived? Examples could be multiplied indefinitely and all of them add up to history itself. Is all history like the ulcer that threw Napoleon off form at Waterloo?

History here gives political philosophy its most difficult problem. Expressed in the most trenchant manner possible, let us say that a sound politics ought to be harmonized with the structure of the real; that the public orthodoxy ought to guarantee therefore the continued well-being of the community. Men and things come and go but being endures. The harmony of a public religion or orthodoxy with the laws of being is—or ought to be and here is the rub—its patent letter to practice the act of existing. But if the gods and goddesses of destiny and of fortune can frustrate the best of orthodoxies and thus bring down the finest of political orders, the thoughtful man must pose the following question: why does not such a polity possess the necessary power and vigor to continue to exist? Paul Tillich insisted that being is one with its proper power to be, its intrinsic capacity to conquer the powers of darkness and of evil.[1] The teaching is as old as Seneca. If virtue, in its proper and primitive sense, is precisely a power to be, a *conatus* which binds men in a community to seek a public good; if virtue is consubstantial with the good life; if the above conclusions be substantially true, we can deduce that a society thus based intellectually on a series of truths that palpate ethically in the life of its citizenry,

[66]

morally possesses the power necessary to grow and perdure in being.

There is nothing contradictory in the theoretical model traced thus far. Historically, however, no such model ever existed. *Virtue has not been the power which conquered the world*. Classical political theory was thus forced to inject in the veins of reality a dosage of unintelligibility and capriciousness which were vested with the mythological robes of the goddesses of destiny and fortune. Given a polity firmly based on an understanding of the structure of reality; given a compact nucleus of virtuous men heading this society and governing it according to good laws; given the ideal of virtue as a public goal acting as a leaven throughout the whole community making good men better, indifferent men good, and bad men ashamed; given the material power and technology necessary to maintain itself against all internal and external enemies; given a level of civilization incomparably superior to that of the rest of the world; given all these things, and then add to them failure, not a failure unforseen but one first adumbrated as the most remote and trivial of possibilities and later sensed as a real menace which ought to be rejected as absurd and even indecent, and then add again a failure now accepted as an inevitable fatality whose sentence of death can only be postponed by rearguard tactics; given all this, and we are given a polity confronted crudely and inexorably with the powers of unintelligibility, the vacant stare of the absurd.

This model society would attribute its historical failure to bad luck, to misfortune. Born to lose, this society can do nothing to snatch victory from defeat. But the urge to live lives on even in the face of inevitable death. The polity we have sketched will want to discover some defence against the irrationality of its own doom. Reason and virtue have failed because they cannot contend with what lies below itself. Sur-

[67]

rounded and menaced by the forces of madness and darkness, of barbarism, the polity in question will try to come to terms with its own enemies as does a sane man who attempts to talk to a psychotic. The more reasonable is the approach, the more inevitable the failure. A sane man can try to astutely infiltrate the mind of his demented opponent but the more successful his own effort, the less rational will be his response. He will be won over! The true power of the powers of darkness resides in a refusal to play the game according to the laws of reality. Abstracting from the ultimate unintelligibility of human evil, of sin, and limiting the discussion to the senselessness of the absurd, we must conclude that the more the model society sketched enters into battle with the irrational, the less virtuous will it be. To mix socially—and even war is a form of social behaviour—with the powers of nonsense is to fall into irrationality and usually into superstition. Superstition is the weapon that men who have never known or who have despaired of reason wield against the occult powers of meaninglessness. Any defence other than superstition at the point of immanent collapse seems beside the point. Reason and virtue have not done the trick. Just as every man dies, no matter how generous and splendid his own life, so too our society will then have to reconcile itself to its own eventual extinction even while it fights a rearguard battle against forces which are beyond the power of reason and virtue. Although all men die, the death of a political community as well as of humanity as such does not seem to be inscribed in the laws of reality. By a curious irony, the model polity which once tried to root its beliefs in the intelligible must now buy a few more minutes of life at the price of trafficking in the obscurity of the irrational.

This paradigm has a certain value for political theory even as a mere abstract scheme illustrative of certain typical problems centering around reason and its counterpart. But the paradigm has a deeper significance because it has been molded by the writer out of the flesh of history. As the reader may have divined, we have been describing the political experience of Rome from its transformation into empire by Augustus, to its high level of civilization under the Antonines, to the outrage committed against it by the barbarians. Rome was virtue and civilization and reason. The Germanic barbarians were their antithesis, at least to the Roman mind. And barbarism won and Rome lost and in losing virtue ceased to be supreme in the affairs of men.

A number of figures and movements in the last centuries of the Roman experience typify this crisis in political conscience. They are of theoretical as well as historical interest. The empire revealed a number of structures that function within the tension sketched between public orthodoxy and historical vicissitude. The reader is free to draw his own parallels between the fall of Rome and the historical moment within which the United States finds itself today. The parallels are uncomfortably close because this nation modelled itself in many ways on the example of Rome. It takes little erudition to be struck by the likeness between Rome battling and losing against the barbarians and America battling and losing against the Communist hordes of Asia and Eastern Europe. Political philosophy is not politics, but a politics not illuminated by philosophy is likely to drift with the changing winds of contemporary pressures and fashions.

Roman politics in the first century of the Christian epoch were already heavily influenced by the image of reality entertained by the Greek philosophical tradition. According to the shrewd observation of the Spanish philosopher, Xavier Zubiri, Greek philosophy was marked by its discovery of nature.[2] Greek thought seized upon something which endures and perseveres through time and which resists the perpetual decadence menacing all things. The Greeks called this something *physis*, a kind of permanence which conquers chaos and decay. Things and men walk rapidly down the road of being towards shadows of death which finally cover them all leaving as a lonely memory nothing but the inscrutability and bitterness of the mystery of an existence that apparently ends in nothing at all. Nonetheless, species or types outlive the fate of the individuals that incarnate them. Things passing through space and time are not stable in themselves but they do reveal a nucleus of principles which permits man to define and understand what they are and what they have been and what their progeny will be. A nature which exists only in individuals can be understood by the intelligence in an abstractive act which yields to the mind whatever there might be of eternity in the flow of time. To abstract is universally human. Without abstraction nobody could function for five minutes, if for that long, after getting out of bed in the morning. To recognize that a shoelace is a shoelace and a door is a door is an abstractive act liberating us from the tyranny of individual existents. Abstraction is the mark of humanity. But the Greeks articulated this universal dimension of human life. Basing itself upon the stability and self-consistency of nature, science emerged for the classical mind as a possibility promising a truly human life for civilized man, for man liberated from the cruelties and caprices of the Hobbesian jungle. The discovery of nature followed the discovery of human nature by Greek thought. This human nature became fully human only in civilization, in the Mediterranean basin. This flowering of civic life was made possible because Greek thought looked upon virtue, human virtue—human power and fullness—as the very spine of an ordered life.

According to Professor Wild in his interpretation of Plato, "virtue is the fitting direction of . . . tendencies towards their natural fulfillment. Virtue is a general ontological category, for each thing has its own peculiar law of sound development. In man, however, it takes on a new importance because of his rational power of guiding incipient action into alternative channels."[3] Virtue, hence, was the highest realization of nature and, although natural law theory was the work of Cicero and the Stoics, man's nature is fulfilled only in the law of virtue according to both Plato and Aristotle.

The tactic of abstraction, as indicated, permitted the Greeks to identify *scientia (episteme)* with an understanding of the permanent and unchanging. The power of scientific abstraction (Aristotle) was engraved within the structure of human knowing. The use of this power was deliberately and freely exercised by Hellenic civilization for the sake of liberating man from the chaos and darkness and flux of the Cave. To the degree to which movement and every class of change can be reduced to laws of being expressed in terms of potency and act, they fall within the scope of science and are considered to be intelligible thanks to their finality, the dynamic thrust of all things towards their plentitude, their *virtus*. Aristotle's noetic represented a considerable advance beyond that of Plato's which contented itself with intuiting a mosaic of static forms of essences, most probably a trick of vision in which images were confused for ideas. The Platonic reduction of science to the frozen immobility of mathematics was a constant temptation for the Greek mind but a temptation resisted with considerable success by Aristotle. According to the Stagirite, science was a network of intellectual habits which cognized that which happens necessarily and for the most part. An authentic science of dynamic nature was guaranteed epistemologically by the universal tendency towards a determined end which formed part of every nature as its promise of future virtue. Virtue, thus, was power, the power of being to be all that it could. Virtue was thought to be a superabounding of being, a fullness of perfection and goodness (*Metaphysics* 4.1027a–1028).

Although this framework was not altered substantially when applied to man, the framework did take on nuances of a highly complex order. A free but evil human act frustrates virtue. Plato reduced human evil to ignorance but Aristotle located it squarely in free will. Both of them developed a sophisticated typology of evil that deduced conclusions from this or that kind of psychological malaise. From this point of view evil does possess some intelligibility because each virtue is counterpointed by its corresponding vice. These vices are open to clinical inspection by philosophers who are aware of the virtues they contradict. To the classical mind, evil was intelligible. We need only recall Plato's brilliant tracing of the progressive degradation from philosopher-king to tyrant in the *Republic*. Tragedy was also intelligible because the Greeks could finger the flaw in the hero. Political failure was understandable when it followed the pattern of man's propensity towards evil. The cyclical theory of governments— good ones yielding to bad ones and bad ones then being overthrown by good polities—was built into this principle.

What remained essentially unintelligible and existentially inexplicable was the totally fortuitous event. Such events seemed to lack causation of any kind and could not be handled by the intelligence. The chance event scandalized the ancient mind and troubled a mentality that could not locate this cosmic caprice within an otherwise well-ordered nature. In its last agony, the classical world simply caved in before unintelligibility and embraced superstition and secret mystery religions as ultimate weapons with which to battle the forces of irrational darkness.[4] Just as an honorable and efficient man of business suddenly ruined in commerce for no fault of his own might take to gambling to recover his fortune, so did the late Roman Empire abandon virtue and give itself over to the Chaldean astrologies and mystery cults that promised success to their devotees.

Aristotle's analysis of the chance event was the very best that the pagan mind achieved in attempting to make some sense out of the senseless, the absurd. The chance event, according to Aristotle, heightens rather than destroys the principle of meaningful finality. If everything happened by chance, we could not know it anyhow! The fortuitious is known as a kind of figure standing out of the background of ordered and seasonable continuity. Good and bad luck are recognizable because final causality exists everywhere in nature and thus is a standard by which man judges whatever falls outside its scope.

Aristotle insisted that chance erupts into the order of being when two determined causal sequences, independent of one another, cross. The well-known example of the merchant from Athens and the thief from Thebes who meet at a crossroad illustrates his thesis. A series of motives reaching back into a remote past move the merchant to be at the cross in the road at a given moment. A parallel causal sequence governs the thief's arrival at the same time. They just bump into one another! The robbery presents no philosophical difficulty: thieves steal from merchants. The rationally inexplicable is the meeting of the two men. Nothing in either causal series *causes* the event. The event is simply fortuitous, sent—according to poetry and popular mythology—by the gods of fate and fortune; sent—according to Aristotle—by nothing at all. The absurd is this very nothing. A chance event does not destroy the teleology of nature but heightens it by opposition. Both philosophy and politics tried to dominate these forces of the Nothing and even to exorcize them but at the end both politics and philosophy had to confess their failure to master history. History is not all that philosophical and reasonable after all!

Cochrane in his monumental and stunningly brilliant work, *Christianity and Classical Culture*, distilled the essence of the effort made by the pagan West to conquer the problem of destiny. Using Cochrane's terminology, we might say that the theoretical center of the enigma looked to the meaning of power, especially political power. The Roman mind "resolved the concept of power into a subjective and an objective factor; the former, character (art and industry); the latter, circumstance (fate and fortune or the gods); tracing its genesis to a combination or, at least, a coincidence of the two" (p. 157). The Romans sought a balance eluding both extremes. A total objectivity of power would have relegated the political order to an irrational destiny which hurtled nations and peoples towards a predestined success or failure without any consideration of the intrinsic merits of the societies in question. Total objectivity would have predestined to ruin or oblivion societies that in truth did incarnate decencies which were essentially human. But a total subjectivity of power would have turned the political order into an elaborate mechanism that churned out honest citizens whose very moral decency and technological industriousness would have permitted them to look ahead serenely into a distant and even indefinite future, assured that their polity would last forever. Subjectivity, as used by Cochrane, means simply that if you play fair you are going to win. It is evident, as the author pointed out in the context of his own study, that a resolution of the problem of power in both directions is impossible within the ontological data given to pagan antiquity: that is, a closed world order composed of nature and its laws counterpointed to an irrational and unpredictable cluster of forces of darkness.

[74]

Both tendencies were at work in the Roman mind at the end of the republican period. There were those objectivists who separated the meaning of destiny from the Roman experience and plainly identified it with irrationality and inevitable ruin, thus patterning political life on the ruin of death which accompanies every individual life. For such men society could do nothing other than confront political and even cosmic disaster with stoic serenity. Civilization and the decencies it incarnates are not absolved from the sordid cruelty and absurdity that lie at the very heart of existence. But Vergilian patriotism drowned out pessimism. Vergil's articulation of the Roman experience and the problem of fortune incarnated the very best in Roman optimism. Interiorizing the powers of chance and fortune, Vergil made of them vehicles through which Rome would achieve its destiny. Provided that Rome cooperate with the gods and make its own work the work of its own gods; provided that Rome return to the virtue of its fathers and the piety of times past; provided that Rome propitiate the gods and thus conserve all things as they had been given her in a past golden age, the future of Rome as the Eternal City and Rome's mission as the civilizing agent of the divine powers of this world—the only world—would be assured. Vergilianism was the first ambitious attempt to discover an immanent meaning to the march of time through history. The destiny of Rome, reposing upon a given people and concentrated as a divine energy in the virtue of this best of all peoples, moved towards a universal goal: the extension of civilization to every corner of the earth that was blessed with the grace of citizenship in the repository of civilization: the Roman Empire.

Rome thus tried to close the gap between the individual and the universal, between history and theory, fortune and virtue, existence and essence. The long centuries of decadence that followed on the Antonines, "the five good em-

perors," forced the Romans to admit that its gauntlet, thrown
in the face of fortune, had been a splendid gesture of defiance but had not been a solution to the basic problem of
political power. The Roman response was the manly and viril
reaction of men who do not whimper, but it was no theoretical solution to the inscrutability of human existence. Rome
hoped. But the hope of Rome involved an implicit theory,
and the theory is not without interest in the context of this
study.

The theoretician was not a Roman but a Greek. This was
typical. Polybius has been accused of being a Greek in the
service of Romans. Polybius, so goes the complaint, was
toadying to his masters, telling them what they wanted to
hear, kissing the hand that fed him. But a man can be servile
and nonetheless be perfectly serious about his theory concerning his masters. A more likely explanation than one
based on Polybius's servility would have this Greek learning
from his Roman lords in order to instruct his fellow Greek
countrymen on the evils of their ways in matters political.
The *polis*, after all, had collapsed under the marching feet of
the Roman legions. In any event, the meditations on Rome
by Polybius were heavily influenced by his Greek philosophical heritage. Plato had faced the problem of the decadence of
political societies in *The Statesman* by way of his theory concerning the typology of six forms of government. The inevitable decay of the three good (relatively good, hence relatively
bad, for that incorrigible pessimist, Plato) gives way to three
contrary forms which are absolutely bad. A healthy reaction
against these evil regimes swings the pendulum back to good
regimes and the cycle merrily (or sadly) wheels back upon
itself through all eternity, a political ferris wheel whose ups
and downs are one with nature itself. The Romans, reasoned
Polybius, locked the three good forms into a simultaneous
synthesis and thus replaced the moving ferris wheel with a

frozen triangle. The proper characteristics of all three good regimes were locked into the vise of a mixed constitution in the Roman Republic and thus they avoided the dangers which the cyclical theory attempted to explain.[5]

The tendency of monarchy to degenerate into tyranny was repressed by the senate and the *comitium*. The propensity of aristocracy towards oligarchy was counterbalanced by consuls and tribunes. The perennial movement of democracy downwards towards demagoguery was checked by both the aristocracy of the senate and the monarchy of the consuls. This interconnection of the instruments of a sensitive politics crafted by the prudence and wisdom of Roman virtue was sufficient by itself to guarantee continuity in political life. Polybius warned, however, that the balanced constitution would work only provided Rome remained relatively small. In this reservation Polybius differed from Vergil, but his prediction of survival based on the mixed constitution when linked with Vergilian destiny are the highest reaches of the Roman will to conquer political irrationality. Vergilian and Augustan *pietas* and *gravitas*[6] chiseled Rome into a community of city and gods. Thus the new empire then aborning was presumed to be guaranteed perpetual existence thanks to its pact with the divine. But the new Rome involved a spreading out in space of the *res publica* under the banner of its own first soldier, the emperor. Civilization and Rome and eternity were one reality.

The theoretical defect of this Roman politics can be detected easily. Human nature is free and a nature placed totally at the service of a marriage between Rome and fortune can scarcely merit the title of freedom. In subjecting Rome to a "manifest destiny" written in historical time, Rome was submitting itself to a law beyond law, to a nature beyond nature. The teaching was embraced by enthusiastic patriots who gloried in the free citizenship of Rome, the corporate

[77]

order and the vigorous civic life found therein. But the latent contradiction was still there, nonetheless, rotting the heart of the doctrine and giving the lie to its putative reality. Personal responsibility and liberty of choice ill fit a theory that gives over political life to an hypostacized Fortune bearing a curious resemblance to gnostic slogans familiar to us today: for example, "the march of progress," "the inevitable victory of liberty," "the future of democracy," etc. These slogans, less heard today in the United States than earlier in the century, bespeak the cruelty of reality towards the idealistic. Inevitable victory for liberty is precisely what liberty can never hope for. Liberty is always a risk. If the power of virtue is inevitable, virtue cannot be free and if virtue cannot be free then virtue ceases to be virtue. The inevitable cannot be chosen in any manly way. In stubbornly denying any respect for contingency and irrationality, the victory of Roman virtue and classical civilization was not guaranteed but rather weakened. If I know that I might fail, I just might possibly succeed because I will try harder knowing that the odds are against me; if I know that I will not fail, if I already have the victory sewed up before the battle, then fail I most likely will. Any overconfident boxer knows that truth after he has been knocked out by his underdog opponent. By a kind of dialectical irony the doctrine of inevitable victory produces its contrary: inevitable failure. In a word: if we have to win, then we do not need to battle in order to emerge victorious in life and if we do not battle then it is probable that we will lose.

Eric Voegelin distinguishes between a long-run gnosticism, "right-wing gnosticism," and a short-term gnosticism, "left-wing gnosticism."[7] Rightest gnosticism locates inevitable victory in a distant future and thus demands of its followers decisions in the present which do not run the risk of being demoralized by short-term setbacks. Rightest gnosticism insists on immediate sanity in the service of a distant insanity.

Leftist gnosticism promises an immediate paradise and, if this paradise cannot be gained by one brief rush against the barricades of the going establishment, leftist gnosticism collapses by the side of the road and awaits the immanent Second Coming. Marxism in its later phases is clearly a right-wing gnosticism which puts off to the future its ultimate goals even while it demands of its followers a crude realism in the here and now. The Youth Rebellion in the United States which burned itself out by 1970 was clearly an instance of a left-wing gnosticism.

All gnostic movements are Christian heresies that preach salvation on earth rather than with God beyond history. Pagan Rome was not in the existential situation of a modern gnostic movement. Rome could not appeal to the "rightest" ruse in order to explain away the exigencies of reality: for example, the loss of a province to the barbarians or a setback by the Persians. Rome was not waiting for the end of history because Rome already incarnated, so Rome thought, the end of history, its fullness and perfection: the present existence of Rome and the full sap of history's meaning were one and the same thing. The virtue of Rome, therefore, was constantly exercised *as a defence, as a conservative strategy*, even when Rome's legions were on the march pushing back the frontiers still farther into the German forests of the north. A doctrine of inevitable victory that claims that the victory has already happened cannot throw dust in the eyes of its faithful by telling them that although hard times are upon us, the millenium will come sooner or later. When victory is already a fact and not a promise, victory can only be defended; it cannot be won. Nothing fails so much as success. The city has already been built and its very extension is a function of the defence. The *limits* of the Empire come from the Latin *limes:* trench! The Romans conquered territories in the middle and late imperial periods only in order to defend themselves the better against the barbarians. From this followed the Roman tactic of abandoning distant posts of defence when the barbarian tide temporarily melted away. To give up territory became a national disgrace only much later in history when politics became confused with spatial boundaries and maps. In Roman times abandoned territory was often a sign that Rome had thrown back another menace to its internal civic life.

The slow turn from inevitable victory to inevitable defeat was blurred for a very long time. The blurring was the work of Rome's flirtation with irrationality. One of these expressions was the traffic in the irrational and in the superstitious which promised victory to Roman civilization at the price of abandoning the personal responsibility for virtue that Rome promised to incarnate. Cochrane refers specifically to the solar determinism of the Chaldeans or *mathematici*.[8] The classical text, reproduced by Cochrane, is from Censorius:

"The Chaldaeans," he says, "hold first and foremost that what happens to us in life is determined by the planets in conjunction with the fixed stars. It is the varied and complicated course of these bodies which governs the human race; but their own motion and arrangement are frequently modified by the sun; and, while the rising and setting of different constellations serve to affect us with their distinctive 'temperature', this occurs through the power of the sun. Accordingly, it is the sun to whom we ultimately owe the spirit which controls us, since he moves the actual stars by which we are moved and, therefore, has the greatest influence over our existence and destiny." (*De die natali* 8)

The same hocus-pocus that hoodwinks millions of modern Westerners who want to handle life as though it were a dice game at Las Vegas ready to be won by the man with a system had already insinuated its oriental face into the heart of Rome. The same nonsense that tricked Hitler and Himmler and that tricks millions of rich and poor today who rush to read the astrology reports before they organize the day's work is already there, for the first time, eating the heart out of the West's commitment to virtue and liberty. Identifying the course of human events with an unalterable and inevitable destiny written in the stars, the astrologers appealed to a Rome whose confidence in resisting the powers of darkness was already undermined. Astrology was a sword at the throat of classical political theory and practice. Aristotelian philosophy, to its eternal credit, had always insisted that human action is essentially the free practice of virtue, of making prudent decisions which always entails risks in the concrete because individuality escapes the scope of pure science and opens the door to good and bad fortune. Many Roman emperors thundered against the astrologers and then meekly consulted them in secret. The perennial temptation to surrender to the stars was to erupt again, much later, in the Renaissance when scientists such as Copernicus and Kepler had to draw up astrological charts for their princely masters. But there was one Roman emperor, whose reign spanned the last attempt to knit together the eastern and western borders of the old Empire, who refused to be fooled by the powers of absurdity. Justinian the Great warned his subjects against those fakes who moved their fingers under lamps and cast mysterious shadows on the wall: watch their fingers before you fall for their shadows! Such was the sage advice of Emperor Justinian.[9]

Vergilian manifest destiny was defective theoretically but it was nonetheless a goal that could be embraced by a viril and soldierly man. It is a shame that Vergil's vision had to degenerate into oriental occultism because the West could not pull off its desired victory by liberty and virtue, the West's very own instruments of action. But neither the old Roman dream nor the eastern surrogates in the fag-end days of empire could appeal to the nascent Christian religion. The new faith was to proffer a totally new solution to the mystery of

political absurdity that englobed both immanence and transcendence. The symbol was the cross of Christ but this symbol was not symbol but reality.

Constantine, the first Christian emperor, was the first
theologian of the politics of transcendence. The emperor
embraced Christianity as the only reasonable solution to the
problem of power. The Christian God had the power and the
pagan gods had lost whatever power they had. Constantine, a
good politician, thought that Christ was the answer to the
mystery of contingency because Christ would guarantee to
His imperial servant the preservation of Roman civilization.

A thing and not a text is the most primitive document of
this politics of transcendence. Unless the meaning of this
Thing be firmly engraved in the minds of students of politics
it is doubtful that the problem under discussion can be clarified with theoretical precision. I refer to the *labarum*, the
awesome standard which Constantine raised over his legions
after his victory in Italy had been promised him in that famed
apparition of a luminous cross in the dark sky. That night the
emperor pondered the battle awaiting him on the morrow
and, apparently, he paced meditatively up and down before
his tent. Constantine saw or claimed that he saw written
under that luminous and heavenly cross the famous words:
In hoc signo vinces, in this sign thou shalt conquer. The
Emperor Constantine might have been duped. This is an
historical possibility that cannot be verified or denied after so
many centuries. Personally I doubt it. He certainly was not
lying because he was looking for an honest-to-god God who
would back his arms. The old gods seemed to have failed
both him and Rome. Constantine was apparently unin-
terested in the zodiac: that road had already led nowhere. A
new politics was being born.

Eusebius has described for us this remarkable banner
under which Constantine's legions were to march from vic-

tory to victory: it "was a long lance covered all over in gold
. . . at the very top was fixed a garland of gold and precious
jewels, and woven therein was the symbol of the Name of the
Saviour, two letters indicating the name of Christ by the
initials of the word X intertwined with the letter P in the
center." [10] This monograph which Constantine made his own
to the dismay of pagan Rome was already known to all the
persecuted Christians of the Empire. Tourists can see it
today in the catacombs of Rome. From the cross bar suspended from the lance "there was draped a purple banner
with the Greek inscription, EN TOYTΩ NIKA which was trans-
lated, as indicated, by the Latin: In hoc signo vinces. The
banner, square shaped, was covered completely with rich
embroideries and encrusted with precious stones. Eusebius,
our best contemporary witness, adds that the labarum was
woven throughout with gold thread and astonished everyone
who saw it in all its blazing beauty and rich splendour. The
cross bar from whence hung the banner was adorned with
medals bearing the images of the emperor and his sons. Fifty
soldiers of the imperial guard, elected for their bravery and
virtue, carried the labarum. Shortly thereafter every legion
went into battle with less elaborate copies of the original
banner.

The labarum was thus recommended to the Roman legions initially because Constantine simply seemed invincible
once he had put his soldiers under the protection of the
cross. Modern investigation has rejected the rationalist and
pedantic opinion of the nineteenth century that Constantine's conversion to Christianity was superstitious, but modern scholars are also largely agreed that the understanding of
Christianity by the first Christian emperor was defective although not formally heretical. [11] The Constantinian notion
of his new faith, expressed for the first time in the Edict of
Milan in 313, repeated and explained in subsequent imperial

[83]

decrees and letters, revealed the Emperor's conviction that "Christ is the God of Power who brings victory to His servants who have not been exterminated despite the most rigorous of persecutions" (*Vita Constantini*). Constantine is clearly speaking about the persecutions conducted by his predecessor, Diocletian.

Fortunately for political philosophy, Constantinianism found its own appropriate political theorists: the court bishop Eusebius of Cesarea and the "Christian Cicero," Lactantius. Eusebius, although widely recognized as a primary source for the history of the first Christian epoch, has fallen upon a very bad press in our days. Cochrane defines him as "the first of the ecclesiastical politicians who shall pass through the European scene."[12] Altaner says that Eusebius "ought to be considered as the prototype of cowardly bishops."[13] Granting that the progeny has been long, we can at least wonder whether these severe judgments do not apply better to Eusebius's namesake of Nicomedia. In any event, nobody can deny that Eusebius was a heretic by orthodox Christian standards. He held a Christological posture intermediate between the Creed of Nicea and Arianism.[14] Excommunicated by the Sinod of Antioch in 325 because he rejected the Nicene Creed, Eusebius later signed the formula but "with a certain mental reservation," according to Altaner. The court theologican subsequently worked vigorously and victoriously towards Constantinian unity in religion through the empire. Years later we find him deeply involved in intriguing against the great Athanasius.

Eusebius's panegyric of the life of Constantine was supposed to repeat the emperor's very words but they probably reflect Eusebius's thought as much as Constantine's. The document is precious for political theory. The *Vita Constantini* is one long hymn of praise to the emperor, "the friend of Almighty God" and "the new Moses." The teaching found in

[84]

this book would have made the Church of God a fifth wheel in the hub of the Roman chariot. In more pedantic terms, Eusebius in chapter 2 reduces transcendence to immanence:

It seems that those who fulfill faithfully the laws of God and reject the breaking of His commandments are rewarded with abundant blessings and are given a solid hope as well as ample power to carry out their goals. On the contrary, the impious have suffered the consequences of annealing themselves in their mistaken election. . . . I personally was the agent whose services God considered adequate for the fulfillment of His Will. In accord with this help of the divine power I have overthrown and destroyed every class of evil under whatever form it prevailed with the hope that the human race, illuminated thanks to my mediation as the instrument that I am, would turn anew to observe properly the holy laws of God and, at the same time, our most blessed faith.

Eusebius begins his program modestly enough, at least in its epistemology. He affirms (through the mouth of Constantine or Constantine through his own) that "it seems" that those who obey the laws of God are rewarded with "abundant blessings." The "abundant blessings" could be interpreted in a purely spiritual sense. In that case they would have an acceptable theological meaning: for example, Eusebius could have simply wanted to say that God rewards those who obey his laws without determining whether this reward is found here in this life or in the next. The following words, however, constrain us to read the passage in an immanentist sense. The goods are not only blessings but the man who has them is "possessed of a solid hope" that he can "carry out his goals" and thus God gives him "ample power" to crown his business with success.

In all, Eusebius makes three propositions: (1) faithful compliance to the laws of God is rewarded with blessings of some kind; (2) good men can entertain a reasonable hope of bringing to a successful resolution their goals; and (3) they are given the power of God to do so. The blessings of God to man are linked, therefore, with goals and aspirations which man places before himself. And are these goals and aspirations the fulfilling of the holy laws of God or are they temporal ambitions whose fulfillment men can expect confidently because they have obeyed the laws of God? The text is somewhat obscure but the character of the thought of Eusebius as well as the rhetoric move us to conclude that he has blurred the distinction between these situations deliberately. If Eusebius had held that our purely temporal aspirations, prescinding from how noble they might be in themselves, have a guarantee to be realized fully because we practice our religion faithfully, he would have denied the scandal which Christianity and only Christianity has confronted with serenity: good men are not always rewarded in this life and the evil all too often occupy the finest and most privileged posts of power and affluence in this world. The parable of Lazarus and the rich man would be drained of meaning. The transcendent mission of Christianity would be disfigured if not totally lost had Eusebius so secularized the religion of Christ. Eusebius would then have totally identified fulfillment of the law of God with human aspirations; he would have erased the distinction between the supernatural and the natural, between what belongs to God and what belongs to Caesar. We must not forget that it is Constantine, the Roman emperor, who speaks to us here through the pen of Eusebius. If the projects of the first Christian Augustus are identified with the will of God and the faithful compliance to His laws, then politics are converted into religion and religion into politics—and both of them into technology, into an efficient instrument for achieving planned effects. Eusebius is wearing two hats here and both of them are somewhat awry on his head: on the one hand, he represents ecclesiastically a hitherto despised religion that gloried in offering witness to the cross and that senses eternity as a flower more glowing

[86]

than all the glories of this earth; on the other hand, he represents an emperor who has stumbled into a religion foreign to his education and to his culture, but this emperor wants to cast the new wine in the old bottles he is accustomed to using; the emperor must advance the new faith to his subjects because it has worked well, not because it is true. The obscuring of the differences between religion and politics flow from the way in which Eusebius focuses the problem. What is at stake is the transcendence of Christianity, as well as the distinction between two orders of being. Granting that politics is not religion, Eusebius so binds them together intimately that God is almost obliged to concede political success to whoever accepts his word and does his will. Religion is thus turned into a game with certain prizes here below for the man or nation disposed to follow the rules. This college football concept of Christianity is so crude that it is difficult to attribute it to so obviously intelligent a man as Eusebius. You win only by losing, by dying to the world: this is Christianity. Eusebius had to know this because he stands in a world soaked in the blood of the martyrs. If you were a Christian you did not win under Diocletian: you got killed and tortured to boot. Your only consolation was your own God: He got the same treatment.

We might accuse Eusebius the theologian of a kind of political Pelagianism. Constantine, through the pen of Eusebius, prides himself in being "the agent whose services God considered adequate for the fulfillment of His will." But Constantine's boasting is a pyrrhic victory according to orthodox Christianity's understanding of the providence of God. Ex post facto, any Christian whose acts were bent to the good and away from evil can say that he is an instrument of God because it is the will of God that good be done and evil avoided. The very abstractness of the proposition removes it from the presumption of private revelation or personal "pipelines" to the Lord. But if a man's acts, although well intentioned and virtuous, produced more harm than good in his life, that Christian man ought to stand by his guns and maintain that even in misfortune he did the will of God. This proposition also manifests the innocent abstractness of a conclusion drawn from a general doctrine. The conclusion, abstractly and even coldly entertained by the nonpretentious Christian, can be symbolized dramatically by the figure of Job: the good man, dispossessed of his possessions, makes no sense within Constantinian theological politics which rewards good service here below with rewards here below. Constantinianism emerges as a curious blending of Pelagianism and popular (not theoretical) puritanism: the Lord will fill my barns if I do his work.

Repeating our overarching thesis, a public orthodoxy in harmony with reality would have worked effectively, in classical theory, had the factors of unintelligibility and absurdity not been thrown as monkey wrenches into the well-oiled machinery of an order of existence presumed to be governed by virtue. We have noted that classical philosophy considered virtue to be a kind of powerhouse in being, the completed perfection of any given reality or nature. This power in man, insufficient to conquer the tragedy and the evil which pululate through the world, was now simply transferred by Eusebius to God. Under Constantinianism, God and his will give the crown of success to the just emperor and the honorable social order. In this first version of "social" Christianity, virtue lacks the power to guarantee its own success in the world but virtue is now converted into a condition for God's benevolence. Hoping to overcome contingency and chance, the theological politics of Constantine placed its hopes in Christian orthodoxy and ultimately in the Athanasian formula of Nicea. (Constantine himself was somewhat bewildered by all the theological fuss.) But this very formula of

Nicea affirms that God is "the Creator of all things visible and invisible." Therefore, God—the deduction is ineluctible—is also the creator of the famed Roman virtue and excellence. This vaunted virtue is not an article for trade which can be negotiated with God. Man cannot sell his own virtue to its owner, God. We are not dealing with some bauble up for sale to the Divine. This thinking is as bad as thinking that a man can be sold his own property. God, bypassing the entire natural order, is really the cause of both dimensions of the real, *virtue as well as chance*. An acceptance of Christianity based on a God who simply blesses our battles and smiles on our enterprises is not any acceptance of Christianity at all. Constantinianism, on this point, is a negation of the scandal of the cross of Christ. In any event, the cruelty of history destroyed the naive pretensions of the thesis. The barbarians kept pouring in until the streets of Rome were choked with weeds. By the fifth century everybody knew that the game was up. Christ could not be married to the Goddess of Victory.

But Eusebius was not the only man who thought that the marriage could be pulled off successfully. L. Celicius Firmanius Lactantius was not called the Christian Cicero merely because he modelled his prose on the master of Roman oratory. Lactantius merits the title because his thought paralleled in a remarkable fashion that of the Roman statesman and philosopher. With Cicero, Lactantius believed in the objective existence of a moral law; with Cicero, Lactantius thought that the reign of justice was the principle object of the state; with Cicero, Lactantius hoped for an age in which the crude roughness of barbarism would be softened by the civilizing mission of Rome; with Cicero, Lactantius marked out the virtue of the Roman citizenry as both an end and a foundation of civil society. Nonetheless, Lactantius was more than a baptized Cicero preaching a Christianized version of the old Roman mores. In Lactantius a thread of fresh thought weaves itself through the old and by then hackneyed themes of *Romanitas*. This thought was a new methodology but it was a methodology which was not to come into its own until Saint Augustine. Nonetheless, certain approaches exploited by Augustine were not as original as we tend to think. They were prefigured by Lactantius.

The method (proper respect for the integrity of the English language precludes my using the pedantic neologism, "hermeneutics") might be called an "epistemological Christianity." Lactantius is a man about the business of reflecting on the consequences of faith for the critical intelligence. Lactantius kept reason and faith distinct, but he proposed to his age, a still heavily pagan age, the following paradox. Classical paganism had not known how to solve a number of typical issues because it depended on a reason not illuminated by the faith of Christ. Reason illumined by faith does not only continue to be reason but such a reason achieves, for the first time in the history of philosophy, the fullness of its own essence. Classical thought was vitiated at its roots because its separation of reason and faith, its hostility to the new faith, led it necessarily into a philosophy which leaned towards a false or imperfect religion and away from the true religion of Christ.

Here in Lactantius is the origin of the *credo ut intelligam* of Augustine and Anselm. Here, in this Roman Christian, is an adumbration of the Thomistic insistence that a reason divorced from faith can theoretically discover many truths necessary for salvation but that in practice reason sinks below its own potential if it is not bathed in the waters of faith. Lactantius's genius is such that he seems to adumbrate the entire tradition of a specifically Christian philosophy. Without entering fully into the theme, it is nonetheless instructive to note that Lactantius does not simply wave a banner. He does not merely draw an abstract sketch of a Christian philosophy. He worked it out in great detail. A philosophy inspired by faith can, insisted Lactantius, demonstrate the inefficacy of pagan justice which is divorced from human affection and the deeper sources of love. The justice of the philosophers cannot existentially move men. It follows that a society based on pagan justice would simply not be just. Classical justice gives to each man his due but this proposition makes sense only if all men are brothers of the same Heavenly Father. Justice to my neighbor is materially inconceivable unless I love him as a brother and I can only love him if I am bound to him by the same creative Power that made both of us. Civil society, therefore, in making justice its end must understand justice as a virtue inspired by Christian charity.[15] Justice can only be grounded on something deeper than merely human virtue. In turn, the natural law can prevail if it is seen as an expression of divine law. The natural law in pagan Rome has not worked, Cicero to the contrary. Lactantius further considered that the famous *pietas* was defective because not based on a love for God. A society which does not recognize that its citizens have been loved by God because created by him lacks a sufficient motive to seek justice and to procure the commonweal. Lactantius did not alter the machinery of the old classical politics; he simply added the oil of Christian love because a machine needs lubrication if it is to run at all. Roman and Greek virtues enter the Christian order complete and entire but completely and entirely changed.

Addressing himself to the origins of civil society, Lactantius attacked both classical materialism and classical legalism. The materialistic reduction of everything human to physical necessity is unintelligible. The physical necessities of men, pressing as they are, cannot constitute an order whose internal principles are spiritual. Although Lactantius did not cite

Plato in this regard, his reasoning parallels that of Socrates in *The Republic* (2), who reluctantly grants to Glaucon that the simple *polis* based on the necessities of life does not satisfy all of man's needs. Legalism thought society to be the consequence of a primitive pact, Hobbes before Hobbes. Lactantius shrewdly destroys that theory by pointing out that legalism presumes that the human elements which are found in any polity were originally scattered. But we never encounter this scattering in experience; it is a gratuitous assumption. It sounds as though Lactantius had read Kant, who emphasized the priority of synthesis over any analytic differentiation or scattering. Finally, the family is the germ of the social order and familial structures are natural and not judicial.

Lactantius literally has something for everybody. Traditionalists can easily warm to his earlier conclusions. Liberals and Christian progressivists will be pleased to find him telling them things they like to hear: the state must see to it that Christians can practice freely their faith and the state is not permitted to impose Christianity or any other religion on its peoples because the acceptance of religion is private and must not be public. Lactantius would have frowned on Charlemagne when he baptized all those Saxons en masse. Christian and other gnostics will be pleased to note that the gradual spread of the faith will produce a slow weakening of positive law. To the extent to which the love of Christ takes root in society the need for positive law will decrease. Such laws will not be abrogated. They will remain on the statutes as parchments without life because the police power of the state will be less and less required. The "law of the love of Christ" presumably will give men the wisdom needed to solve all litigation! Lactantius avoids this embarrassing situation in a part of his theory which sounds curiously like a civilized

[92]

version of latter-day Jesus-freakery. In any event, the state will not disappear totally because vice and ignorance can never be dominated completely. Lactantius is thus a conservative and a liberal, a gnostic and a traditionalist, even a Christian radical, by turns. He surprises us still further by subsequently sounding like Martin Luther: the political order is a consequence of original sin. The reader has before him seminal solutions to a host of political problems whose elucidation was to occupy the attention of thinkers and even civilizations through a millenium and a half of meditation on the meaning of political existence within a Christian context.

The most crucial point Lactantius makes for the subject under discussion here is his insistence that "the love and piety of Christ" will resolve automatically the problem of political power. We can turn towards a future full of millenarian possibilities if we turn to Christ. In effect, he traces a direct relation between the supernaturalization of natural virtues in charity and the ultimate victory of political power. This is his orthodoxy. Not surprisingly, Lactantius dedicated his *Instituta* to the protector of his mature years, Constantine the Great. The martial *labarum* of the imperial Christian soldier now melts into the sweetness of the love of Christ. Both, after all, promise victory here below.

The Christian Cicero, certainly more than a baptized Cicero, nonetheless missed many of the implications of his own baptism. Some evidence leads us to think that his understanding of Christianity was even less satisfactory than that of Eusebius. It is well known that Lactantius did not distinguish the Holy Ghost from the Son of God. His comprehension of evil is Manichean and his gnosticism is evident from the teachings sketched above.[16] He believed that the universe had existed 5,800 years and only 200 more remained until the reign of Antichrist. (This numbers game, however, was quite common in early Christianity and seems to still disturb certain enthusiasts.) Christ would then come and rule another thousand years which would be followed by the Final Judgment and the definitive separation of Heaven and Hell. A man cannot help wondering where they had been all that time! The reign of Antichrist will be brief because the Christian utopia which preceded it will have so humanized and civilized the entire world that the devil will be overthrown with ease as humanity swiftly returns to civility and grace. The Apocalypse is an embarrassment to the Christian Cicero.

The paradox of Christianity simply passed him by. The cross had no permanently historical meaning for Lactantius. The cross is to be embraced but gotten rid of on this side of time. The power of evil—positive and Manichean but still puny for Lactantius—can be thrown back by muscular Christian virtue. Christianity is a technical solution to a technical problem. Unintelligibility, chance, the absurdity of sin, tragedy, the scandal of evil crowned and goodness scorned, the constant pressure of disorder and the ever tumescent indecency of failure, are existential factors which Christianity and its cross explain but do not explain away. Lactantius was united to Eusebius and hence to the entire classical tradition when he affirmed that human virtue ought to carry all before it and thus assure a permanent and peaceful existence for people living in a Christian polity. Both Eusebius and Lactantius knew that virtue was a creature of God. No Christian who takes creation seriously could argue to the contrary. The Christian Cicero did have a deeper insight into the meaning and limits of virtue than had his pagan fathers. Lactantius understood the importance of love for justice. He stole Augustine's thunder on this one—but, after all, he lived before Augustine. Lactantius sketched, inside the limits of

[94]

his possibilities, the relations between Christian faith and a Christian political theory. Nonetheless, Lactantius did not settle the problem of chance or unintelligibility in politics. He was not an Augustine—but then again, few men are.

The solution to the problem of power within the context of Christian politics was the work of Augustine of Hippo. His reasoning on the business is concentrated within the famous chapters 21–26 of Book 5 of *The City of God*. From these pages Charlemagne learned the proper role he had to play as a Christian emperor of Rome restored. Augustine plants the problem of power within a sensibility and intelligence annealed totally in a fully Christian vision of the real. The bishop of Hippo at first simply contents himself with reporting the classical ideal of virtue as the end of man (chapter 20). He then grounds this ideal in a personal relation between God and man and thus bypasses the immediate exigencies of the commonweal. The personal-divine and personal-human relation transcends the artificiality and only thinly masked materialism of classicism in which "Prudence leads nowhere, Justice distributes nothing, Temperance moderates nothing, except to the end that men may be pleased and vainglory served."[22] St. Augustine tells us here that virtue spelled with a capital goes nowhere: capitalized *Excellence*, without a goal, is a Rube Goldberg machine, going round and round and going nowhere at all. Augustine here totally transcends the Platonism that crippled his Christian genius. Nor can the philosophers defend themselves by saying that they seek the praise of no man because this judgment means that they seek their own praise: they "seem to themselves wise, and please themselves. . . . For their virtue—if, indeed, it is virtue at all—is only in another way subject to human praise; for he who seeks to please himself seeks still to please man." But the Christian "with true piety towards God, whom he loves, believes, and hopes in, fixes his attention more on those things in which he displeases himself, than on those things, if there are any, which please himself" (5.20).

Virtue guarantees neither failure nor success, in personal life nor in political life. These are gifts of the Divine Will and fall absolutely within his power: "We do not attribute the power of giving kingdoms and empires to any save to the true God, who gives happiness in the kingdom of heaven to the pious alone, but gives kingly power on the earth to the pious and to the impious, as it may please Him, whose good pleasure is always just" (5.20).

When a man accepts the concept of a Providence which cuts across the conventional opposition between natural intelligiblity or meaning, virtue, and the senselessness of chaos and chance and evil rewarded, a philosophy of history is possible which ex post facto can see the hand of God working through virtuous men but which can believe as well that this divine hand is also working through the powers of darkness because these powers, which would annihilate God if they could, are nonetheless moved—by unknown ways—towards a final design sketched by God for history. Evil, after all (the discovery was Augustine's), is a fissure in being, a lack, nothing positive, hence a wound in being which is under the government of God. The God of Augustine is the Lord of history. An analogy has been drawn in this connection from a chess game: even though the play seems to be going against the pawns and knights of the Lord, they know in faith that they will win the game. The analogy limps, of course, because this victory is beyond the confines of the chessboard of the world.

Augustine is not satisfied that we deduce these conclusions from his text; he hammers them home for us: "He who gave power to Marius gave it also to Caius Caesar; He who gave it to Augustus gave it also to Nero; He also gave it to the cruel

Domitian; and, finally, to avoid the necessity of going over all of them, He who gave it to the Christian Constantine gave it to the apostate Julian, which gifted man was deceived by a sacrilegious and destestable curiosity" (5.21).

Augustine, in a splendid instance of his grisly good humor, dwells gleefully on the efforts of Julian the Apostate, that rather priggish second-rate intellectual who thought himself to be the reincarnation of the old Roman values plus Greek wisdom, to achieve the success of Roman arms by way of an appeal to the occult forces of nature:

And it was because he was addicted through curiosity to vain oracles, that, confident of victory, he burned the ships which were laden with the provisions necessary for his army, and therefore, engaging with hot zeal in rashly audacious enterprises, he was soon slain, as the just consequences of his recklessness, and left his army unprovisioned in an enemy's country, and in such a predicament that it never could have escaped, save by altering the boundaries of the Roman empire, in violation of that omen of the god Terminus of which I spoke . . . for the god Terminus yielded to necessity, though he had not yielded to Jupiter. Manifestly these things are ruled and governed by the one God according as He pleases; and if His motives are hid, are they therefore unjust? (5.21)

The pure classicism of virtue against barbarism was not up to pulling off the trick of victory. The putative heir to philosophical wisdom put his hopes in his traffic with the powers of superstitious nonsense by listening to "vain oracles." They caused the man to burn his ships and provisions behind him. Augustine is delighted: do these frauds expect us Christians to sell our inheritance for the sake of a bankrupt virtue or, even worse, for the sake of the oracles?

Augustine insisted constantly that ultimate political meaning rests solely in the will of God. In this way the Christian Doctor can walk both sides of the street. The Catholic emperor whose dominions enjoy prosperity, whose enemies have been routed, whose sons have multiplied, can thank

God for these gifts given him. But the Christian emperor who does his duty to God and the state and who sees all his projects collapse before his eyes, can take consolation in the truth that in some inscrutible manner he too has fulfilled God's will and has participated in the mystery of the cross and will receive his reward in the next life. Even the absurd wraps in itself an obscure meaning read only in heaven. Sometimes looking back on disaster, we can trace dimly an intervention woven in the thread of history, a will which is not capricious but wise with a wisdom surpassing the limits of human comprehension: "For neither do we say that certain Christian emperors were therefore happy because they ruled a long time, or, dying a peaceful death, left their sons to succeed them in the empire, or subdued the enemies of the republic, or were able both to guard against and to suppress the attempt of hostile citizens rising against them. These and other gifts or comforts of this sorrowful life even certain worshippers of demons have merited to receive, who do not belong to the kingdom of God to which these belong" (5.24).

Augustine is not the partisan of religious neutrality by the state that Lactantius seemed to have been. The Christian rulers ought "to make their power the handmaid of His majesty by using it for the greatest possible extension of His worship" (5.24). Quite evidently, Augustine would not warm the hearts of the latitudinarians of our day. But it is also evident that Augustine did not advance Christianity as a solution for any concrete political problem. Christianity can act politically as a kind of final meaning within historical existence. It does so for reasons advanced in this study. Possibly Constantine's unfolding of the *labarum* won him victory for his arms. What Christian can deny to God his favorites, especially if they be his friends? A man or a nation or a society can go into battle under the banner of Christ. Augustine admits that God decided to bless Rome because Constantine turned towards Him, but Augustine warns against any emperor (read: any political leader or order) from converting to Christianity in order to receive the same recompense. God granted Constantine the honor of founding a city which was to be the eastern companion of imperial Rome, a "daughter of Rome herself." God gave Constantine a long rule as unrivalled emperor who possessed the power needed to sustain and defend the Roman world. But, warned the African bishop, "lest any emperor should become a Christian in order to merit the happiness of Constantine, when every one should be a Christian for the sake of eternal life, God took away Jovian far sooner than Julian, and permitted that Gratian should be slain by the sword of a tyrannt" (5.25). Granting that Augustine may have interpreted the thoughts of God as though the Divinity were a theologian, his doctrine is nonetheless admirable for the skill with which he distinguishes issues blurred by the classical tradition.

Nowhere is his teaching better revealed than in the well-known chapter 25 of Book 5 concerning the faith and piety of the emperor Theodosius. These pages were to become the model of the "Mirror of the Christian Prince" literature of the Middle Ages. In ending his panegyric of the good emperor Theodosius, Augustine—as though he feared that his overarching message would be lost—returned anew to the theme of eternal bliss being the reward for honorable political service. God is the giver of this gift and he gives it only to those who are sincerely just. All other blessings and privileges of this life he gives indistinctly to both good and evil. Among these blessings our author lists light, air, the earth, water, fruits, the soul of man, his body and his senses and his mind and life. And among these blessings there is to be counted as well the possession of an empire which is ruled always by Him in accordance with his providential government (5.25).

Augustine's resolution of the problem of power is theological but the theology implies a psychology, a metaphysics, and a philosophy of history.

Augustinian psychology accuses the older classical political theory of holding to a human philosophy which lacked sufficient subtlety in its elaboration of the primacy of virtue within the commonweal. Classical virtue lacks sufficient motivation to act practically on its own. Man is free with the liberty needed to reject or accept his own perfection. Unless a man be given a motive for being prudent, generous, chaste, honorable, and just he will make no effort to be so or he will make only a half-hearted effort. To make a clarion call to fulfill your nature ethically through virtue is like asking a man to die on the battlefield for the third law of thermodynamics. An appeal to an abstraction just will not work and Augustine knew it would not. Plato tried to pump some motive into the moral life by appealing to its beauty, but he soon dropped the effort when he realized that there are many beautiful things and acts which are not particularly moral at all. Aristotle appealed to generosity but Augustine quickly pointed out that Aristotle's generosity is defective on two grounds: it cannot be preached to the mass of men and to the minority it simply promotes pride and insufferable self-sufficiency, priggery, both fiercely condemned by Christianity. According to Augustine virtue becomes a concrete historical possibility when the call to virtue is converted into something personal and not civic, when I desire my own perfection because God desires it and I love God. The love of God is the forge in which pagan virtue is tempered and thus transformed into an effective political instrument. Did not the same Saint Augustine taunt the pagans on their own grounds? We Christians are braver than you are and hence make better soldiers than you do and we are more honest and hence better tax collectors! Don't talk to us about virtue!

Augustinian metaphysics involves a rejection of the pre-

sumed absolute status of nature and hence implies a rejection of nature's enemy as absolute: that is, chance and
fortune. Thomas Aquinas's exposition of the issue is possibly
superior technically to Augustine's but it adds nothing essentially new. Aristotle, the reader will recall, based the problem
of chance within its unique status of being the only uncaused
kind of event in the universe, an intersection of two intelligible causal series having nothing essentially in common with
one another. Aquinas did not reject this Aristotelian teaching concerning the unintelligibility of the fortuitous. For
Thomas chance continues to be an event without any cause
in the order of finite causality. The immanent absurdity of
chance is not negated by Aquinas nor is it explained away as
it is in the solar religion of the Chaldeans or in Marxism
today. Not produced by a series of finite causes, the chance
event nonetheless has a transcendent cause, God. The Lord
is the cause of the two or more causal series that intersect and
is hence the cause of their intersection. God is the sole cause
of the chance event, be it good or bad luck. Fortune, unintelligible within the context of this world, is known to be intelligible when situated in a context in which the entire order of
finite causation depends on an intelligence and will which
form no part of this order but which makes the order itself
exist. In a word: I know that chance is intelligible but I do not
know the intelligibility. All Christian reconciliation to the
absurd depends on the truth of that proposition.

If a political order fails due to bad luck, despite the virtue
that it incarnates, this failure has been decreed by the will of
God for motives known only to Himself. A polity quickened
by this sense of the transcendent mystery of divine providence can only unfold its banners under the shadow of the
cross, a scandal whose ultimate meaning is hidden in the
heart of the Triune God. No political philosopher is constrained to believe in the truth of Christianity, but every po-

litical philosopher who has done his thinking after the advent of the Christian thing is obliged to take account of the Christian response to absurdity. To the inquiring mind even of a civilized skeptic, the Christian response—be it true or not—makes it possible for men to live within the inscrutable.

Augustinian philosophy of history sees history as moving towards Apocalypse and the end of time but this movement, linear and not cyclical as for the pagans, is guided by the finger of God and that finger is hidden even as it takes the pulse of a history beating in harmony with its own unknown will. Let the good man, we must say, whose will is conformed to his Lord's will take consolation even in defeat and ill fortune because his ill-fated destiny has also contributed, in ways unknown to him, to God's mysterious government of all things in being. He works through crooked paths, but they all lead to ultimate felicity for the man who surrenders himself to His will. If he was born to lose, so too was his God.

A fundamental principle of Thomistic political philosophy states the following: particular goods are to be sought by particulars and common goods or commonweals by those to whose care they have been given. The principle, couched here in an old-fashioned scholastic jargon, can be illustrated easily by a few homely examples. We might consider the case of a French professor in a university whose enthusiasm for his subject and whose brilliant teaching have swept half the student body into majoring in French. Now let us consider the situation of the president of that university who is well aware that it would be a disaster if half his students majored in one subject, thus upsetting the intellectual ecology of his school. What are the respective duties of these two men, the professor and the president? According to the Thomistic principle at play, the president ought to prevent such a large influx of students into one tiny department but the professor—says the principle—should go on teaching with all the verve that marked his work in the past. The commonweal of the school as a whole pertains to the president: his business. The particular good of the French classes belongs to the professor: his business. Should the professor take on his shoulders the role of the president, then his own teaching will suffer: he will teach less well and with less enthusiasm because he is now taking into account his superior's obligations. Those obligations are not his: he ought to try to beat the president and the president ought to see to it that he is not beaten! Consider, now, the case (it is classical within the context of Christendom) of a woman who pleads for the liberty of her husband, a condemned thief, before a judge. His duty consists in keeping the man in jail but her duty consists in trying to spring him into freedom because his family needs him. Should she assume the judicial robes of the state, she takes on a responsibility not her own; she thus shirks her particular responsibility to her family. According to the principle at play, the commonweal cannot be achieved unless particular goods are sought by particulars.

This principle, hammered home with brilliance by the late Professor Yves Simon in his classes at the University of Notre Dame when the writer had the privilege of studying under him, ought to be evident to any observant spectator of political history: any overly politicized society collapses because nobody does his own work; everybody is too busy trying to settle affairs of state and the polity degenerates into a debating society at best or into a mob at worst. Nobody goes about his own business of being a corporal or a sergeant because everybody wants to be the captain. A final example, also famous, ought to suffice to make the principle clear. My father is dying tonight and I am trying to keep him alive. An angel appears and tells me that it is God's will that my father die tomorrow. What should I do? According to the principle in question, I should go on trying to keep my father alive. If

God wants him dead, that is God's business but God Himself has given me the duty of attending to my ill father. Unless God abrogates that responsibility through his angel, then God wills me to try to accomplish what he wills me to accomplish even though what He wills me to accomplish will be swept into a providence that wills that I lose: my father dies despite my efforts.

God governs the common good of the entire universe. Any given political order is charged with the particular good of its own society, a society falling under the jurisdiction and authority of a regime presumed to be legitimate. If the achievement of this good (the reasoning is my own and I attribute it neither to my old teacher Yves Simon nor to the tradition within which both of us have philosophized) demands the destruction of civilization, then political theory ought to draw the conclusion that such a destruction would be the will of God because he has willed that this society stick by its guns and do its duty. God wills that regimes do their duty: the rest he reserves to himself. If governments took to themselves the common good of the globe itself, they would be easy targets for any international pirate who would then know that he could get his way simply by threatening an atomic holocaust. Political terrorism in the world today is predicated on the assumption that any political order can be blackmailed because the consequences of refusing to pay the tab are greater than the risk taken by refusing to surrender. The situation is frightening because the electric technology of our age permits just such a situation to arise at any moment. A psychopath captaining a Polaris submarine could cow a continent into submission if that continent let him get away with it on the grounds that surrender to insanity is better than chancing the destruction of civilization and blowing us all back to the Stone Age. But sound political morality demands that this chance must be taken in these circumstances. I cannot assume into myself the entire burden of historical consequences and possibilities; I must act morally and as a man in the here and now in which God has placed me—cost whatever it might cost! Any other attitude is totally destructive of both corporate and personal morality.

The issue is theoretically important; it is also practically important today for politics and statesmanship. The late Roman Empire, as pointed out, confronting chaos and barbarism, tried to commerce with the forces of the irrational, with the psychotic, in order to buy a little more of the precious metal of existence. Rome failed because existence cannot be bought at such a price. Today the Western World, the shrunken husk of what was once Christendom, wracked from within by doubts and betrayals, is faced with an incomparably more formidable enemy than old Germanic barbarism. A new orthodoxy which threatens to make itself the public doctrine argues today—in government; in the academy; in the organs of international politics; even through the spokesmen for world religions—that the West must traffic with this Monstrous Leviathan, International Communism. The West must do so, so goes the argument, for the sake of peace and survival. But the survival of decency cannot be bought by emptying its own treasury of the money that has made decency to be decency. God does not ask the West to consider the problem of survival as some ultimate end: after all, all life and death are in his hands. God asks the West to do its duty, come what might. This conclusion belongs to the common public orthodoxy of civilization. Life is not to be bought by dishonor. The Roman world had an understandable excuse for dialoguing with the unintelligibility of the powers of darkness. The Romans were confronted with an authentic scandal because it seemed that virtue could not conquer and thus assure the Roman Empire of survival. But we know something different. The ultimate triumph of goodness and, therefore, of the political order, simply is not known as something guaranteed here below. Definitive triumph belongs to a power on the other side of the order of being and is open only to the man and polity whose wisdom has been wrapped within a wisdom which conquers the things of this world.

This principle must be understood with all the delicacy involved in political speculation and action. The principle does not urge us to abandon astuteness when we treat with the enemies of civilization, be they the Turks before Vienna in the sixteenth century or the Russians in Berlin and Angola and Cuba in the twentieth. The principle does not insist that we hurl all our troops and all our resources into the breach in a desperate cavalry charge against barbarism, although the principle does not discount this possibility. The principle does not goad us into a politics of international suicide. The principle does not countermand and negate the subtlety and even the deviousness demanded in the actual practice of the arts of diplomacy. It rather commends all of these things and presses them upon us in the name of political prudence. But the principle does insist that these arts be seen for what they are, techniques in the service of something deeper than themselves: the preservation and the enhancement of civilization and therefore the ultimate destruction of civilization's enemies. Should the arts of diplomacy convert themselves into a general foreign policy whose very end is the preservation and perpetuation of political evil, then politics would have renounced its own proper finality, a common good shared by those of us who have thus far escaped falling under the heel of slavery.

Western foreign policy here and abroad has thus entered in these declining years of the twentieth century into an implicit pact with the enemy just as many Roman emperors in the centuries of decay, despairing of ultimate victory over barbarism, threw themselves in the arms of oriental superstitions in the hope of saving some shadow of civility from the surrounding doom.

Political irrationality is always symbolized in terms which appeal to the imagination and thus soothe the outrages suffered by reason. In late Roman times, the irrational was often symbolized by the stars. Let the stars save us because we cannot save ourselves! There are over thirty million Americans today who have turned to astrology and other occult and eastern conundrums in search of the same security against the risks of life as the age is shaken to its foundations. In our times this escape from the absurdities lurking in history often takes form under the cloak of gnostic dreaming about a total elimination of poverty from the face of the earth. An eerie unreality seduces by its myths of historical determinism. This principled insanity has confused us now for thirty years by turning means into ends and by proposing in the United Nations and elsewhere anticolonialism and antiimperialism and democracy and similar nostrums as though they were in truth ends worthy of rational consideration. More recently, neoisolationism has told us to go home in a world without roofs or walls. The West has seized upon this rosary beaded by the hands of a bankrupt secularism because the West has lost the courage to face up to the only political end which can really interest any decent man in the last quarter of the century: the business of beating Communism or getting beaten at the try.

A heresy as old as ancient Rome pullulates through our world. This heresy urges on us a politics of surrender, in part or in whole, before our enemies. These heretics believe that an atomic conflict is inevitable unless we perpetually yield at every point where we are challenged. The Cuban missile crisis in the Kennedy years proved that they can yield and yield dramatically when their bluff is called. But even there

[107]

we won only by promising to never interfere again in internal Cuban affairs: in a word—we lost and Cuba lost with us. World conflict, say these men who yield on principle, would carry with it the destruction of our civilization and that of our enemies. Because these conditions would render human life intolerable, reducing mankind to a pitiful remnant of burnt-out cave men grubbing for a living on the crust of a ravaged planet, we men of the West must give up our hopes of re-conquest, not only in Eastern Europe but everywhere. We abandon reconquest as a goal although we all know that Communism will never give up total victory as its goal.

This teaching urges itself upon us in a dozen ways: it insists that we always retire, whether it be in Hungary in the mid-century or in Vietnam yesterday; it demands that we concede to them, whether it be in Cambodia or in Portugal or in Angola. These gospellers of despair dismantle our intelligence networks; they hamper the executive at every turn. Embarrassed by sporadic victories against the enemy as in Spain or Chile, the teaching can always demonstrate that such and such a retreat is demanded by world opinion and counseled by moderation. They urge upon us, with success, that we bail our opponents out of economic and financial straits that otherwise would have brought down their empire years ago. Russia stands, a mighty tyranny—because propped up by western economic aid. Against any stiffening of opposition, the heresy raises the specter of atomic war and its horrors. Against every spontaneous reaction to Marxist brutality, the dogma raises the cry of chauvinism or fascism. Detentism would never dream of surrendering the world all at once to the enemy: it does so little by little, hoping thereby to soften the harshness of the new world being prepared for our children. The doctrine is thus spared the embarrassment of preaching surrender openly and crudely to a world still penetrated heavily by Christian morality. The heresy domi-

[108]

nates the media wherein it finds some of its loftiest oracles. It occupies governments. It is the new orthodoxy of an intellectuality purged of hope and altogether without chivalry. It is the yellow banner of the academy and the arts.

Were we to unfold the presuppositions lying behind this flag of defeat, we must find the same fears that worked towards the weakening of the Roman Empire. They—the Communist enemies—will never lay down their arms nor give up their dreams of world conquest because they are crazy with conviction—a very unhealthy but disturbingly real state of mind. We live in a better world and enjoy a more humane society than they do, but we know that there is no ultimate meaning to life, that our centuries of blood spent in the name of liberty and religion have yielded nothing dearer to us than the comfort and ease that we enjoy today. We like this comfort and ask only that it be expanded and shared by the rest of the world. If we yield constantly to the enemy and even surrender to him completely when he demands that we do so, we may well be permitted the continuous exercise of our pleasures and our complacency. At the very least we will not die—right away, that is—and thus cease to be. Possibly we might even teach our barbarian conquerors the manners of civilization if not the morals in which we do not believe anyhow. In any event, we survive.

Saint Augustine and the Christian tradition say something else. This tradition, formed as it is of swords which flash down the ages touching one another in comradeship, tells us that ultimate survival of this our beloved civilization is hidden in the wisdom and will of God. He has not entrusted us with the destiny of history, but only with the duty of making it. To him belongs the victory, to us the battle. Our fathers wrought the city out of the catalyst of time. They fenced this city all around and they set up sentinels and to each they gave a sword. They ordered us to defend the city, and it were better for the whole cosmos to go up in flames, unto the very last star and the most remote moon, burnt out—the whole of existence scorched and reduced to a cinder blown away into the awful wastes of the void—than that dishonor should unfold the banner of Hell within our walls.

[4]

SIR JOHN FORTESCUE AND THE ENGLISH TRADITION

◆§ A number of years ago the distinguished professor of Roman law, Dr. Alvaro D'Ors, noted a decline in interest within philosophical and political theory concerning speculation on the forms of government. D'Ors proceeded to indicate that, in his opinion, this indifference was due to the excessively mathematical and even geometric fashion according to which traditional classical theory on the topic had developed: that is, forms of government were divided according to how many men governed—monarchy: one; aristocracy: a few; democracy: the many.[1] Granting that the one-few-many theory was fleshed out in Plato and Aristotle by a qualitative principle of distinction according to which the many of democracy stood for liberty and the few of aristocracy represented virtue, the mathematicizing of political distinctions then seemed to D'Ors to lack sufficient interest for a world in which political realities are not fashioned by them, even though they continue to function residually within politics. Expanding on the professor's observations, we might note that whether the Soviet Union is governed by one man, Stalin, or whether it be governed by a clique makes little difference to the structure of the society itself. Internal battles and maneuvering for positions of power are personal wars fought at court, but they do not substantially change the political structure of the society in question. Greece could remain a monarchy in name for several years before converting itself into a republic but that conversion has not changed the nature of political life in that nation. The issue is complicated further by the preservation, well into the late twentieth century, of the classical liberal distinction between a head of state and a head of government. The symbolic head of state can be an hereditary king as in the Scandinavias, or he can be elected or chosen president as in Ireland, Germany, and Italy. In no case does he govern: he merely reigns. Power lies in a parliament itself dependent on a rigid party system and the head of government comes out of that system and is dependent on it.

But today, some years after D'Ors's seminal lecture, there does seem to be emerging a renewed interest in the very question itself of governmental forms and their relation to politics. The Watergate crisis quickened a lively discussion on questions circling around executive clemency, executive immunity, and the respective roles of the three branches of American government. Some commentators, including ABC's Howard K. Smith, openly expressed their discomfort at the union of chief of state, chief of government and head of party in one and the same person. Others even suggested a constitutional reform which would make the president directly responsible to the legislature as is an English prime minister. Some of us recalled the late Willmoore Kendall's insistence, made at the height of presidential pretentions, that the real power in the United States was vested in Congress. Others, such as the author of this essay, pointed to a return to the dynastic principle in American political life and to the subsequent decline in democratic individualism: that is, the rise of the Rockefellers, the Percys, and the rise and fall of the Nixon-Eisenhower dynasty. These issues and others as well point to a reemergence of questions centering on power and power's relationship to constitutional forms. This chapter hopes to be a contribution to this conversation.

Sir John Fortescue (1385–1479) lies at the watershed of English constitutionalism from whence the United States inherited. The constitutional issues facing this nation today grew out of an historical tradition that had its roots in medieval England, in an England not yet divided into Cavalier and Roundhead, Tory and Whig, loyalist and legalist. Nonetheless the ingredients for these political schisms were already present in fifteenth-century England. Fortescue meditated deeply on them and an understanding of his teaching ought to throw light on the nature of medieval government and it ought to be of service to the political philosopher in his search for political models or paradigms. Sir John was Lord Chancellor of England (for a very brief period of time) and I intend to probe his teaching on the nature of English kingship and its relationship to the laws of that kingdom. Fortescue warns the king against abusing the laws of his realm and prophesies that disaster is promised the king who would traffic in illegality. The moral is evident for Americans in the declining years of the twentieth century.

English constitutional history has evolved in such a way that Fortescue's notion of a "royal and political regime" bears only a peripheral relation to the existing political system in Great Britain today. There is no independent or quasi-independent executive in the United Kingdom anymore than there is in West Germany or Denmark. Therefore the problems that arise in the context of a strong executive versus either legislature or courts simply do not occur in contemporary England. They have been erased by time. By a curious irony the reality of an independent executive, a medieval inheritance, has lodged itself on the western shores of the Atlantic in the United States of America. Fortescue's teaching has more relevance for a political philosopher of the American experience of today than for the English.

Locating Fortescue within the sweep of Western political speculation, we find that he has engaged the attention of historians of English constitutional law and of political philosophers as a relatively late flowering on English soil of the political thought of Saint Thomas Aquinas. It behooves us, therefore, to examine in some detail the dependence of the lord chancellor on Aquinas. There is a striking text very early in his *De Laudibus Legum Anglie* which suggests that Fortescue knew Thomas in a systematic detail unsuspected by many scholars. The *De Laudibus*, of course, is cast in the form of an exercise in teaching in which the old chancellor, an aged knight, himself in temporary exile, puts the Prince of Wales to school in the meaning of the laws of England and in the structure of English kingship. Gently urging the prince to give up some of the time he heartily spends on martial exercises, prudently and rapidly amending his admonition with praise for the prince's soldierly and knightly interests, Sir John asks the prince, rhetorically, "But how shall you be able to love justice, if you do not first somehow grasp a knowledge of the laws by which justice itself is known?"[2] Noting with Aristotle and Fabius the Orator that "nothing is loved unless it be known" and that which is not known is "usually not only unloved but spurned," Fortescue launches into a short disquisition on how "learned experts" fall into this trap (p. 15):

For, if a metaphysician tells a natural philosopher, who has never studied mathematics, that his science considers things disjoined from all matter and motion according to reality and reason; or a mathematician tells him that his science considers things conjoined with matter and motion according to reality but disjoined to reason, the natural philosopher, who never knew anything disjoined from matter and motion in reality or reason, rejects their sciences, though nobler than his own, and derides both of them, albeit they are philosophers, for no other reason than that he himself is utterly ignorant of their sciences.

This doctrine was by no means a classically Aristotelian statement of the division of the sciences. Grafting both Aristotelian and Boethian elements into his own strikingly original teaching, Aquinas had elaborated this position technically in his *Commentary on the Trinity of Boethius*.[1] The precise epistemological sense of the Thomistic distinctions between natural philosophy, mathematics, and metaphysics falls outside the scope of this investigation. The fact, however, that Fortescue knew this noetic and used an ignorance of it as an analogue to the ignorance of the laws by a king indicates that our lawyer was no mean philosopher in the Thomistic tradition. Fortescue did not merely dip into Aquinas for texts to buttress his own position. Fortescue had absorbed Aquinas.

Nonetheless, the question of Fortescue's dependence on Thomas cannot be settled quite so easily. Fortescue refers constantly to Aquinas when he advances the "royal and political regime," historically incarnated in England, as the optimum political regime. Briefly, the *regimine politicum et regale* refers to a polity governed by a king, by one man, but governed according to laws which he does not make principally but which he discovers in the institutions, customs, usages, and statutes of his kingdom. The *regimine politicum et regale* was contrasted, by Fortescue and others, to the *regimine regale*, the simply royal regime in which a kingdom was governed by laws which depended on the intelligence and will of the ruler himself. Sir John, in both his explanations of, and his panegyric to, the royal and political regime expresses his dependence on Aquinas. Most particularly we find him citing the *Opusculum de regimine principum* (chap. 2, art. 18–19).[6] This short treatise was widely quoted in the fourteenth and fifteenth centuries and it was attributed then to Saint Thomas. Although Carlyle suspected that this work was not vintage Aquinas but was probably the work of Ptolemy of Lucca, it was not until 1949 when Eschmann revised the earlier translation made by Phelan, that it was definitively established that someone, probably Ptolemy, shattered the unity of Aquinas's genuine treatise *On Kingship, To the King of Cyprus,* and sprinkled its paragraphs here and there throughout a new work written by the anonymous author himself.[4] Every passage dealing explicitly with the royal and political regime are from the hand of the later writer. He evidently had an interest in pushing this regime against princely pretentions. A careful scrutiny of Saint Thomas's own study on kingship indicates that he was not formally interested, in this treatise, in the question of checking the power of the king by the laws. Although he admonishes against tyranny and insists that the king be so educated that he not fall into this perennial temptation of rulers, Aquinas tells us nothing about how tyranny is to be avoided. The Common Doctor is concerned, rather, with the duties of a king in the pursuit of a common good; of his relations to the Spiritual Power; and of the ways in which a king can establish a kingdom or city. In a word: *On Kingship* is a positive treatise on kingcraft and no clearly stated teaching on the difference between kinds of kingdoms are to be found in its pages. *On Kingship* was not written from the angle of the independence of the laws from the will of the sovereign.

This absence of any specific reference to the royal and political regime does not argue that the doctrine itself is spurious Thomism. In Aquinas's commentary on *The Politics* of Aristotle, he specifically discusses the difference between a political principle and a royal principle.[5] Earlier, Aristotle had been puzzled by the paradoxical nature of the purely royal form of government. In one sense absolutely royal government is the absolutely best government because it best imitates, as Charles McCoy has pointed out, the command of the free passions by a rational soul annealed in virtue. (This theme was to be played on by medieval rhetoricians who saw in the purple robes of the king an external symbol of internal virtue.)[6] In another sense, however, this theoretically best government cancels out the notion of citizenship as previously elaborated by Aristotle. To be a citizen involves both obeying and commanding. But a simply royal king only governs; he never obeys. His subjects, in turn, never govern but only obey. How can a type of rule be advanced as the best polity which sets aside the very nature of man as a political animal, as a citizen? Saint Thomas dances around the objection: there is something better than being a good citizen and that is being a good man; the virtuous man who relates himself positively to a law which he has not made and who obeys that law is better than merely being the good citizen who helps make the law. It follows that "the assumption that only a citizen may rule does not hold for the royal polity, which is that which is best simply speaking."[7]

Behind this Aristotelian and Thomistic teaching there loomed the doctrine elaborated by Plato in *The Statesman* (269–301a) of government by a philosopher-king which would be superior to government by men subject to laws. Plato's reasoning, which was not quite that of either Aristotle or Thomas, was based on the presumption that justice is achieved only in the concrete whereas law always obliges universally and in the abstract. Whereas the laws generally achieve justice, they err at times because of existential peculiarities which cannot be distilled into the clarity of legal propositions. Given, however, that nobody this side of paradise is all that wise, legal government is the best we can hope for in an imperfect world. On this point, all three of the West's most preeminent political philosophers are in accord. In fact, Aristotle in his *Politics* (1288a) goes further than Plato in insisting that where there is no one man with heroic or godlike virtue, it would be against simple justice "that one man should be lord of all."

Despite the absence of explicit reference to the nature of the royal and political regime in *On Kingship*, the doctrine definitely does figure within the total sweep of Saint Thomas's political philosophy, although I think it fair to say that the doctrine is not central to his principal political preoccupations which are generally concerned with the unity of political action (hence his preference for monarchy) and the achievement of the common good. In capsule form: a regime is political when the power of the ruler is constricted by the laws; it is simply royal when the ruler governs "everything"; it is "mixed"—hence both royal and political—when the prince rules "only over certain things which fall under his authority" and is also "in part subject—with respect to the things concerning which he himself is under the law" (ST 1–2, q. 105, a. 1).

The passage just cited is the most remarkable single passage in Aquinas on the "mixed regime." Given its relevance to Sir John Fortescue's later teaching, we shall comment on the text in some detail. In respect to the "proper ordering of rulers in any city or people, two points are to be taken into consideration. One is that all should take some share in the government." Thomas's reason for sharing the government with all men is not based on any consideration drawn from justice. No demonstration of any putative right of all men to participate in government can be drawn from a mere consideration of justice. Saint Thomas argues to the same effect from the public peace that issues from a common love: "in this fashion the peace of the people is conserved; and all men love and cherish such an ordering of (public) things." The Common Doctor is not telling us that a share in government is a requisite of justice; this sharing in government is based on something deeper than justice—love. Men preserve what they themselves have made, and unless the polity be loved it cannot enjoy durable peace. Sir John Fortescue will repeat the same conclusion although he will angle the conclusion from a consideration based on the need to avoid tyranny, "which only comes to pass when the regal power is restrained by political law." Referring to pseudo-Thomas in the *De Regimine Principum*, Sir John insists to the prince that this restraint upon his power by law "will provide no small security and comfort for you and for the people" (p. 27). Returning to the text of Aquinas, we now find him shifting from the universal to the particular. The best way to set up the kind of order he proffers as necessary for any sane government is by way of a certain form of government: "the first place is held by a kingdom, where the power of government is vested in one man." Saint Thomas's preference for monarchy grew out of his conviction that the very end of civil or political government was the common good of the whole. This common good cannot be achieved capriciously but needs a principle of common political action. The unity of the end is best achieved when the principle of political action is itself fully one. Aquinas finds this principle exemplified at its highest in monarchy.

The reasons for his preference are buttressed if we compare *Summa Theologiae* 1–2, question 105 with *Summa Theologiae* 1, question 103 where St. Thomas addresses himself to the question of "Monarchy and The Divine Government of the World." Given that monarchical government looks to the best, the essentially good ("quod est essentialiter bonum, quod est optimum") because government is nothing other than directing the governed to their end and this is a kind of goodness; given that unity belongs to the structure of the good, it follows that the most unified government will yield the highest political good. We could hardly expect Thomas or any other Christian doctor to opt for anything other than divine and hence monarchical rule for the entire world of things and men. But Saint Thomas roots his teaching here in metaphysical rather than theological principles.

A report—no more is permitted by the economy of this

[119]

study—of Saint Thomas's philosophy of being will clarify his reasoning. Being seeks its own unity as it seeks its own good. The good is being as desirable, as perfective. Unity is the indivision of a reality from its own existence.[8] In seeking their unity things seek simply to be and not to dissolve into the chaos of their own constituent parts to say nothing of nonbeing. This unity in existence is a kind of peace, Saint Thomas teaches, in which all the parts of any whole are harmonized in being. These propositions must be linked further with Thomas's understanding of *to be*, of *esse*. Existence is not only ultimate act without which there is nothing at all; existence is also a synthesizing or composing act which anneals all the constituents of any reality into its unity in being.[9] This togethering of the complexity of the real (nowadays we might call it interfacing, a metaphor drawn from physics) is being as an active synthesizing into unity. Where the unity of the whole encounters a principle which is itself unified, then the whole is the more unified. Politically, this means that the goodness of the being of a polity is better achieved by the monarchical principle than by principles which are divided in their own very nature. The corruption of monarchy is tyranny and the corruption of the best is the worst. Saint Thomas was not blind to the weaknesses in monarchy but as a political philosopher he simply insisted, in these passages, that if all goes well monarchy will yield a better polity than either pure aristocracy or pure democracy, even under the hypothesis that all goes well with them.

Returning to the text (*ST* 1–2, q. 105, a. 1), we find Saint Thomas calling aristocracy a kind of rule "which signifies government by the best, where the power of government is vested in a few." Here Aquinas shifts rapidly from his monarchical point of view to a broader vision which englobes other political forms. "The best form of government," therefore, "is found in any city or kingdom wherein one is given the power to preside over all, while under him there are others having governing powers." The earlier emphasized principle of unity of action is now wedded to the desirability of vesting the virtuous with a ruling function. "And yet a government of this kind is shared by all." Thomas, who first emerged as a principled monarchist and who then shifted to an aristocratic bias, now proves himself far more a democrat than Fortescue was ever to be: "because all are eligible to govern and because the rulers are chosen by all."

Does Thomas opt for an elective monarch and is he thinking of the papacy as a paradigm for civil government? Or does he mean, rather, that the aristocratic representatives are elected? If so, by whom—by the people at large or by their own kind, their peers? Or does he mean that popular representation will be achieved through the political representation of a society's institutions? This last possibility seems more in keeping with medieval society than the others. The issue is unresolved but the text as it stands could apply equally to the American or French presidency or the medieval hereditary kingdom. (The dynasty, after all, in a sense is elected by the society that it represents and governs.) Thomas ends here still playing a democratic theme: "in so far as the rulers can be chosen from the people," the people should choose them. Granting that the text bristles with problems, the overarching thrust of Aquinas's preference for a mixed regime is annealed in his preference for monarchical government: the mixed polity helps preserve the peace of the community and this peace works towards the unity that monarchy presumably guarantees: achieve unity of action through a king; see to it that the best men are represented in government; draw the democratic principle into this structure and thus preserve its viability and avoid its pitfalls.

Sir John Fortescue's approach to political theory was basically Thomistic but it was Thomistic with a significant difference. Saint Thomas had neither axe to grind nor polity to cherish. His political speculations have about them a disinterestedness that suggests a monastic detachment from the world. Unlike Plato and Aristotle who are both frank apologists for the *polis* as the best form of political society, Thomas wrote his political philosophy from a distance. One senses the attitude of a monk towards the things of this world. They are weighed and found to be very good indeed, but their good is something which this man has renounced for himself. Aquinas appreciates patriotism but he is the patriot of no earthly kingdom. But Sir John Fortescue was a quintessentially English patriot. A reader of his works need only turn to the chapters in the *De Laudibus* in which Fortescue defends the English jury system and insists that it can work only in England—not in France, the bête noire and the counterpoint to his English paradise—and it can work in England because only in England are there free and hearty yeomen in abundance who can drop their work and assemble when called to deal justice in the courts as jurymen. And in England the trees grow taller; the fields yield a richer harvest; the food is better; the climate more propitious; in a word, all things have been worked by Providence that Englishmen in England live better than other folk, are better than other folk, and are altogether worthy of the superiority of their polity over that of lesser breeds. Every annoying trait of English xenophobia that the modern world has attributed to Englishmen is found in this fourteenth-century theoretician of constitutional law. Christendom is still a living reality. The Renaissance has not yet penetrated England with its siren call to classical reaction. But England is already England, better than France and better than the Holy Empire and its adherence to the civil law (Roman law). Sir John takes the Italian friar and bends an entirely disinterested political philosophy to the defense of an historic polity. He writes for his prince: both are exiles. Both yearn for the shores of England.

Sir John Fortescue stands in the same relationship to Thomas Aquinas that Cicero stood to Plato.[10] Cicero and Sir John are both patriots but they are also philosophers, heavily in debt to men who had no stake in their political communities: Plato had abandoned Athens in spirit and Saint Thomas belonged to Saint Dominic and to God. Granted that Plato writes as a frustrated politician and out of a kind of bitterness that accompanies ex-politicians; granted that Thomas writes altogether without any political bias whatever, neither man belongs to any *patria*. But the senator belonged to Rome and the lord chancellor to England. They had in common the task of bending philosophical conclusions to concrete political exigencies; they had to demonstrate that philosophical models or paradigms already had found an historic existence in their own soils. They had to cancel the perennial split between absolute paradigmatic excellence and lived historic experience, loved personally because it is a man's very own being.

The prince, begins the chancellor, must not study the laws of England with an eye to evaluating their merit. The chancellor lays it down squarely that he is not going to demonstrate the principles making up the laws of England. "Principles . . . are not known by force of argument nor by logical demonstrations, but they are acquired, as it is taught in the second book of the *Posteriora*, by induction through the sense and the memory" (p. 21). Nothing could be more Aristotelian, nor, in this case, more English. The principles of law and political prudence do not descend upon the mind from on high as though they were Platonic ideas hovering in a void. They are not captured by a rationalist intelligence in some privileged and unique intuition. They are garnered "by induction, through the sense and the memory" (p. 21). Fortescue does not dogmatize here nor does he indoctrinate his pupil. He appeals to Aristotle's contention that a principle—in any order of the real—is that from which something else proceeds. Therefore there is a priority to principles which prevents their being proven or demonstrated by anything presumed to be anterior to themselves. "For that reason, Aristotle says, 'there is no arguing with those who deny principles', because, as it is written in the sixth book of the *Ethics*, 'there is no rational ground for principles'" (p. 21). The prince of England need not busy himself with the details of the law; he has judges and advocates, serjeants-at-law, and others who dedicate their lives to this enterprise. An understanding of the principles of English law is sufficient for the monarch.

And these legal principles must be known by an English king because he "is not able to change the laws of his kingdom at his pleasure, for he rules his people with a government not only regal but also political." Here Fortescue counterpoints, as he does throughout the entire treatise, English law with the civil law of the continent and most especially of the Empire. Under the civil law "what pleased the prince had the force of law" (p. 25). Should such a prince govern arbitrarily, his people will grumble and his regime will be threatened by sedition. These evils are avoided by an English king whose will is disciplined and limited by the law and whose government is thus a joy to his people. Both king and people are secured and comforted by this pact and the people buttress the royal power and the royal power sustains the commonweal. Fortescue grants, with Aristotle, that "it is better for a city to be ruled by the best man than by the best law" (p. 27). Granted the almost universal absence of this "best man," the next best regime is one governed by a king whose "regal power is restrained by political law" (p. 27). An unrestricted prince is made of clay like the rest of us and his power easily degenerates into tyranny.

It is extremely important that we pause here in order to weigh the import of Fortescue's teaching on this business of the laws and the royal power. There is nothing in Sir John of the liberal superstition of "government by laws and not by men." Democratic mythology would have it that politics is an order constituted by processes and not by human content, by machinery and not by mind and will. A moment's reflection is all that is needed to dispel the illusion. No law ever governed anybody. Laws do not govern but men govern in accordance with laws and the laws are in the service of justice, not justice in the service of the laws. This is the constant teaching of the Western tradition. On the unlikely hypothesis that wisdom would incarnate itself politically in a man to whose care a political community was entrusted, that community would be better governed by him than by laws. Laws are guideposts to justice, no more. But the man of total wisdom and virtue simply does not exist for pure reason. Aristotle's "best man" for kingship without laws does not mean the best man available but the absolutely best: this king, in the Christian tradition, is Christ, the King—and he is not the King under discussion in either the Thomistic or the Fortescuian texts.

The artistic and psychological genius of Sir John Fortescue flourishes at its highest in chapter 10. The chancellor has urged the prince to rejoice that his "regal power is restrained by political law." This very restriction "will provide no small security and comfort for you and for the people" (p. 27). The chancellor, in a word, is asking of his prince—let us give him his name, Edward—no small thing: that is, that he be happy precisely because his power is checked. There are few men indeed engaged in governing others, even in modest enterprises such as universities or commercial firms—who exult in the diminution of their own power over those they command. They may agree to be bridled by the law but it is almost beyond the capacity of fallen man that he rejoice in being thus humbled. He may take it as a discipline upon himself but that he positively like it is asking very much indeed! But this psychological act of almost superhuman virtue is exactly what Fortescue is asking of his prince. Sir John wants the prince to love the laws of England, not merely give his consent to them. Sir John's strategy at this point consists in letting the prince complain about his power's being limited and in then developing, as a counter move on the chessboard, a theory according to which such a limited power is just as powerful as the supposedly unlimited power exercised by his continental cousins in purple. But first let us hear the royal complaint: "Then the prince said forthwith, 'How comes it, chancellor, that one king is able to rule his people entirely regally, and the same power is denied to the other king? Of equal rank, since both are kings, I cannot help wondering why they are unequal in power' " (p. 27).

Fortescue's immediate answer is cryptic and unexplained: "It is sufficiently shown, in the small work I have mentioned, that the king ruling politically is of no less power than he who rules his people regally, as he wishes" (p. 28). Fortescue refers to his earlier *Opusculum de natura legis nature et de eius censura in successione regnorum suprema*.[11] The answer is by no means self-evident and Chancellor Fortescue postpones any demonstration of its truth. The authority of kings ruling politically and those ruling simply royally differs thanks to the origin of that authority. But political power, in the mind of Fortescue, is unitary and in his medieval world that unitary power was lodged in the person of the king. The exercise of royal power could be specified by laws made by the people as in England or it could be specified—as Fortescue indicates—by more capricious formalities such as the greed and passions of the ruler; but specified, power will always be.[12]

[126]

Power in a vacuum totally without content is a contradiction in terms.

We are a long way from the liberal shattering of power into the trilogy of executive, legislature, and judiciary and we are a long way from Donoso Cortés's critique of that theory. In England power was snatched from the king by the new middle classes in the late seventeenth century and the king's role was reduced to executing the will of Parliament. A share in the implementation of power by the crown gave credence to the liberal illusion that power had been divided, as well as giving false hopes to High Tory defenders of the preeminence of the Throne. The Marxists are not altogether wrong in their insistence that political power at bottom is economic. Hilaire Belloc demonstrated that the English monarchy died effectively when it became dependent on a new capitalist class which fattened upon the spoils of the Church.[13] He who controls the purse more often than not not only controls the power but is the power. In England, by the late seventeenth century, and on the continent by the nineteenth in the apex of classical liberalism, power was exercised by the upper middle classes, often aided or fitfully frustrated by older landed nobilities and royal houses. This new political power always found itself checked and specified by laws and customs, by religion and by tradition even when it bridled against these fences to its willfullness. The new economic power was all the more effective, powerful, in that it masqueraded itself under the banner of a tripartite division of power. In eighteenth-century England we find a precious case illustrative of these propositions. King George III, stirring himself from customary Hanoverian lethargy, reasserted a royal influence in Parliament and thus attempted to specify a political power which no longer pertained to the crown. George could do so, for a time, by buying support in Parliament and by using the still extensive royal control over patronage. George tried to bend the already established power of the aristocracy, of Commons and Lords, to his own policies but there never was any serious possibility that the Crown could—or even wanted to—subvert that power which then paraded under the banner of the Constitution.

We will not understand Sir John Fortescue if we read him as though he were a defender and expositor of parliamentary supremacy, of a kind of polity that was still generations aborning in the middle of the fifteenth century. For medieval Frenchmen and Englishmen as well, power is still royal. But, adds Fortescue, the source of power is different in both and these distinct sources are what distinguishes the regimes found in the two kingdoms.

Formerly, men excelling in power, greedy of dignity and glory, subjugated neighbouring peoples to themselves, often by force, and compelled them to serve them, and to submit to their commands, to which in time they themselves gave sanction as laws for those people. The folk thus subject, by long endurance, and as long as they were protected, by their subjection, against the injuries of others, consented to the dominion of their rulers, thinking it better to be ruled by the government of one, whereby they were protected from others, than to be exposed to the oppressions of all those who wish to attack them. And thus began certain kingdoms, and the rulers of them, thus ruling the subject people, usurped to themselves the name of king, from the word 'regendo', and their lordship is described as entirely regal. (p. 29)

Thus, continues Fortescue, Nimrod, not himself a king but a mighty hunter, "secured for himself a kingdom": hunters subdue beasts and kings subdue the beast in each one of us, thus curbing our liberty and bending us to obedience. So too did the Romans assume "the government of the world." And "when the sons of Israel demanded a king as all people then had," the Lord, after explaining to them that such a law was nothing more than the pleasure of the king, gave them over to their own folly (p. 29).

We find in chapter 12 of the *De Laudibus Legum Anglie* a foreshadowing of *The Leviathan* of Thomas Hobbes. The main lineaments of Hobbes's contract theory of the origin of government are already ticked off by Sir John: these are, a jungle of snarling men and nations at each others' throats; the dominance of those who excel "in power, greedy of dignity and glory"; the subjugation of the weaker; the final consent by peoples to be governed by men who would protect them against their enemies; royal law within the pact promising protection (p. 39). If the *De Laudibus* looks ahead to *The Leviathan* of Hobbes it also bends back to Book 2 of Plato's *Republic* (358e–359a). Plato recounts there the opinion of those who believed that the rule of law originated as a compromise between men who could not successfully wreak injustice on their fellows (p. 31). Whereas Hobbes identifies the existential situation prior to government as a "state of nature," Plato relegated it to the realm of opinion or *doxai*: that is, this is what men say about the origins of society, especially the origin of justice. For Fortescue, the Hobbesian jungle is not the "state of nature." Nature and its laws are the same for all men. From this point of view, "The laws of England in those points which they sanction by reason of the law of nature, are neither better nor worse in their judgements than are all laws of other nations in like cases." Nothing could be more Thomistic and nothing could indicate more forcefully that the Englishman could transcend his xenophobia when the chips were down. The author presses Aristotle as well into the service of his argument. The *lex nature*, hence, is deeper and more universal than are circumstances which give birth to either a royal or a royal-political regime. The lord chancellor understands the *lex nature* to be a natural law which is a permanent condition for moral behavior. Forms of government cannot be deduced from nature but must be understood as products of history. But we have no reason to think that Fortescue relegated the origin of the simply royal regime to Platonic *doxai*. Sir John apparently thought that this was really how such societies got going.

And this moves him to speculate on "How kingdoms ruled politically first began" (chapter 13). Fortescue commences by citing Saint Augustine's famous definition of a people found in Book 19, chapter 23, of *The City of God*. "A people is a body of men united by consent of law and by community of interest" (p. 31). But Fortescue does not work with this definition as did Augustine. Augustine, dissatisfied with this fundamentally Ciceronian teaching, interjects into the body politic the dynamics of love, as did Aquinas after him. "A people is an assemblage of reasonable beings bound together by a common agreement as to the objects of their love. . . . In order to discover the character of any people, we have only to observe what they love."[14] A common love, as the final cause of political existence, was not without interest to the English barrister. What marks the true Englishman is his love for the laws of England. But a treatise on politics and love was not central to the point Fortescue was making in the *De Laudibus*. Augustine's people "does not deserve to be called a body whilst it is acephalous, i.e., without a head."[15] Here Fortescue launched into his justly famous analogy of the English body politic with a living organism, with the human body:

Saint Augustine, in the 19th book of the De Civitate Dei, chapter 23, said that A *people is a body of men united by consent of law and by community of interest*. But such a people does not deserve to be called a body whilst it is acephalous, i.e. without a head. Because, just as in natural bodies, what is left over after decapitation is not a body, but is what we call a trunk, so in bodies politic a community without a head is not by any means a body. Hence Aristotle in the first book of the *Politics* said that *Whensoever one body is constituted out of many, one will rule, and the others be ruled.* So a people wishing to erect itself into a kingdom or any other body politic must always set up one man for the government of all that body, who, by analogy with a kingdom, is from 'regendo', usually called a king. As in this way the physical body grows out of the embryo, regulated by one head, so the kingdom issues from the people, and exists as a body mystical, governed by one man as head. And just as in the body natural, as Aristotle said, the heart is the source of life, having in itself the blood which it transmits to all the members thereof, whereby they are quickened and live, so in the body politic the will of the people is the source of life, having in it the blood, namely, political forethought for the interest of the people, which it transmits to the head and all the members of the body, by which the body is maintained and quickened. (p. 31)

The chancellor is now close upon his binding of the king of England to the laws of his realm and he is close upon answering the prince's complaint about the presumed superior power of his continental rivals. The analogy of the political order to a living body was by no means foreign to medieval rhetoric but nowhere is there to be found a more striking analogy of the political order to the Church as the mystical body of Christ than in the *De Laudibus*. Although the appropriate passages from Paul are not mentioned in the text (pp. 32–33), they had to be present in Fortescue's mind because of the operative adjective *misticum*. As in every true analogy, the differences are absolute and the likenesses are relative: the Church is the mystical extension of Christ but the king is the extension of the people and grows out of the people as "one man" which governs and from whence the king, its head, has erupted. (Sic ex populo erumpit regnum, quod corpus extat misticum, uno homine ut capite gubernatum.) King and people make one body, one *regnum*. But "the heart is the source of life . . . having . . . the blood which it transmits to all the members . . . which it transmits to the head." The English king gets his kingship, his title, from the people and the people is the heart, a heart needing a head.

The analogy is extended to laws and nerves. The body "is held together by the nerves" and the law emerges as the corporate nerve binding together all the members of the body and annealing them into unity. Law is derived from *ligando*, binding, and as nerves knit bones and flesh into one body so does the law knit community into kingdom: the commonwealth is "sustained" and preserves its rights through the laws "as the body natural does through the nerves" (p. 33). The king, true enough, governs the body politic but "just as the head of the body physical is unable to change its nerves, or to deny its members proper strength and due nourishment of blood, so a king who is head of the body politic is unable to change the laws of that body, or to deprive that same people of their own substance uninvited or against their wills" (p. 36). The king of England does for England what any human head does for its body but the king can do so only because his very role as head of the polity is dependent on the laws as is the existence of a physical head dependent upon a network of nerves that comes forth from the heart of the physical body. When the nerves function well, the head functions well; when the laws flourish, the king flourishes. When the head looks after the nerves, all goes well with the body; when the king heeds and protects the laws, making them his laws, all goes well with the kingdom.

Sir John is now close upon answering the prince's objection concerning the inequality of his power as a future king of England in comparison to the power of European (read French) kings. The difference between continental royal power and English royal-political power has been rooted by Fortescue in history and not in the nature of power itself. Fortescue appeals to Diodorus Siculus, in his second book of the *Ancient Histories*, where it is written that "the kings of Egypt . . . were restrained by the laws; nor were they thereby displeased, but thought themselves fortunate . . . for they considered those who indulged their own cupidities did much which exposed them to dangers and perils."[16] The lesson is not lost on the Prince: "The power of the two kings is equal, since the power by which one of them is free to do wrong does not increase his freedom, just as to be able to be ill or to die is not power, but is rather to be deemed impotency because of the deprivation involved. . . . For the holy spirits who, already confirmed in glory, are unable to sin, are more powerful than we, who with a free reign take delight in any deed" (p. 81).

It is typically English to compare the laws of England to the bliss of the angels! The author here has shifted the conversation from the plane of what nowadays is called comparative government to that of metaphysics and even theology. The ability of man to work his own will even at the cost of sin does not increase his power but diminishes it. The pertinent passages in the earlier work by Fortescue bear this out. Pride and cupidity, when unchecked, lead to the ruin of power. Sin is the death of the soul and if the freedom to sin were the essence of human power, then only a dead man could properly be called a man (p. 95). Not to be able to fall easily into tyranny is an advantage and not a limitation to the power exercised by a king. It is evident that Fortescue here appeals to a liberty which is higher than that of mere choice: the liberty which in truth is liberation and that liberty frees the man and it frees the king to do the good. Liberation from an easy temptation to tyranny and caprice is what the laws and customs of England confer on their king, thus steadying him and rendering him all the more effective in the exercise of that political power which is his and his alone. But "those ancestors of yours," insists the chancellor in the *De*

[133]

Laudibus, "endeavoured to throw off this political yoke, in order thus to rule merely regally over their subject people, or rather to rage unchecked, not heeding that the power of the two kings is equal" (p. 95).

But these laws of England do not only bridle the passions of the king; they bridle those of all men. Fortescue makes this point when discussing the subject of the legitimation of bastards. The chancellor is no friend of these unfortunates. Whereas the civil law of the Holy Empire permits the legitimation of bastards, the law of England does not: "for the law of England in this matter does not encourage sin, nor favour sinners, but deters them and threatens them with punishment lest they sin" (p. 95). For Sir John the laws are the webs of the wings of power and the laws ought to be as tough as is the power that it specifies.

The entire trick in understanding Sir John Fortescue's argument on the equality of power in the two kinds of regimes consists in thinking oneself back into a Christian world in which the ability to work harm on others and to follow the wisp of one's own desire are not understood to be marks of power but are looked upon as wounds in human nature and hence in human power itself. Sir John exalts the liberty of Englishmen over all comers, but the liberty in question is always disciplined by the laws, customs, and usages of the realm. A purely moralistic approach to the treatise is insufficient to capture the delicacy of the reasoning. A moralist, in the modern sense of the term, would have faced the prince's complaint that his power is limited by the laws of England and is therefore inferior to the power of the king of France or the Holy Roman emperor and would have granted the complaint: yes, your power is less than theirs and so what! But Fortescue has argued exactly the contrary: the specification of royal power by laws independently come by through inherited tradition does not weaken that power but rather strengthens it from the debilitating influence of individualistic idiosyncrasy. The king's power is not the cloakroom simulacrum of the same found in the White House of Mr. Nixon—a power petty in its exercise and pitiful in its attempts to circumvent the laws of the land. Medieval royal power in England is public and is joined to the laws of the realm. Fortescue's reasoning thus joins that of his master, Thomas Aquinas, in the latter's insistence that giving a piece of the pie of politics to the governed, letting them share in the decisions of the realm, is not a dictate of justice but a council of political wisdom: the subjects or citizens of a political society are likely to be happier in a situation created, at least in part, by themselves than in one simply imposed upon them. Such is the thrust of Aquinas's reasoning. Fortescue argues the other side of the coin: the contentment issuing therefore strengthens the king's hand in the use of the power he has inherited. Rather than being drained of his role in government, the king is fortified therein: he has a united kingdom behind him, a kingdom whose first servant he has become by his very role as king. Not the facade for a locus of power hidden from public knowledge, the crown is its open repository and when something goes wrong we know where to seek redress. Hilaire Belloc called this "The Popular Monarchy" and insisted that its restoration was the only guarantor for the liberty of the subject.[17] In such a royal and political polity the king stoops to conquer. This suggests Christ's teaching that he who humbles himself will be exalted. Fortescue thus joins the pragmatic argument of any prince who wants more power as do all men with his own lawyer's commitment to the laws and to liberty. Sir John walks both sides of the street—the king's and the subject's—and his argumentation is all the more brilliant and convincing for having done so.

There is nothing in this fourteenth-century treatise that

smacks of the divine right of kings which flourished under the early Stuarts. There is nothing even hinting at parliamentary supremacy. The medieval constitution transcended both poles of this essentially modern dialectic. Fortescue has elaborated a theory of power which understands power to be unitary. The same metaphysics of power was to be resurrected centuries later in Spain by Donoso Cortés.[18] Fortescue has foreshadowed Hobbes on the origin of government but, unlike Hobbes, Fortescue has not made the law of the jungle the law of nature. Fortescue has articulated with his symbol of head and body a theory of political existence in which governed and governor are bound together not by some social contract or pact but by an organic unity comparable to the unity existing between the limbs of a man's body and his head. Fortescue has restricted the Hobbesian temptation to submit to arbitrary rule to the exhaustion that plagues any society that no longer senses itself to be a unity but that rather experiences the weeds of the jungle as they crawl over the ruined walls of the city and poison the wells of decency within.

Fortescue, the philosophical theoretician of the body politic, has bent his model to the prescriptive inheritance of the medieval English tradition. Fortescue's England was not all that good; it could not have been the paradise painted in exile for Prince Edward. But England was a paradise for lawyers! Wracked by rival claimants for the throne; bereft of stable government from on high; torn by feudal conflict, England turned to the law for what little stability could be woven into the chaos of the times. The royal and political regime was more a model than a reality because government was often neither royal nor political in the struggle for the throne. But philosophical models of the best regime are not blueprints for immediate political action; they are stars by which statesmen can guide the always imperfect ship of state. Beneath the Heraclitean whirlwind of the Wars of the Roses a certain stability based upon custom and law kept knit into historic continuity the life of the nation. And the warp and woof of that fabric was the quasi-sacral character of the common law. Sir John Fortescue bent Aquinas to his own English constitutional model. The synthesis was to have a very short life on English soil because of the Reformation and the shift in power that it effected. The royal and political regime had a much longer run for its money in the Spanish kingdoms than it did in England. Debilitated by the French influence of the Bourbon kings, the royal and political regime lingered on as reality until Napoleon and as hope within the Carlist tradition: *fueros y rey*—"the laws and the king."

Fortescue's independent executive found a home in the American experience but the ultimate question as to where is the power to be found in America has yet to be answered. For decades the American presidency played at being the power but that power was brought down by Congress with such an astonishing rapidity that we are left free to wonder whether the presidency was only play acting a reality that was never its own.

Sir John's regime expired in the West. For a description of modern Western politics we might be better served by Aristotle's insistence that most governments are a cross between democracy and oligarchy. Sir John's prince himself never mounted the throne of England. Both prince and chancellor could well haunt the English speaking world in this moment of total crisis in our institutions, in this moment in which men once again find the question of the form of government to be at least a puzzling question because these forms are often totally bereft of power. I confess my admiration for Sir John Fortescue as well as my admiration for the polity he

[137]

defended with such brilliance, and I declare that I am confident that a study of Fortescue in our times might help us toward an understanding of where we are. Without understanding there is no effective action permitted man on this earth.

[5]

DONOSO CORTÉS AND THE MEANING OF POLITICAL POWER

◄§ The Christian politics of Sir John Fortescue is totally bereft of pagan illusions concerning any putative power in power to deliver to man the goods of eternal life and the happiness that is written as a hope in his nature. If Sir John's king exercised a moderate and limited power he was thereby cheated in nothing. This kind of power is the best that any man called to a throne could have and it is the most that he ought to desire. Even should such a king violate the laws of the land through surrendering to the perpetual temptation to have more of everything and thus more of the power that is already his own, his deed will work him no good. His power will eventually wither and his sceptre will become a reed because the presumptuous of this world are always humbled, and if not humbled in life then humbled in the grave. Christian politics are the work of men who live in two cities and one of these cities, the one of this world, is tolerable only if the itch to play God is relieved by the salve of laws annealed in man's very own nature.

Both Fortescue's prince and his chancellor are long gone and so is their Christian polity. But philosophical questions are not subject to the laws of mutability and decay. Metaphysics, as Gilson once said, buries its own undertakers. Fortescue's limited polity, the work of a quintessential Englishman of the late Middle Ages, was to emerge again as theory in the mind of a nineteenth-century Spaniard, Don Juan Donoso Cortés. There is no evidence that Donoso ever heard of Fortescue. It is highly unlikely because the first modern English editions of Fortescue postdate the death of Donoso. That both men angled the question of power from strikingly similar platforms is illustrative of our thesis that Christian questions produce Christian answers.

Power, in the context of the secular politics of modernity, is identified with the problem of success. Power is exercised publicly by the prince in the service of the perpetuation and expansion of an already existent *res publica*. Successful power, therefore, justifies itself. Machiavellian cynicism resurrects, under a new form, the ancient classical conviction that power equals virtue but Machiavellian virtue is naked *virtus* in the primitive sense of the word: strength, such as the *vis* of a boxer's arm. Nothing could be more distant in theory from the Augustinian insistence that power is ultimately God's and that success is at bottom a gift and not a consequence of the skillful and even virtuous manipulation of the techniques of politics. If the fruition and crowning of power are effects which simply cannot be planned into existence by man, then the focal problem of power in a Christian context ceases to be the glory of the prince or the presumed eternity of the polity. Men look elsewhere when they question power and ponder its meaning because they know by experience and believe by faith that no power can justify itself, that the most decent of political orders can be wrecked by contingency, that human power is marked with the mortality dooming mankind itself. Christian political philosophy has always tended to seek out the source of power in order to fence it in with a thicket of limits that bend power to the common good and thus keep it humble. We Christians suspect power because we believe that whatever authority guides power is always derived from on high. No power, be it political or otherwise, justifies itself. It is as contingent and as dependent as are all creatures of God. Even more: if power is bound to fail in the end, if no society can claim an eternity reserved to God, if paradise is not the earthly fruit of politics, then our questions concerning power must necessarily shift their focus. Let us sin no more as we renounce gnosticism. This renunciation moves the question of power away from success and over to the ways in which power can be exercised and hence limited. Power in itself is as good as is being, but this goodness demands an ordered specification. Fortescue's ordered specification was the royal and political regime. For him this form of government, while doing justice to the responsible use of power, was worth the bet of those men who fear power's perpetual tendency to bully us in the name of millenarian promises or tyrannical insanity.

Whether a man be a believing Christian or not he cannot fail to note that the Christian reservation of absolute power to God entails the limiting of power in the political order. The decline in belief in such a God necessarily entails, in its turn, the releasing of power here on earth and its expansion into a simulacrum of a God now thought to be dead or so remote that his death or life is irrelevant. Early modern political theory worked, often obscurely but sometimes consciously, towards a doctrine that secularized power and thus altered its relations to authority, both human and divine. Three men mark this break with the classical and medieval past and we can mark off mentally their roles in the history of modern man by following the example of Aristotle and using the domestic household as an analogue of political existence. The master of the modern political house is the creation of the genius of Machiavelli. Hobbes fashioned the servant. Jean Bodin supplied the roof which we have known since as the state.

Neither Machiavelli nor Hobbes conceived of political existence as though it were an entity, a thing. Even Hobbes's Leviathan is an aggregate and not a being. The concept of

[141]

the state as something sovereign unto itself and hence constituting a fusion of both authority and power was the invention of Bodin. Although there are analogies to the modern state in both the Greek *polis* and the late Roman Empire, it is not correct to refer to the state as having existed in any strict sense before Bodin and the centralized absolute French monarchy whose theoretician he came to be.

Jurisprudence in the early centuries of the Roman Republic rested authority in the wisdom and prudence of the judges. But the judges themselves remained silent until society asked them to render an opinion on some concrete case. It follows that Roman law, before its transformation and corruption at the hands of the Hellenic mind, was constituted by an act of judging which was always an act of answering, a *respondere*.[1] This response was simply the answer given to the questions put to wise men by the community. Thus it was that Roman law clearly distinguished between the concepts of authority and power. Public power, whose concrete expression is government, waited upon the voice of the repositories of the law. It followed that the authority of the judges was sharply differentiated from the power of the magistrates. We can even assert that not only was the Roman judiciary independent of the power of the executive but that power itself was subordinate to an authority that was respected so highly it could stand without any buttressing it might have received from the executive. We have trouble today even articulating the distinction because we live in a political order that has accepted Bodin's state as though it were as natural as the rise and fall of the tides, a political order in which authority is identified with public power and in which power is sovereign.

Classical thought recognized very early in the game that there was a link between the authoritative and the personal, between judgments and judges, but it did so only in an obscure way. We refer, of course, to Plato's elaboration of the doctrine of the philosopher-king. Although tyranny is government in defiance of the laws, the rule of the philosopher-king is government which transcends the laws. Because his intervention in time is a quasi-providential event whose mystery is heightened by the rareness of the occurrence and by the impossibility of even preparing for its advent, government by law is superior to rule by men in the normal course of history.[2] The *absolute* superiority of the politics of the wise king is located within the laws' necessity to legislate in the universal and in their occasional failure to reach complexities which are consubstantial with individuality. It follows, according to Plato, that the very universality of the law frequently misses the particular and thus does violence to the justice due particular men. Nonetheless, the marginality of this possibility justifies government by the impersonal majesty of the law.

Historically, the theory of the natural law grew out of and perfected the previously elaborated philosophy of natural justice. Natural justice, conceived by Plato and Aristotle, was expanded into the natural law philosophy of which we have spoken earlier. Natural law theory, as expanded beyond its Stoic and Ciceronian origins by Aquinas, involves the following: (1) a moment of reflection in which a man meditates on the exigencies of his own nature, be they prohibitions or commands, be these exigencies indemonstrable first principles consubstantial with the ontological nature of humanity or secondary precepts deduced from these first principles; (2) a moment of decision in which he embraces or rejects, in the fullness of his freedom, the demands he has discovered in himself.[3]

Although, according to natural law theory, natural law is nothing other than nature itself—we have argued the thesis earlier—man's articulation of the law—a slow and laborious

[143]

business which depends on both ethical maturity and intellectual sophistication—is an attempt to fuse in consciousness that which is already fused in reality. Given that law must legislate in broad and very often properly universal terms; and given that law as understood in the human mind can never totally reach the concrete complexities of existence, it follows that the law as theory can never identify itself completely with reality. Law as known and formulated must remain a mere map of reality and is never a perfect reflection of the road it charts. Aristotle's virtue of prudence was a bridge between universal law and its concrete application.[4] The prudent man, according to Aristotle, knows how to read the map. Something similar happened in the early flowering of Roman law under the Republic. Authority pertained to the law but only to the law as interpreted and rendered concrete in cases by the judges. Thus the relation between authority and the personal, reserved by Plato to the mythological reign of the philosopher-king, inserted itself more modestly if more effectively in the theory underlying Roman jurisprudence.

The medieval experience made its own the teaching of the early Roman jurists but it did so according to a radically new political situation introduced by the new configuration given society by Christianity. The break-up of the Roman Empire in the West gave birth to a new civilization which was highly decentralized in government, which rested upon a feudal basis, which abandoned any attempt to identify ultimate authority and sovereignty within itself because it located both in a transcendent God; a civilization which was marked by the autonomy of religious orders, by the virtual independence of towns and cities from royal or imperial power and by parliaments in France and England and Cortés in Spain which held the power to grant or to withhold subsidies from the national government. Authority in medieval Christendom was broadened beyond the authority proper to the judges until it was diffused throughout a whole host of institutions that marked the medieval world and made it the unique political thing that it was. Authority was as pluralistic as life itself. Public power, government in the plain sense of the term, grew out of a society whose complexity exceeded the experience of classical politics. Sovereignty was reserved to God.

The medieval checking of political power by authority—more exactly, by a host of authorities—resident within the very tissue of the community, is crucially pertinent to any theory of power. Suffice it to say here that the theoretical problem posed by Plato in this regard found its solution in what might be called, with some reservations, the Christian politics of transcendence. Plato's complaint that the wise and the good are without power and that power is more often the perquisite of the evil or the stupid, his insistence that an absolutely good political order depends upon the identification of power and wisdom, and his pessimism about the possibility of this union being found in history were theoretically solved by the Christian identification of power and authority in God. The subsequent scholastic teaching concerning the power of God as ordained by his goodness and wisdom simply pointed to the divine government of creation by the Lord of History. But the Christian dispensation heightened rather than diminished the distinction between authority and power written into early Roman jurisprudence. If sovereignty pertains to the fullness of authority, then only God is sovereign because only he speaks with an underived authority. The political order for medieval man was even less "sovereign" than it was for classical antiquity. Authority, wheresoever it might be found, was thought to be participation in a divine attribute and in no sense a property belonging restrictively to the public power of the political order, the medieval kingdom or *regnum*. Expressing the issue more exactly, we must say that if power or its representatives did possess authority in medieval times their authority did not accrue to power simply because of power itself. The Two Swords, although symbolically valuable, inadequately expressed the relations between Church and Empire. What theologians were wont to call Peter's indirect power in things secular was not power at all but simply authority. Medieval man saw clearly, as did the Roman jurists, that all authority is moral! A breakdown of authority is always a breakdown in the moral order. A papal interdict, for instance, worked just as long as men respected Rome's authority. As soon as men and nations ceased to respect that authority, it became ridiculous for Rome to hurl its thunderbolts. In a word, authority can do nothing other than speak.[5] The execution of its commands depends upon a power humble enough to listen. Moralists will find here a deep paradox which strikes at the heart of hierarchy and which suggests, to this author at least, the parable of the humble being exalted and the lords of this world being laid low. In any event, medieval man neither respected nor obeyed any authority that could not trace its origins to, and legitimize them in, the authority of God. This no doubt irritated kings, for they proclaimed their sovereignty all the more because they really had so little of it.

The same cannot be said of the national French monarchy at the time Jean Bodin was reflecting upon the meaning of political power.[6] France was by then already a highly centralized political unit and all Europe was following in its footsteps. The old medieval order was in full decay. Sovereignty was made immanent by Bodin, who located it within terrestrial existence, within politics as such. The *res publica* came to be the thing that we understand today under the rubric of the state. According to Bodin, that grouping of families which forms the basis of society is governed by a highest political power, a *summum potestas*. This power is

[146]

both absolute and perpetual: "power—One, Absolute, and Perpetual" (pp. 25–36). This power is also sovereign (pp. 40–47). Should power lose sovereignty, the republic would cease to exist (pp. 47–48).

The politics of absolute power and the politics of the modern state depend, as do all politics, upon metaphysical presuppositions. Medieval man never had to face the problem of an absolute power in politics because he could never have conceived of its possibility. The arbitrary use of power was discussed only within the classical context of tyranny. But tyranny as such has nothing to do with the absoluteness of power but with its unlawful use. (It can even be argued that the classical Platonic and Aristotelian tyrant can *never* exercise absolute power because such an exercise would involve satisfying the tyrant's passions which are assumed to be necessarily incapable of being gratified. It is for this reason that the classical tyrant is always unhappy). The unlawful use of power might be good accidentally because occasionally the law might violate the concrete good in the existential order. A tyrant can get things done at times that the laws prohibit him from doing. In any event, the term *absolute* as applied to power means, within medieval presuppositions, the following: power is totally unconditioned either from within itself or from any extraneous factors upon which power might exercise itself; in this sense only God's power is absolute because only he can make things be altogether without fashioning anew some preexistent subject.[7] Medieval thought, therefore, tended to locate the treatise on power in the context of the treatise on creation as did Thomas Aquinas in his *De potentia dei*. Absolute as applied to power could also mean a power absolved or divorced from any other dimension of the real. This is suggested by the very term, *absolvere*. Medieval speculation tended to talk about a naked and lonely power stripped of every other consideration in terms of the possibility or impossibility of God's annihilating the human soul once he had created it.[8]

Some theologians settled the problem by distinguishing between God's absolute power and that same power as ordained by his wisdom and goodness. Absolutely speaking, according to this theory, God could annihilate the human soul because it depends totally on him for being. Given, however, the truth that God's power always harmonizes with his wisdom and goodness, God would not do so. Probably the distinction between *could* and *would* breaks down in this case because of the unity of power, wisdom, and goodness in the being of God: that is, to say that God could but would not is not to say anything about God at all. In any case we have grasped the point at issue when we see that medieval Christian thought was so suspicious of any absolute power that it felt constrained even to hedge that power when found in God himself, hedge it around with these attributes which precisely make God sovereign: his wisdom and his goodness, the providence of his divine government. The issue has enormous political consequences, as we hope to demonstrate, but it suffices to note here that Bodin's elevation of the political order to the status of an absolute of perpetual power was another step along the road to the divinization of political existence.

Although Bodin's understanding of his own religion was defective, he was a Christian of sorts and he did hope that the sovereign would exercise his power in harmony with the moral and divine law.[9] But this hope could only have been, and in fact was, little more than a pious exhortation. If political power is absolute—it behooves us to take Bodin's use of language as seriously as he took it himself—it cannot be conditioned by extraneous considerations drawn from the moral order. Such a conditioning would limit power and strip it of its supposed absoluteness. Any harmonizing of power and the wisdom from which comes authority is possible only under two conditions: (1) either power is identically wisdom (and, a fortiori, goodness) as the theologians had taught; or (2) power is limited from outside itself. Power can remain absolute and good only when it is divine. If power is to act other than in a merely powerful way, blindly, if power is to act wisely and prudently in harmony with justice and truth, then power must be specified or limited by dimensions of being that are not formally identified with power as such. (In metaphysical terms drawn from the theory of being in Aquinas, we can say that power is existence, act, exercise, doing; authority is essence, specification, content. Identical in God, these dimensions are distinct in creatures.) Medieval political experience found these structures of reality in the community which was regarded as the repository of an analogical incarnation of authorities themselves derived from God.[10] But Bodin's public power is really absolute. No matter how much he might speak of the sweet reasonableness of a sovereign power as exercised by a Christian prince he cannot square this reasonableness with his insistence on the absolute character of the sovereign. That Bodin is serious in what he says we know because he not only revindicates for the *res publica* the *imperium* of the Hellenized Empire; he not only preaches a sovereignty which is one and indivisible and hence superior to any other authority either religious or social, but he also teaches that the state is the substantial form of civil society, its animating principle.

We here witness the birth of the modern state. The comparison of public and political sovereignty with the Aristotelian substantial form is decisive, so decisive that modern men often find it difficult to understand what the politics of Christendom were all about because Bodin is a wall separating that age from our own. Medieval Christendom was so firmly structured through a series of self-governing institutions, each of which claimed an analogous participation in authority, that public power—the power of the crown—as usually restricted to leading the political community that it crowned in fighting the enemy from without or in fighting with it in an effort to reduce its pretensions. The king could put his sword at the service of his kingdom or turn it against the kingdom, but he could not absorb that kingdom within himself by his own power. No one phrase better sums up the limitations placed on royal power by the medieval political community than the warning read Spanish kings in Castille upon the occasion of their coronation: "Thou shalt be King if thou workest justice and if thou dost not do so, thou shalt not be King."[11] The medieval public power, incarnated in the person of the king (more accurately, in his family: medieval monarchy is dynastic), did not constitute the *res publica christiana* but crowned it so that the society in question might act corporately in history.[12] The legitimate power of the king was the fruit of a hundred pacts solemnly entered upon by princes and subjects, themselves represented by a thicket of institutions which were the work of generations and even centuries of common experience.

When Bodin published his *Six Books of The Commonwealth* in 1576, the medieval kingdom was just about dead in France and in plain agony in most of Europe. A new thing had come into being: the state. Most of the old medieval institutions still gave an appearance of life but the heart had gone out of them. Townships and guilds, provincial parliaments, regional charters and the rest were being reduced to so many quaint relics from a past age, preserved as facades because they were still dear to men who had grown up among them and who looked upon them as the flesh of corporate life and the sign of an older liberty.

Bodin's use of the symbol of substantial form to define the role of the state in civil society is not without interest. Aristotle's substantial form was understood by the intellectual community of Bodin's time to mean more or less what Aristotle himself intended it to mean: that is, the substantial form is that interior principle of growth and specification (*dynamis*) which quickens a reality from within and makes it to be what it is. It follows that hylomorphism could never have been used in any properly symbolic sense to describe medieval politics. The articulation of public power into government in the older Christendom grew out of the community in the sense of crowning that community, as indicated, or of serving as the community's representative for secular ends. Public power or government, conceived as an active harmonizing of an already heavily differentiated and institutionalized society and understood as being enjoined by the community with the specific function of seeing that justice was done or the law fulfilled as well as repelling invaders and securing the peace of the realm; public power, limited to these crucial but still moderate roles, would not be spoken of by serious men in terms of an Aristotelianized substantial form. Medieval man preferred to draw analogies from human anatomy. Thus Sir John Fortescue, as noted in the previous chapter, compared the *res publica* to a body which could not function without a head.[13] Public power became absolute only when it truly did become the substantial form of the republic. The community, reduced to an amorphous dough without any institutions with significant political representative functions, was shaped this way and that by power which absorbed all authority into itself and proclaimed itself sovereign. In this fashion the modern state—conceived in France, suckled in Germany, and matured in Russia—replaced the *res publica christiana*.

The theoretical problem of power from Montesquieu to our day has been a problem of the possibility and desirability of setting limits to power's tendency towards absolutism.

Montesquieu deduced the desirability of limiting power from man's imperative to be free.[14] He tried to find freedom within the context of the state he knew, Bodin's. His dilemma was this: how can we avoid tyranny within a political situation in which the republic has become sovereign and the sovereign has been identified with perpetual and absolute power? Unless we understand the factors which went into the drama of freedom as seen by Montesquieu, by Sieyès, by the Encyclopedists and by the European liberal tradition that grew from them, we cannot understand either Montesquieu's solution or the theoretical weaknesses found therein by European traditionalism in the person of its most eloquent and profound spokesman, Donoso Cortés.

We can provisionally define European liberalism as the continental system of political thought and practice which grew out of the French Revolution and dominated the entire nineteenth century excepting the years of the short White Reaction in France (1814–1830) and in Germany (1814–1848). Dedicated to the doctrine of national sovereignty, buttressed by the religion of progress, and bent upon the secularization of society, European liberalism's preferred form of government was a highly centralized parliamentary democracy based on the party system and tempered by an allegiance to commercial and industrial interests. The poor voted and the rich governed. While linked to the Jacobin tradition of the previous century, nineteenth-century liberalism was more comfortable than crusading, more oligarchic than egalitarian. In all cases, however, European liberals firmly opposed any restoration of the ancient authority of either Church or Crown.

Montesquieu and the liberalism that looked to him for guidance never questioned the presuppositions of the sovereign state endowed with absolute power, even though liberalism wished to use that power sparingly in the service of a wider distribution of liberty. If we assume that power is sovereign, if we assume further that authority has lost its independence and has been absorbed into power, if we postulate the national state as the substantial form of the republic, it follows that any limitation of power must come from within power itself. Society could not limit power because society, on the assumptions in question, would not possess the independent institutions with the requisite authority to speak in the name of wisdom and truth and thus demand that they be heard. Montesquieu wanted the sovereign to listen carefully to the people and to govern in accordance with prevailing customs. But custom in Montesquieu and in liberalism had already lost the force of law that it possessed in the medieval world.[15]

Neither custom nor any public orthodoxy exercised any political role in the liberal commonwealth. They are not authoritative voices in the liberal republic. Although the liberal commonwealth must listen to society, it is under no obligation to heed any authority society may claim to enflesh in itself. It follows that public power, be it democratic, aristocratic, monarchical, or any combination thereof, can offend the liberty of the subject and most probably will do so unless we can discover *within* power some possible principle of limitation.

Montesquieu's solution is so famous and has influenced both politics and history so profoundly that it suffices here merely to state again in capsule form a teaching that can be found in any manual of politics published in the Western world in modern times, a teaching which history has honored by permitting it to pass into folklore. Liberty is assured a permanent role in the commonwealth when power is limited through its separation into legislature, executive, and judiciary. A built-in system of checks and balances assures the citizenry that any tendency towards tyranny will be curbed. But let us permit Montesquieu to speak for himself:

The political liberty of the subject is a tranquility of mind arising from the opinion each person has of its safety. In order to have this liberty, it is requisite the government be so constituted as one man need not be afraid of another.

When the legislative and executive powers are united in the same person, or in the same body of magistrates, there can be no liberty; because apprehensions may arise, lest the same monarch or senate should enact tyrannical laws, to execute them in a tyrannical manner.

Again, there is no liberty, if the judiciary power be not separated from the legislative and executive. Were it joined with the legislative, the life and liberty of the subject would be exposed to arbitrary control; for the judge would be then the legislator. Were it joined to the executive power, the judge might behave with violence and oppression.

There would be an end of everything, were the same man or the same body, whether of the nobles or of the people, to exercise those three powers, that of enacting laws, that of executing the public resolutions, and of trying the causes of individuals.[16]

The theory has its antecedents in Polybius's analysis of the constitution of the Roman Republic, but Polybius was less concerned with the problem of the liberty of the subject than with the impossibility of fitting the Roman constitution into the Greek tripartite division of governments.[17] Montesquieu, however, found in his ideal constitution, the English, an explanation for the freedom of the subject. The English crown, according to the French Anglophile, functions as executor of the law and as commander in chief of the armed forces; parliament legislates; and the judiciary is in the hands of the people because juries are drawn from the populace at large and at random. Most historians of politics agree that Montesquieu would not have approved of some of the subsequent developments in English constitutional law because the executive has virtually lost its independence except in moments of crisis. Nor can we imagine Montesquieu's approving of a ceremonial monarch whose functions are reduced to opening Parliament and presiding over Derby Day. But notwithstanding these vicissitudes of history, Montesquieu would recognize in contemporary England substantially the same division of power he praised when he wrote *The Spirit of the Laws* in 1748.

The doctrine of the separation of powers was more descriptive in Montesquieu than prescriptive, but European liberalism seized upon checks and balances and separation of powers as a theoretical justification of the majoritarian parliamentarianism that ever since has been looked upon as the *conditio sine qua non* of democratic liberty.[18] The conviction was substantial with the dominant mood of the liberalism that occupied the continent in 1848. The identification of free government with the separation of powers had by then become a settled conviction within the galaxy of judgments forming the liberalism of the times. This conviction was written into the French Constitution of 1830, which gave the throne to Louis-Philippe (who agreed to be the policeman of the Revolution, thus proving himself a true heir to the traditions of his House.) The separation of powers was behind that aping of British institutions indulged in by the heirs of Napoleon and it is among the ironies of modern history that continental liberalism found a model for its political institutions in the very country and tradition that brought to heel the first soldier of the Revolution.

It was in opposition to this spirit that Juan Donoso Cortés wrote his famous letter to the editor of the *Revue des Deux Mondes*, November 15, 1852, in answer to an attack made upon him by the liberal (Orleanist) royalist, M. Albert de Broglie.[19] His answer contains a theory of power which is the most serious challenge to the presuppositions of liberalism as we have inherited them from the nineteenth century. That this theory has hitherto not been studied dispassionately and with philosophical detachment is due largely to the calumny heaped upon the head of its author by the entire liberal tradition.

The student of political philosophy, upon approaching the text of Donoso Cortés, must keep in mind that he is about to be instructed by the finest intelligence that placed itself at the service of what we tend to call today the Counter Revolution in contradistinction to English and American conservatism. Donoso belongs, therefore, to what continental political thought simply calls "traditionalism."[20] The student ought to make an effort to locate Donoso Cortés within the context of his times: Donoso, an architect of the Spanish Pragmatic Succession; an early pillar of the liberal monarchy of Isabel II; an opponent of the claims of Don Carlos Isidro of the principle of legitimacy and of a nation at arms against the imposition of the centralizing radicalism of Madrid; in short, a man who owed everything, his title of Marques de Valdegamas as well as his own career in diplomacy, to the liberalism he came to loathe in the last brilliant years of his short life. The reader newly come to Donoso will also want to know that he is about to meet the man most hated by the European left and most especially by the Catholic left, hated with a venom that so puzzled Carl Schmitt that he concluded that its intensity was "not normal and proper to political opposition," that it must spring from "motives which are deeper, metaphysical"[21] and which cause his contemporary Spanish biographer, Don Federico Suárez, to wonder why it was that the enemies of Donoso—they are legion—would have preferred him to have been a "romantic or a primitive"[22] rather than an elegant diplomat who graced with equal ease the salons of Europe from Madrid to St. Petersburg. The reader must also set aside any propensities he might entertain about academic and scientific departmentalism. To the theologian, Donoso looks like a political theorist; to the political philosopher, he seems a theologian; to the man of action, a theoretician; to the academician, a politician. In truth he was all of these things and yet were we to seek a formula capable of defining the man we could do no worse than call him the absolute negation of the Revolution in all its forms.

Broglie had accused Donoso of worshipping the Middle Ages and of urging upon the Church "an absolute and universal domination" in European affairs, of "inculcating in the minds of men the need for a restoration of the Middle Ages." It was this last accusation that Donoso considered to have been the most significant of them all and it was the spur moving him to write the letter of 1852. Donoso begins by candidly pleading guilty to the charges as far as political principle and not historical form is concerned. The Middle Ages, he begins, were set in motion by a tendency which sought "to constitute Power in accord with the principles making up the public law of Christian nations." Modern Europe, however, is engaged presently upon the task of shaping Power according to "certain theories and conceptions . . . foreign to Catholic norms."[23] As a consequence we in Europe will soon come to know, in a future not distant, a "Power infallibly . . . demagogic, pagan in its structure and satanic in its grandeur" (p. 462). So that this prophecy may be intelligible to his readers, Donoso proposes to develop rapidly in his reply to Broglie a theory about the nature of power itself.

He advises us that "God has imposed upon the world a sovereign law in virtue of which it is necessary that the very unity and variety found in God Himself be found in all things" (p. 462). Although not articulated in the letter, it is clear that Donoso here refers to the orthodox Christian doctrine of the Trinity of Persons and Unity of Nature of the

Christian God. In his famous *Essay on Catholicism, Liberalism, and Socialism*, published one year earlier in 1851, Donoso had explored a paradox that recalls the mind of the Patristic Age and that would not be emphasized again in modern times until Chesterton wrote his *Orthodoxy:*

The same God who is author and governor of political society is author and governor of all domestic society. In the most hidden depths and in the highest places, in the most serene and luminous of the heavens there resides a Tabernacle inaccessible even to the choir of the angels: in that inaccessible Tabernacle there is worked perpetually the prodigy of all prodigies and the Mystery of all Mysteries. There is the Catholic God, One and Triune: unity expanding itself, engendering an eternal variety as well as variety condensing itself and resolving itself into an eternal unity. . . . Because He is One, He is God; because He is God, He is perfect; because He is perfect, He is most fecund; because He is most fecund, He is Variety and because He is Variety, He is family. In His essence are contained, in an unerring and incomprehensive way, the laws of creation. . . . All has been made in His Image and because of this, creation is one and varied. (p. 220)

This law of unity found in variety and variety in unity, the metaphysical character of which Donoso does not leave in doubt, works within the heart of the family where the unity of the child is born of the variety of the parents in a circularity which prohibits our affirming that variety is prior to unity or unity to variety.[24] This last clearly cuts Donoso away from that kind of individualism which at bottom denies all reality to social relations and separates him from Hegelian organicism, which sees the individual as growing out of, and as constituted by, society considered as a preexistent whole. We might be tempted to seek Donoso's law of variety and unity in the Thomistic analogy of being were it not that a reading of the Donosian texts fails to reveal any systematic dependence on St. Thomas.[25] Furthermore, we must remember that the intellectual climate of the early nineteenth century, even when Catholic, was not dominated by Thomism. Thomistic studies were revived some four decades after Donoso's death. Donoso's conviction represents, perhaps, an obscure awareness that if being is not ultimately pluralistic in structure the West would have to embrace the lonely God of Islam.

"Who does not see in this law," insists Donoso in *The Essay*, "a high and hidden mystery: unity engendering variety perpetually and variety perpetually constituting unity?"[26] Not content with stating his law, Donoso is constrained to explore it further: this is "the hidden law presiding over the generation of the One and the Many which ought to be considered the most high, the most excellent and the most mysterious of all laws since God has subjected all things to it, human as well as divine, created as well as uncreated, visible as well as invisible" (p. 236). Nor must this law be thought of as though it were a univocal formula which applies to all things in the same way as do mathematical proportions. The law of variety and unity is, paradoxically enough, subjected to itself:

Being one in its essence, it is infinite in its manifestations; all things that exist would seem not to be at all except to manifest the same law; and each and all of the things that are manifest this law in a different fashion: in one way it is in God, in another way it is in God made Man; now in a new way it is in His Church, in the family, and then in another way the law is in the universe; but it is in all things and in every part of the whole; here in one place it is invisible and an incomprehensible mystery and there in another place it is a visible phenomenon, and a palpable fact. (p. 239)

The sovereign law of unity and variety appealed to in the letter, therefore, is understood by Donoso to be a philosophical principle in the most rigorous sense of the term, a law he had explored with the most exquisite care in the early chapter of *The Essay*. This law must, however, remain unintelligible to any reader who approaches it with the prejudices moder-

CHRISTIANITY AND POLITICAL PHILOSOPHY

nity has inherited from the rationalist tradition. We are not
concerned here with a law either intuited by the intelligence
or deduced from undemonstrable first principles. Donoso's
law of variety and unity is a consequence of his own acceptance of the Christian doctrine concerning the Trinitarian
God. On this point at least Donoso is closer to the Augustinian than to the Thomistic tradition because his *episteme* or
political knowledge is the fruit of his meditation upon a truth
which transcends the naked capacity of the human mind.
Once the Christian teaching on God is accepted, however, it
becomes capable of illuminating a whole area of experience
far more intelligibly than would a purely immanentist political philosophy.[27] All things partake of unity and variety but
man is able to see this truth clearly only in the light of a
doctrine, a dogma, which he does not see but believes.
Donoso is clearly in the *credo ut intelligam* tradition of Saint
Augustine.

With so much said we can proceed to affirm that whereas
uniformity and univocity govern the rationalist and liberal
universe, variety and unity rule the Christian traditionalist
world of Donoso Cortés. Donoso finds his supreme principle
of being working within political existence in the following
fashion: "In society unity manifests itself through Power, and
variety manifests itself through Hierarchies." Both are inviolable and sacred. "Their co-existence is simultaneously the
fulfillment of the will of God and the assurance of the liberty
of the people."[28] The burden of the argument of the letter is
Donoso's demonstration that political sanity involves an essential unity of power on the one hand and the essential
variety of hierarchies on the other hand. The marriage between power and hierarchy (our principle of authority, as
shall be seen) is the *conditio sine qua non* for a Christian
political and social order.

The careful reader will note that Donoso insists that unity

is found within power. Although of itself this does not constitute an antiliberal and anti-Montesquian position it does
suggest the tack that Donoso actually will take. The sugges-
tion is heightened by Donoso's distinction between the
medieval and the absolute monarchy. The former reflected
proper relations that ought to exist between power and the
hierarchies. "Power was one, perpetual, and limited; it was
one in the person of the king; it was perpetual in his family; it
was limited because it was checked forever by a material
resistence encountered in an organized hierarchy" (p. 462).
Donoso denies flatly that medieval assemblies such as the
Spanish Cortes or the English Parliament formed part of the
public power. When monarchy was strong without being absolute, representative assemblies were a dike to the tendency
of power to expand itself indefinitely; when monarchy was
weak, these assemblies were a field of battle which reflected a
society in chaos. He insists that those historians who see in
medieval representative institutions the source of modern
parliamentarianism are "ignorant of what a parliamentary
government is and they know nothing of its origin" (p. 462).
Donoso thus denies any strict continuity in the experience of
Western man between the autonomous political institutions
of the Middle Ages and the liberal parliamentary system of
nineteenth-century Europe. Historically it seems difficult to
gainsay the Spanish thinker despite the fact that the revolt
against absolutism was often mounted by men who used
medieval limited-government rhetoric as a cloak for their
own revolutionary goals. Modern civilization—returning to
our analysis of the text—owes its decadence in the moral,
political, and religious orders to its failure to obey the tensions that ought to exist between power and hierarchy,
between—reverting to our earlier discussion—power and
authority.

The absolute monarchy had the good fortune, according

to Donoso, of having conserved the unity and perpetuity of power in the person of the king and the dynastic family. Absolute monarchy, however, sinned in that "it despised and suppressed all resistances" to power by destroying those corporate hierarchies in which these resistances had grown up and which incarnated them. Absolutism thus "violated the Law of God." In so doing it violated the law of variety and unity. What follows in the text is an eloquent defense of freedom foreign to the rhetoric of liberalism: "A Power without limits is an essentially Anti-Christian Power and it is simultaneously an outrage done the majesty of God and the dignity of man. A Power without limits can never be a ministry or a service and political Power under the imperatives of Christian civilization can never be anything less. Unlimited Power is also an idolatry lodged within both subject and king: idolatry in the subject because he adores the king; idolatry in the king because he worships himself" (p. 462).

But if Donoso finds much to condemn in the absolutism that culminated in the Enlightenment, he finds even more to attack in the political system that grew out of the French Revolution. The absolute monarchy "although negating the Christian monarchy" in one fundamental aspect, did affirm it in two other fundamentals: power remained one and perpetual and thus obeyed the metaphysics of political power as understood by our author. Parliamentarianism, however, violated the structure of power in all of its essential notes and hence in their consequences. Liberalism, writes Donoso:

denies power's unity because it converts into three through the division of powers that which really is one; Liberalism denies this principle in its *perpetuity* because it grounds the principle itself in a contract and no power is inviolable if its foundation is variable; Liberalism denies Power's *limitation*; this is so because this political trinity in which Power resides either cannot function due to its impotency, an organic sickness itself the result of Power's division or Power acts tyranically not recognizing outside of itself, or discovering around itself, any legitimate resistance. It thus follows that the parliamentary system which denies the Christian monarchy in all of its conditions of unity also denies that institution in its *variety* and in all the conditions producing variety because the parliamentary system suppresses the "social hierarchies." (p. 462)

Wherever the liberal system has taken root, all corporations tend to disappear along with the hierarchical order within society that they establish. By *corporations* Donoso does not mean any specific kind of institution but that analagous whole which includes an aristocracy; free guilds (themselves heavily attacked and ultimately destroyed by liberalism); self-governing townships; regional assemblies representing regional interests (what we in this country call the principle of states' rights); free universities belonging to ecclesiastical or other private interests and not extensions of the state (the state university was the creation of the continental European system of liberalism); a strong free peasantry whose concrete rights rest upon customary law; in a word—that whole complex of autonomous institutions that disappeared upon the continent due to both absolutism and liberalism and that has survived, if only in a truncated way, within the Anglo-Saxon world. Free institutions naturally group themselves within a hierarchy and their destruction involves the leveling of the whole community and the disappearance of the principle of hierarchy from political order. The theory of parliamentary supremacy, involving the concentration of power in a body which claims to be sovereign, admits of no dialogue between executive and deliberative assemblies except the one which is carried out through cabinet ministers who are themselves nothing other than ambassadors of parliament and its will. Donoso insists that no discussion can be found between the liberal parliament and the people that is continuous. The lone exception admitted is, of course, the dialogue expressed by free elections, but these elections are exercised at limited concrete moments. (Donoso knew, being no fool, that democratic elections are not all that free in fact: masses are manipulated by money; nonetheless, Donoso did not use this argument and preferred to take on the liberals on their own assumption which he knew to be shaky and possibly downright false, that elections in truth are free.) The brief cohesion, heady and fleeting, which society finds on election day falls back into either the indifference of men who one day later have lost their role in the political order or into that chaos which follows on the refusal of the defeated to buckle under to the decision of the polls.

Donoso, the politician and the historian, attacks the Revolution: the drying up of the vestiges of medieval liberties at the hands of the centralizers: that is, the abolition of what little remained in Europe of regional liberties; the division of France into administrative units dependent on Paris; the suppression of the last of the free trade unions in both Spain and France and the reduction of artisans and laborers to a lumpenproletariat with no economic or political voice in the land; the sale of municipal and church properties under the government of Mendizábol in Spain which saw a quarter of Spain's land under the auctioneer's block in less than a year, thus creating a new rich middle class "which was less a political party," in the words of Menendez y Pelayo, "than a bad conscience"; the steady war of attrition against religious orders; the flattening of Latin Europe into a grey field administered by ever more centralized governments dominated by party ideologues hostile to the Christian tradition. Donoso adds that those who see any significant difference between liberalism and socialism err. Whereas the former violates power in matters political, the latter does so in matters social.

Donoso does not, of course, deny the existence or value of political contracts. He could hardly have done so in the light

[164]

of his own nation's history. The supremacy of the crown of Castile gained legitimacy in the eyes of Spaniards because it was the product of an intricate network of pacts contracted by Castile and the other Spanish kingdoms, counties, and lordships. This legitimacy was written into the law of the land and it lingers even today in Navarre which enjoys a number of state rights *(fueros)* that are a thousand years old and that were reluctantly respected by the centralist Madrid government during the Franco regime. Navarre's contract with Castile involved the sanctity of these ancient laws and customs, of a juridical corpus as venerable and as complex as any in the civilized world.[29] Donoso's contention is not, hence, a denial of the juridical validity and factuality of contracts but rather a denial that political power can be understood philosophically to be constituted by a contract.

Power can always be seized from the ins by the outs but political power itself—understood as a dimension of human existence—persists in being perpetual except in moments of total breakdown within a society. The absence of power is anarchy. In a word: wherever there exists a political society we find there a power that is just as perpetual as is the society. Donoso's note of perpetuity as belonging to power does not mean eternity nor does it exclude an ethic of revolution. The issue is really self-evident. There can be many public powers successively in time, many governments, the one following the other due to the disappearance and appearance of new political societies produced by invasion, revolution, decay of the old public orthodoxy, or any other cause capable of altering the fabric of an existent community. Power itself, however, must be conceived as coterminal with any given political society. Behind Donoso's contention lies his own reiterated conviction that power is simply a necessary expression and representation of a living historical community. An admission that power is nonperpetual within some existent

[165]

community involves a denial that political society is a temporal and psychic continuum. Nineteenth-century liberalism did just this, however. In its excessive reaction against the absolutism whose ape it was, liberalism so shattered the unity of power that it reduced society to a battleground or a boxing ring. It follows that liberal theory not only denies the limitation of power which is the fruit of hierarchical variety but it shatters society from within, fragmenting it, denying it the coherence which is the product of what I have called throughout this work and elsewhere a "public orthodoxy."[30]

Let it be noted clearly that Donoso is elaborating here a metaphysics of power in total opposition to that prevalent in the rhetoric which fills the literature of liberalism, a rhetoric which drew—as indicated earlier—on its own understanding of what Montesquieu had written about the British constitution. We have already seen that the liberal insistence that the subject or citizen finds freedom only when power is divided into three was deeply ingrained in the European mentality at the time Donoso composed the letter. We have noted that the political model buttressing the theory was thought to be England. It followed, therefore, that Donoso had to face the imposing fact of the English constitution, come to terms with it theoretically in the light of his own teaching on power, or abandon the field.

Donoso was keenly aware of the fact that his political theory on the issue at hand stood or fell with his own analysis of the British experience. He begins his attack by pointing out that these men who "attend only to appearance and to forms" will conclude that parliamentarianism has existed "in all times and places." These forms can be found "in England where the nation is governed by the Crown and the two Houses of Parliament; and they can be found in past times in all the nations of Europe where clergy, nobility, and cities were called together to deliberate over affairs of a public nature."[31] But, he insists, if we suppress appearances and attend to "the spirit" animating them, we must conclude that the medieval parliaments as well as the modern British constitution have nothing to do with European parliamentarianism.[32] His words are better than any gloss:

If, beginning with the British Constitution, we set ourselves the task of examining not only its external organization but also and principally its internal organism before the late reforms, we shall discover that the division of Power was altogether lacking in reality, being nothing other than a vain appearance. The Crown was not a Power nor did it even form part of Power: it was a symbol and the image of the nation; to be a king there in England was neither to rule nor to govern: it was, purely and simply, to be adored. This passive attitude of the Crown excludes by its very nature the idea of government which is incompatible with the idea of a perpetual inaction and an eternal repose. The House of Commons in both its composition and its spirit was a younger brother of the House of Lords. Its voice was not a voice but an echo. The House of Lords under this modest title was the only true Power in the State. England was not a monarchy but an aristocracy and this aristocracy was a *Power which was one, perpetual and limited: one,* because it resided in a *moral Person,* quickened by a single spirit; *perpetual,* because this moral person was a class endowed by legislation with the necessary means to endure perpetually; *limited,* because the Constitution and the traditions and the customs obliged the House of Lords to behave in accordance with the modesty of its title. (p. 267)

The British constitution that emerged from the Protestant Succession and the defeat of the Stuart cause in no sense broke with the essential structure of power within medieval Christendom: if medieval political power was one in the king, perpetual in his family, and limited by a hierarchical variety of institutions, modern Great Britain possessed, in the mid-nineteenth century, a similar structure, the unity of power reposing in the aristocracy, perpetuity belonging to the hereditary nature of that aristocracy, and limitation to the traditions, customs, and laws guaranteeing Englishmen their

[167]

rights. These rights—we must admit—decayed considerably since the high Middle Ages under the pressure of Tudor centralization and the loss of independence by the Church. Guild principles were in full decay by the time Donoso commented upon England: in fact they had been effectively dead for a century and a half. Nonetheless the rights of Englishmen, as the Burkeans quite properly insist, were largely guaranteed and respected. So far as the crown is concerned, we need only note that its illusions of power were unmasked as hollow when the Stuarts tried to take them seriously. What Hilaire Belloc was fond of calling "the popular monarchy" was dead before Charles I raised the royal standard at Nottingham.[35] The Restoration politics of Charles II were a series of brilliant delaying tactics by a crown already fighting a hopeless battle against a new aristocracy that was the repository of the Reformation Settlement, of a new public orthodoxy that was the Power in the land.

The apparent division of power in the English constitution was simply a division of labor in the business of government, a division called for by the complexity of the tasks at hand and by the highly desirable need for the agents of power to debate among themselves and with society at large before exercising their mandate as corporate representatives—as a moral person in the words of Donoso—of a regime or a public orthodoxy. Power (the point is not specifically made by Donoso) has two instruments to implement its will, neither of which is identically power itself: violence and persuasion; both require a plurality of agents and even of institutions. Donoso's nervous fingering of the essential unity of political power made him contemptuous of the forms of debate and of dialogue. In this he may have erred but he can be forgiven his error for having struck at the heart of the affair, that is, the British constitution was the representative of a nation led by an aristocracy whose rule was accepted as proper and just by the people at large. This power, unlimited from within its own structure, was definitely limited or checked from without by the common law, by custom, by prescription, and by a thicket of traditional rights and duties which were inherited by the American colonies and thus incorporated into the American tradition. Donoso's contribution here was strikingly original: that is, there simply is no organic link whatsoever between the Whig tradition and the French Revolution. If the Anglo-American whiggish tradition has any link whatsoever with the political thought of modern Europe, that link, by a curious irony, has to be with the counterrevolutionary philosophy of the nineteenth and early twentieth centuries. That both tend to abominate each other is an issue belonging to the substantives of politics and not to the metaphysics of power.

The French history illustrates Donoso's insights by contrast. The Bourbons of the eighteenth century had attempted to limit their own power from within that very power by appealing to parliaments for an impartial reading of the legality of royal actions. This attempt was frustrated at its inception because the supposed limitation was either false, in no sense serious due to its having come out of a royal sovereignty which itself accepted no source of law beyond itself except a vague appeal to the Christian conscience of the king; or because, when serious, the limitation tended to identify itself with the class interests and doctrinal predilections of the lawyers who interpreted the law, thus creating a special interest lobby, so to speak, inside the total machinery of government which was bent on securing its own advancement to the detriment of the presumed impartial majesty of the law. Had the French crown been led consistently by the lawyers instead of only by fits and starts, power in France would have shifted to the new bourgeoisie before the Revolution instead of afterwards. The crown would thus have become the agent of a new liberalism some one century or more before it actually did so in the reign of Louis-Philippe from 1830 to 1848. The Orleanist king's refusal to be crowned by Rheims as had the Capetian dynasty from time immemorial indicated his willingness to serve the Revolution whose power base was the rising industrial middle class.

Donoso's metaphysics of power is thus buttressed by an historical phenomenology which brushes away any illusions about power's effective limitation from within its own structure. Donoso, unconsciously, bends back to Sir John Fortescue whose symbol of the head—the king, the power—meshes splendidly with Donoso's own insistence on power as unitary. Fortescue's symbol of the laws as the limbs of the body politic meshes just as well with Donoso's understanding of power as specified by authorities existing in institutions thrown up organically by society itself.[34] The medieval English lawyer lived in a political order articulated by himself in a strikingly similar way to the Spanish diplomat's articulation of that same order in retrospect. That the one man did not know the other because of the accident of time and that the second did not know the first because of the accident of space is a striking confirmation of the vigor of a Christian philosophy that can be coherent with itself simply provided that it attend carefully to the existential exigencies out of which theory must emerge.

We have already mentioned that, according to the letter, medieval assemblies must not be understood as though they were political powers. They represented the principle of authority and not power and hence kings had to dialogue with them and had to listen to their desires and complaints. These assemblies crystalized the natural resistance to power found in the community and hence they chastened kings and humbled crowns. When the purse strings depended on society, power was given an additional motive for heeding the authority incarnated in the commonwealth and power was forced to come to terms with that authority. Medieval parliaments were, says Donoso, a "social force, . . . an organic resistance and a natural limit to the indefinite expansion of power."[35]

Liberal parliamentarianism, on the contrary, developed according to the theory that power must be perpetually divided, thus placing it—according to Donoso—at the mercy "of a hundred parties." The resultant chaos turned the parliaments of the last century and of this one into battlefields. The French Republic of the reforms of DeGaulle which restored power, or has tried to restore power, to the executive is old enough for us to affirm that it snatched France from chaos; it is too young for us to affirm that it has shaken France out of the dream of the myth of parliamentary democracy. In the scorching words of Donoso, written at the acme of liberal mythology, parliaments "by suppressing the hierarchies which are the natural and hence divine form of *variety* and denying to Power its indivisibility which is the divine, natural, and necessary condition of its *unity*, produced an open insurrection against God as far as He is the creator, the legislator, and the conserver of human societies" (p. 474).

In the grim, steely world of political and social unrest produced by liberalism, God permits the combat but he "denies the victory" (p. 474). Donoso here pushes his philosophy of power to its final consequences. If the law of unity and variety is true to the ultimate order of being it follows that any attempt at violating its structure must be self-defeating. We would miss the significance of Donoso's critique were we to reduce his study to an analysis of political institutions, some of which he approved of and some of which he disliked. Donoso's preference for the traditional Catholic kingdoms of the Middle Ages can be read this way and political philosophers ought not to deny to their fellow practitioners existential and historical preferences. Nonetheless, behind Donoso's predilections there lies a philosophy which transcends them because it purports to teach us something about power as power, no matter where, or in what historical moment of time, or under whatever form it might exist, including— of course—under the form of democracy. The division of power and the centralization of society are twin ontological monsters for Donoso Cortés. The decentralized political community that diffuses authority through a variety of autonomous institutions is a dictate of the law of political existence. In our time, as pointed out earlier in this book, Professor Alvaro D'Ors discovered this law at work in the early Roman distinction between power and authority. "In general terms, authority is the truth recognized by society and it is set off against *potestas* which is force or power recognized by society."[36] Both grow out of and represent the same political order or regime but they ought "to remain permanently separated because if authority resides in the same organ that possesses *potestas* it follows that authority could never serve as a limit or brake."[37]

The alarming collapse of Christianity today in a society bent upon secularizing itself so profoundly that it even makes of Christianity a tool in the desacralizing of political existence[38] has left the West without an effective representative of the authority of God and of the moral law. Institutional tinkering with the instruments of power in some vain attempt to play them off one against another is no effective scalpel for ridding the body politic of the diseases of tyranny and chaos.

Politics which sin against the laws of being do so at their own peril. They fall into either a tyrannical power which violates the body politic or into a chaos within whose vortex every faction within the community vies with all comers for the palm of a power possessed by none. Donoso's phenomenology of power, the basis of his metaphysics of power, today works out its tragic destiny in the new African and Asian countries where the disintegration of tribal loyalties follows the centralizing of power and its identification with sovereign authority. Authority, no longer centrifugal, diffused throughout the community by way of a plurality of institutions that repose ultimately upon some final representative of divine truth, some last voice which speaks with the wisdom and even the thunder of God, loses itself in the insane pretensions of a tyrannical egotism (isolationist America today) or gives itself over to gnostic or totalitarian dreams in the name of a supposed fiat written into the flow of history (Russia and China). The French Revolution which has destroyed us all was ushered into the West by its outriders and its visionaries from Machiavelli through Bodin and beyond to Marx and Marcuse. Don Juan Donoso Cortés, unlike Montesquieu, refused to tinker with the body of the West. By then it was too far gone in disease. He called for the surgery of the counter revolution.

THE NATURAL LAW TRADITION AND THE AMERICAN POLITICAL EXPERIENCE

❧ I have a very good friend who insists that he rejects murder because his prescriptive experience has taught him that murder is evil: his rejection is historical and cultural. In turn, I have often asked him if there was nothing in the very act of murder, abstracting from the Mount Sinai prohibition and from our civilized abhorrence of such an act, that made him reject it. Granted that Mount Sinai makes you look at murder, does not the very look itself tell you that murder is intrinsically wrong, wrong altogether without the divine prohibition engraved in the tablets? My friend has always refused to ground his rejection of murder on any intrinsic evil presumed to inhere in the act: his rejection, as indicated, is traditional and not rational. Now the difference between determining that murder is evil by confronting the act and judging it to be intrinsically wrong and determining that murder is evil because our inheritance says that it is evil is the entire difference measuring the abyss between natural law philosophy and all other philosophies of law, including legal positivism and conservative historicism.

The business ultimately is one with the enormous separation between those who accept political constitutions, be they written or unwritten, as moral absolutes and those who, discovering or thinking that they discover some discrepancy between the constitution and the natural law, appeal to this superior dictate. Socrates made this appeal a classic test case of one man against the public orthodoxy of the community.

My purpose here is not to explore the reasons advanced by the friends of reason, the advocates of natural law theory. My purpose is political. I wish to locate the issue within the framework of political philosophy. The construction of a political model helps us understand natural law in its relation to practical politics in all its stark nakedness. If any man holds that there exists a law which transcends the written statute; if he holds that such a law is both thoroughly reasonable in itself and authored by God, man's Creator; if, further, he insists that any conflict between written, positive law (or unwritten, customary law) and this transcendant law must be adjudicated in favor of the latter—then the political society in question must draw up its options in dealing with such a fellow and he must draw up his options as well. If the polity in question holds that the natural law is already woven into the written statutes, then an appeal to the law books or, more rarely, to the spoken tradition will be an appeal to the natural law. If the society—more commonly—grants the existence of a natural law but looks upon it as something reposing in the bosom of prescription, custom, and tradition, then the natural law can be expected to guide, from the moral background of the people, the writing of positive law. (In Spanish law an appeal to the natural law can be made by a lawyer in court because natural law has equal status with positive law; the study and expertise in natural law is a legal profession in Spain. Spain, however, is always a notorious exception; in England and the United States a lawyer and a judge can appeal and adjudicate above the positive law in rare cases but the right to do so is not officially recognized.)[1]

But what happens in case of a conflict between natural law theory and positive law, most especially positive law written into legislated statutes? If the natural law gives way to the positive law, then the society has effectively abandoned natu-

[175]

ral law theory as a guide for behavior and has relegated it, at least, to an individual norm of behavior. But this last will not wash because the very theory of natural law itself insists that its dictates be norms for the common good of the community. Natural law theory is not individualistic, it is corporate Natural law insists that pornography, for example (abstracting from the thorny epistemological and legal question as to what really is pornography in this or that case), is bad and that it is bad not just for me but for everybody, and it equally insists that not only must I not invade my neighbor's property but that he must not invade mine nor anybody else's. If the society, on the contrary, wishes to safeguard the natural law in a political fashion, then it must contrive some institution, itself having the force of positive law and the power of the sword, entrusted with ensuring the public acceptance of natural law. The alternatives are either the abandonment of natural law in favor of legal positivism or an invitation to rebellion.

Let us give these propositions a contemporary flavor. The natural law insists that abortion is murder. Society A has a horror of abortion because Society A has an overarching commitment to natural law theory; this commitment is so strong that the society does not need to legislate against abortion. For Society A, the natural law is so profoundly grounded in the viscera of the people that it would seem absurd to write down a law against such a crime. That abortion is a peculiarly hideous crime belongs to the prescriptive inheritance of the community; nobody has to write laws about it. Society A might very well distinguish between what could be called first class and second class murder and it could conclude that abortion belongs to the latter category, but such a society would never inscribe in its written constitution any positive prohibition against murder as such. For such a society a written prohibition of this nature would be as absurd as a written promise by a bride and groom not to kill one another. Another society—we call it society B—possibly because its people are more vocal or dramatic or possibly because it is menaced by dissenters from within, might well write into its constitution a commitment to the natural law. But, in order to do so, the community would have to make it the business of some institutions, all of which had legal and official status in the polity, to defend the natural law: for example, to prohibit the killing of the old people in the name of their being a nuisance, or to prohibit the killing of unborn people under the same rubric. The issue is complicated in the case of a supposed democratic community. I do not refer here to a society that simply uses democratic procedures in order to get about its business, but rather a society that exalts the goddess Democracy into an ultimate principle of the Good in things political. The first society might well opt to use democracy as a political instrument up to, but no further than, ultimate questions on right and wrong. The second society considers that the democratic principle itself is the ultimate in such considerations. The democratic society, as defined here in the second instance of a democracy, must test any possible commitment to the natural law by appealing to the electorate. This last suggests, of course, that there is a law superior to the natural law, the law of the will of the 50 percent plus one. This last law within what we call an ideological rather than a procedural democracy, becomes then the very first of laws.

How then does the natural law tradition fare within such an ideological democratic ambient? By a curious irony the enemies of the supposed immutability of the natural law always appeal to the immutability of the democratic principle. Philosophically, this means that democracy is exalted to the status of an absolute. Aristotle tried to refine this situation in his conviction that over the long run justice would prevail simply because people, taken in the large and by the handful, tend to be more decent than perverse. In the short run, however, Aristotle held that injustice often prevails in the majority at any time, and this majority might very well be acting viciously out of passion or irrational self-interest. In some Orwellian tomorrow it will be small comfort indeed to tell some old chap just before he is to be snuffed out by the clinical executioners of the state that things will get better tomorrow because folks, after all, are usually decent—tomorrow. Democracy would seem, on the surface, to be a shaky ally of natural law theory, which always defends and condemns, in the concrete now. In truth, ideological democracy is a deadly enemy of natural law theory.

These philosophical models are not simply logical antinomies. They have had historical existence, and the passage of time reveals to the political philosopher a kind of inner logic dictated by the very nature of politics. In order to understand that logic and then apply it to the American experience in our day, we might well turn to the history of natural law in the Western world.

If we accept the articulation of the political philosophy of Thomas Aquinas as somehow typical and even paradigmatic of natural law teaching as known in the West, we can see in his very teaching (ST 1–2, qq. 91–97) the causes for the decadence of natural law theory in our time. The theory of natural law and its deeper roots in classical antiquity are found in Plato and Aristotle. Injustice for Plato (*Republic* 2) is ultimately a refusal to mind your own business, to order your own business, your own life, according to circumstances intrinsic to your own life. In Aristotle (*Nicomachean Ethics* 3) there emerged the notion of justice as giving to each man his due: proportional justice. But only in Cicero did a theory called natural law emerge which was to have a massive impact on the subsequent history of European man (*De republica* 1.6; *De legibus*).

Ciceronian natural law transcended the law of the peoples. It was, he insisted, a law that governed all men simply because they were men. In *De republica* (1) Cicero was very sparing in his enumeration of what fell under the natural law: contracts must be fulfilled; oaths must be honored; no man may kill another on his own authority; men in a foreign nation must not profane the customs and beliefs of their hosts; lies are abominations. This is indeed a thin list of what constitutes law. The *Didache*, an early Christian list of abominations against nature, added significant prohibitions: children in the womb may not be killed by their parents; children outside the womb may not be killed by anybody. The prohibition was important because the Greeks (but not the Romans) were notorious for murdering girl babies. Buttressed by Paul's teaching in chapter 1 of his Epistle to the Romans, the *Didache* insisted that there was a law that was not based on statute, that was not dependent on any formal revelation, but that was one with any intelligent and properly willed insight into the very exigencies of human nature itself.[2] The important truth here is the growing conviction in the West that there was a trans-positive law which bound all men—and liberated them as well—and that concrete political societies must bind their own legal codes around this law, one that comes forth from God but that is known by reason. We might add here that this gradual unfolding of natural law was an immense relief to European civilization, a liberation. Although the demands of the natural law can sometimes grate against the grain of human weakness, more often than not natural law frees. Often it frees men to live. I have never yet met an advocate of abortion who wishes that he had been aborted.

Ciceronian natural law was wounded theoretically because

the law had no lawgiver. It was a law without teeth. Behind the teaching of Thomas Aquinas we encounter the almost mordant critique of pagan and classical natural law by Augustine. We have already spelled out, following Cochrane, how Augustine dismissed the pretentions of any law without a lawgiver on the grounds that such a law or appeal to virtue is purely abstract. (*City of God* 5). I can, insisted Augustine, appreciate justice in the large, but this does not move me existentially to be just in the concrete to this man I encounter in the street. I can understand the goodness of temperance or fortitude as abstract ideals, but these ideals do not of themselves urge me to be temperate or strong in the concrete order. In the real order men act well or badly because they love. To a Christian immoral behavior is another nail hammered into the cross of Christ. A coward can turn brave because he loves his wife who is being menaced by a prowler; a drunkard can reform because he loves his children; a strong man can become stronger, a weak man can become strong, and a bad man can be made to be ashamed because of love. Love, in the Augustinian vision of existence, is the gasoline that puts into motion the machinery of classical natural law.

Saint Thomas, as well as the great Baroque Age natural law theorists who gave us international law, did not bypass Augustine's insistence on the preeminence of love. But they did shift their attention to another issue, that of authority. The natural law, be it as natural and open to discovery by reason as it might be, nonetheless demands an interpreter, and this interpreter must be an authority concerning the content of the law itself. All men know the primary principles of the natural law such as "do good and avoid evil," but few men are sufficiently educated to apply such a principle in the concrete intricacies of moral decision. In the Catholic tradition the interpreter was the voice of Peter, descendent of the Apostles, the pope. In some Protestant confessions the natural law was rejected along with a general rejection of human reason. In most Protestant confessions, however, the interpreter of this common moral legacy of the West was the inheritance itself of Christian morality, speaking through its wisest representatives and incarnating itself in living political and social institutions. This survival of natural law tradition within Protestantism has been vigorous and far more powerful than the sixteenth-century theological rejection of any exercise of reason upon matters moral. In both the Catholic and the dominant Protestant traditions the interpretation of natural law was left to the caprice of no brilliant individual, no matter how illuminated he might have been.

I repeat the tension and paradox: as natural, the law can be understood by reason, but we cannot trust just anybody's reason to do the job: we need an authority. The tension is less a tension and the paradox less a paradox when we draw analogies from less controversial areas of life: Euclid's elemental geometry or the geography of the State of Wyoming are understandable to anybody, understandable theoretically, but they are actually understood only by authorities in the two disciplines of geometry and geography. An authority is principally a person who knows the truth in some area of reality. Authority is always personal because authority affirms some truth, and only a flesh and blood human being, a man, can state that this is so and the other is not. Were it otherwise, we would have to assert the absurdity that abstract propositions or laws justified themselves. Abstractions do not do anything; they do not act. It is man himself who uses abstractions in the service of making judgments about things. The truth is always a personal possession because truth is always the function of a mind. Outside of a mind there simply is no truth.[3] Authority, according to the tradition guiding this study, is the personal possession of truth in some order of being.

[181]

The crisis grew out of the English roots of American politics, and these roots are deeply embedded in the Middle Ages. In the Middle Ages there was a vigorous effort made to identify natural law with the common law, customary law, the law which was not written down but which was handed on by word of mouth.[4] I have already indicated in detail Sir John Fortescue's attempt to apply to the English constitution the natural law teaching of Saint Thomas Aquinas. According to Saint Thomas (ST 1–2, q. 97, a. 3), customary law is reducible to an application in the concrete of the natural law, unless there are grave reasons leading competent authorities to think otherwise. The law is good not because it is ancient, but its antiquity is a sign of its probable goodness. Law, according to Fortescue, as pointed out earlier, is not something which men make in England; law is something which we Englishmen principally discover. To make a new law was a grave and serious business which the crown was urged never to do without exercising much caution and prudence. The king, insisted Fortescue, ought to do this only after consulting the authority of the judges.

And it was about that very time that there entered into the Anglo-Saxon experience the ambiguity of the relations between natural law and political society. The English king in theory was the supreme judge in the kingdom, but in fact he usually knew only enough law to carry out his royal duties. He depended on the judiciary in order to get the counsel he needed to dispense justice. But the judiciary slowly made itself independent of the royal power until the king depended more and more on his royal prerogative to suspend written laws which he deemed to be not in the service of the common good. The dispensing power, undoubtedly often badly used in the concrete, was nonetheless based on the natural law insistence that the common good of society is society's ultimate end; should some concrete law, considered by the

king to be a bad law or to be bad in this or that set of circumstances, violate the common good, then it must be at
least suspended. English kingship, of course, consisted in
that crossing of Germanic kingship as soldier and Hebraic
kingship as judge that marked the Middle Ages. Enemies of
the prerogative always cried out against it as tyranny but then
again what else could they do? The royal prerogative survives
today in English constitutional theory as a mummied relic; its
exercise would demand the immediate abdication of the
sovereign user thereof.

This suspending right of the crown was based in theory on
the conviction that there was a law superior to positive law
and that the king of England, in some remote metaphysical
and theological sense, was the representative of that law. In a
word, the crown was the repository of the authority of the
natural law in English constitutional theory, a last recourse
for justice for the poor man against the rich, until the late
seventeenth century.

Natural law theory floated in the air as a kind of inheritance from the Middle Ages, vaguely embedded in the common law, but undefended by any authority possessing the
power of the sword. The theory survived in the system of
granting paroles and suspending sentences when the ends of
justice were thought to be better pursued in this manner than
through strict enforcement of the letter of the law, but these
remnants of older convictions about natural law and justice
were muted with the increasing domination of the supremacy of Lords and Commons. England today is a moral
chaos because of this failure to find some political voice for
the natural law—either a judiciary trained philosophically in
its tenets or the restoration of the authority of an independent crown. It was in the name of this thirst for an ultimate
recourse to justice that made Hilaire Belloc and his friends
launch the banner of "Popular Monarchy" in the early

decades of this century.[5] The quixotic nature of their politics bespoke the confusion into which England's venerable adherence to natural law theory had fallen. The natural law possesses the authority of reason, but without an authoritative voice interpreting that transcending dictate the natural law might as well be relegated to the sphere of private opinion. To incarnate that voice in a personal authority superior to the vicissitudes of party opinion and the humiliations of partisan spoils was both philosophically reasonable and historically justified in the context of English political history. Nonetheless, it was quixotic—and when Edward VIII looked as though he might just be that kind of a king, he was swiftly sent into exile, aided—we must admit—by his own foibles.

The American revolution against Crown and Parliament was a middle-class revolt. There was no Parisian Terror when this nation broke from England. There was no rule in the street by the mob even though Tories were roughly handled or uprooted. The American Revolution was calculated, premeditated, thought through, and launched by the first men and economic interests of the colonies. Everybody involved knew what he was up to. What the Constitution and *The Federalist* sought was a consensus among the citizens of the new republic. Let us, so went the theory, set aside ideological differences and religious divisions and let us get about the business of minding our own businesses and tending our own gardens. The country was vast and there were few urban concentrations of potential political dynamite. The so-called theory of the extended republic adequately fitted the desires of colonists who wanted to expand, make their fortunes, and let their own kind live in peace to do the same.[6]

The United States was not born. The United States was made; it was a work of art. This, at the very least, was the theory that won the Civil War and it is upon the victorious theory that I build the following observations. For a political philosopher this experience is extremely significant because it corresponds to what was little more than a dream for Plato and Aristotle: to model a political society, not by way of preexistent tradition and custom but totally out of the cloth of the minds of its founders. We are a nation because a number of men wrote us down on foolscap. Even though we were created out of the minds of the Founding Fathers (so goes the victorious theory), their world was that of men in whose spirit mingled, in varying degrees, the traditions of the older natural law theory as well as those of eighteenth-century Enlightenment rationalism. The American Constitution was an instrument which attempted to resolve fundamental problems not by creating a tribunal which represented the natural law in its universal and ultimate character, but by placing in tension the diverse interests of the people. Bouncing the ball back and forwards in such fashion that nobody or no institution had the final word was worked into the very genius of the system. This is the thesis of L. Brent Bozell in his monumental work on the history of the Supreme Court.[7]

According to *The Federalist*, the Constitution threw into an orbit of tension differing factions and interests in order to avoid any one of them, pretending to represent the "Truth," from submitting the nation to its own peculiar ideology. The system was organized in such fashion that all groups and interests could develop their corporate personalities without disturbing one another. Geography played a crucial role in this development: the first North Americans faced land spaces which were inconceivable to Europeans. Given that economic interests quite naturally predominated in the early years of the Republic—everybody was trying to make his own fortune—the free development of the land demanded that no group preaching an exclusive corner on the "Truth" could take over the government. Laissez faire: every one to his own

[185]

and let nobody bother his neighbor. Let us make a new world and see to it that the structure of the Constitution will prohibit any ephemeral majority from taking over and launching the Republic into rash adventures.

These convictions quickened the definitive interpretation of the Constitution as well as shaped its writing. The document that emerged from the deliberations in Philadelphia was a model of thinking which reflected, possibly unconsciously, the philosophy of Montesquieu: we must divide power if we are to avoid tyranny. In this attempted division of power based on the fear of tyranny, natural law was to be the casualty. But even natural law men did not wish to yield its definitive interpretation to one of the three branches of government for fear of arbitrary rule.

There was a further ambiguity in the Constitution. This document grew out of American religious pluralism and philosophical eclecticism. The confusion which worked its mischief into history is intelligible only if we return to the natural law tradition at its very roots. This tradition, both classical and Christian, was based on certain metaphysical presuppositions: man has a nature, as dynamic and changeable as it certainly is, which nonetheless perseveres through the ages. Any kind of historicism is hence an enemy of natural law philosophy. Unless human nature enjoys a certain stability the center of which is intrinsically good and not corrupted by sin, it is useless to speak about a common good rooted in a finality supposedly inherent to the substance of man. Evolutionism denies the first proposition. Northern Calvinism, with its emphasis on a supposed total corruption of man by original sin, denies the second proposition. In short: if there is nothing constant in human nature, if man is a sheer process of becoming, the only law possible for him would be law not merely conditioned by history but part and parcel of history. This negation of a human essence implies

[186]

that there is no law which transcends the historical moment. Coupled with the Calvinist theology of New England, which insisted on total human depravity without grace, the natural law philosophy was menaced by a deistic and free-thinking eighteenth-century rationalism allied accidentally with an older and very rigorous form of European Calvinism.

The natural law tradition mingled with these contradictory strains in the American experience as an older legacy from the English tradition. Natural law theory was by no means the exclusive property of Roman Catholics. Both Russell Kirk and Peter Stanlis have demonstrated the natural law roots of Burke's conservatism.[8] Behind Burke there looms the prestigious figure of Hooker whose *Ecclesiastical Polity* advances a natural law doctrine which is frankly Thomistic and which formed part of the English public orthodoxy.[9] Everything, therefore, was confused. Most people talked about a natural law but it might have meant anything from Hobbesian natural law, the law of the jungle, to Locke's natural law, an invitation to get rich. Government welcomed the friends of the older natural law, mostly Anglicans, but it also welcomed its enemies. Obscurely, government sensed that it wanted no clear-cut victory by any tradition on this score. Our constitutional institutions were so structured that no one of them could dominate the others for long. Congress supposedly braked the power of the Presidency. The Presidency braked Congress. Both were checked by the Supreme Court; but the Supreme Court, selected by the President, was itself braked by Congress, elected by the people. The aristocracy of the Senate was braked by the presumed democracy of the House and vice versa. In a word: there was no ultimate authority in the whole Federal system capable of defending the natural law. The system was built to avoid an appeal to an ultimate authority.[10] The confidence of the Founding Fathers reposed in their conviction that out of this network of tensions and restraints there would emerge a free and decent society. The system certainly has worked reasonably well, and it was buttressed by the hope that no single institution, such as an absolute king or a church or even a parliament, would usurp the liberties of free citizens.

Today the system itself is in danger for a number of reasons which fall outside the scope of this study. So far as our purposes are concerned, the system of checks and balances no longer can guarantee rights discovered in the natural law. If public opinion, manipulated as it is by the mass media, is in favor of the natural law tradition, then that tradition will prevail. If, on the contrary, public opinion—always molded and manipulated by the electronic and printed mass media—is opposed to the natural law tradition on this or that issue or even on the existence of such a transcending law, then the tradition will die in this land.

If the defenders of natural law appeal to the people, then they are doing either one of two things: (1) pragmatically garnering support for substantive issues commanded or forbidden by the natural law; (2) or laying the truth of the natural law before a popularity contest. If natural law defenders are doing the first, then it simply means that they act out of desperation because there exists no institution in the land whose specific role is the defense of unwritten rights and duties. They are then fighting a lost cause because of the increasingly hostile attitude towards any law whose authority is presumed to be God. The spirit of the age is against natural law teaching. The Establishment itself is either covertly or openly hostile to any public defense of a transcending law. If natural law defenders have opted for the second possibility, if they truly believe that such a law can be defended favorably by a show of hands, then they have sinned against the tradition that they espouse. A democratic show of hands does not demonstrate the reasonableness of a law, whether the law states that one must not murder the unborn or the aged or the law that insists that one may not directly will the death of civilians in wartime.

Democracy, not as a procedural method to get on with the business of government, but as an unquestioned political and philosophical absolute, is ultimately incompatible with the pretensions of the natural law tradition. Once a society sets up a public authority or watchdog charged with safeguarding duties and rights thought to be themselves untouchable absolutes, that society has declared that it is not an ideological democracy. We did not do this when the nation was founded for a number of understandable reasons. It is difficult to see how we could possibly do this today in a climate of opinion that is substantially more secularist and materialist than was the opinion dominating the late eighteenth century. The democratic principle (not procedure, as pointed out) is unwritten orthodoxy in the United States. It may not be challenged publicly under threat of excommunication from the society. This principle has simply taken the place of all older orthodoxies and today plays the role that natural law once played in Western civilization.

I am not interested here in exploring remedies. I confess that I have none. As a philosopher, it is my duty to explore causes. An insidious form of immorality consists in proposing action without exploring causes.

Therefore I shall content myself here by restating the thesis. In the Middle Ages the English crown stood for a justice based on the naturalness of the law. The crown did this in theory at least. Therefore the crown could and did suspend positive or written legislation if it deemed that this legislation went against the intrinsic rights of the King's subjects or disturbed the common good of the realm. This older constitutional role disappeared as reality even though it survived as a mummified relic in theory.

[189]

A preoccupation with the possibility of tyranny prevented the Founding Fathers from reposing the natural law in the law of either executive or judiciary or legislature. Madison, for example, argued in a letter to Monroe that justice ought to prevail even against a majority, and justice ought to prevail, not because it is expedient that justice be done, but because justice is an absolute. But this healthy American love for the inviolability of the human person formed a tension with the equally healthy American fear of tyranny. That both the love and the fear might conflict could not have been predicted at the dawn of the Republic. Tyranny today does not wear one hat; tyranny does not come from any one institution. Tyranny grows out of a new barbarism bent on self-indulgence and passion. The new barbarism mingles with legal positivism and sheer materialism as well as older rationalistic and scientistic understandings of human nature. Natural law convictions are heavily operative in the United States, but they are operative viscerally, and the media as well as the courts are generally against them. That a million children can be aborted in New York in one year with hardly a ripple of protest and that the Watergate bugging case, a moral triviality, can produce a storm of protest around the nation indicates that our moral priorities are somehow perverse. Venial sin has become mortal sin and mortal sin has become venial: the world has flipped morally.

The violation of a written law moves Americans to indignation but the violation of an unwritten and higher law cannot arouse Americans institutionally. In the battle against abortion, for example, the only possible protest is in the streets. But this protest, if aimed against the slaughter of children in abortion clinics, is itself aborted by the police, the public repositories of the written law permitting the slaughter. Any man who takes the natural law seriously on an issue of this gravity; any man who insists that murder not be done and not be done now—the written law to the contrary, will find himself, as some have already found themselves, in jail. We have come, corporately as a people, to hold the proposition that justice equals statute.

A natural law man today, if he wishes to stay out of jail, must content himself with urging his convictions within his own sphere of influence in the hope that he can accomplish something on a limited scale. But he cannot hope to win publicly and politically. The political model sketched early in this chapter finds here its ultimate relevance; without political teeth the natural law can never be made to function publicly in any society. Our constitutional system, from the standpoint of natural law convictions, is a Hamlet without the Prince of Denmark. An appeal to the natural law will gain no lawyer his case in court—unless he is a spellbinder arguing before a jury uncorrupted by legal positivism and higher education, nor will such an appeal protect the rights of man before the higher judicial courts of appeal. The Supreme Court is possibly the highest repository of the denial of natural law in the nation.

The natural law in our land, as in England, floats in the air, a kind of vaguely remembered inheritance upon which we act naturally, if we are basically decent people, but without any voice in the body politic. Nobody flatly denies that there might be something out there called a "natural law." But the children of this generation are wiser than the children of light. They usurp the very rhetoric of the tradition they despise. Every new law nowadays is passed in the name of somebody or another's rights: rights for homosexuals; rights for women "over their bodies," etc. These "rights" are usually positively prohibited as evils by the natural law and they are as ephemeral as is the majority that hurries them into statute. By a curious irony the fears of the authors of *The Federalist*—government by a faction in the name of some gnostic nostrum—joins hands today with the fears of the defenders of a tradition of law much older than this nation, in truth as old as God's creation of Man; and this law is being violated in the United States of America and it is being violated in the name of written or positive law. This violation, if continued, will destroy the race itself. Poor Americans! threatened by a dagger before you are born and threatened by the same dagger before you are called to die, you will pass your lives under the shadow of clinical and white-robed barbarians who own your very existence and who will tolerate you, if indeed they do tolerate you, because you pass inspection, like horses or dogs, before a legalized tribunal that has forgotten what it means to be a man.

PROFESSOR VOEGELIN AND THE CHRISTIAN TRADITION

This study opened with the observation that political philosophy tends to flourish in moments of crisis and decay. When all goes well with their world, men do not question the presuppositions of their own historical communities. Questioning follows on the experience of doubt or the premonition of impending disaster. Political philosophy is flourishing today in the United States. And political philosophy flourishes because the nation is passing through a grave crisis of self-identity and self-recognition. The absentminded loss of our victory in World War II and the subsequent failure to establish a "Pax Americana" (which would have lent substance to our Roman and Republican pretensions); the frenzy of masochism that surrendered half the world to Communist slavery; the partial defeat of our arms in Korea; the total defeat of our arms in Vietnam; the burning of our universities and cities in the sixth decade of the century; the abdication of Cambodia and Angola; the neoisolationism of the American left and the establishment; the decay of our military strength, a decay come upon consciously and deliberately because of our preference for an easy and even opulent life; our hypocrisy before political scandal at home and our apathy before political tyranny abroad—all of these factors and others have compounded a fracturing of the American soul. As with all sick men, we now worry about our health. Political philosophy is rarely curative but, when theoretically sound, is diagnostic.

The diagnosticians are upon us. The formidable School of Chicago, begotten by the even more formidable Professor Leo Strauss, urges upon us a return to classical antiquity for the philosophical wisdom needed to understand the straits upon which the Republic has fallen. Strauss's emphasis upon natural right has won him friends in all those circles that deplore our mindless collapse into positivism and historicism. But the disciples of the late Professor Strauss, retaining always the piety and reticence proper to the Master of Secret Writing, ignore two thousand years of Christianity even while avoiding any public expression of their thinly disguised conviction that the whole business of the religion of Christ was a fraud. These lads are fond of Averroes, Master of the Double Truth: one public truth for all of you nonphilosophers which will permit you your superstitions which, after all, do yeoman service in our time for the preservation of a civilized polity; one private truth for those of us, an elect few who have read the Greek texts, who know that your Christian civilization was built on a lie, is an affront to the Greek wisdom of Aristotle, is an obstacle to men who seek to think seriously about political things.

For these reasons I have chosen to examine the Straussian school through the prism of the thought of Professor Harry Jaffa. With that consideration this book shall end. But the Straussians represent only one pole of the philosophical-political spectrum dominating American conservative thought today. The concept of American conservatism has not figured in my study because it has been without importance to the issues raised in this meditation on things political. It is of importance, however, in evaluating the curious bifurcation of conservative political philosophers into followers of either Strauss or Voegelin. Against Strauss, more accurately, in olympian unconcern for the Straussian school, Eric Voegelin raised the banner of a political philosophy that took

history seriously, that saw history and its order as an inseparable synthesis. His excoriating and brilliantly definitive attacks against gnostic dreaming and positivist pretension
gained him Christian allies everywhere. And I take this op-
portunity to publicly express my profound gratitude for Professor Voegelin's earlier work in this country. I learned from
him and so did many others. Whatever strictures follow in no
sense detract from the gratitude that students owe masters.
But, to quote Aquinas, although I love Plato, I love the Truth
even more.

If Straussianism is a danger to Christian political theory,
Voegelinianism is an even more subtle danger and more
dangerous because of its very attractiveness to Christians
who look once but who fail to look twice. Voegelin respects
history and he respects the Lord of history, Christ—but Voegelin does not believe in him, or, at least, he does not believe
in him as historic Christianity has believed. Hence Voegelin
has not believed.

Sound Christian political philosophy must shake itself free
of the academic authority of both Strauss and Voegelin even
while it absorbs their genuine insights. To this purpose these
final chapters have been written.

Professor Voegelin's ambiguous attitude towards Christianity can be traced, at least with hindsight, to his almost
worshipful attitude towards Plato and the entire classical tradition at large. But the learned scholar did not really tip his
hand until he published the fourth volume of his series, *Order and History*. The book, as with everything Voegelin does, is
stunning in what it achieved.

But what Professor Eric Voegelin did not do with this the
fourth volume in his monumental *Order and History* is almost as intriguing as what he actually did. I am giving away
no secrets when I report that this long awaited book was
anticipated by a plethora of speculation by Voegelin watchers

in this country. Eric Voegelin, come to these shores from the Germanies, has been the scourge of positivism in political science, the hope of Christian conservatives in the restoration of the dignity of philosophical meditation on the structure of history, and the living symbol of a new and fresh synthesis of disciplines in the service of our common Western tradition. I, for one, hailed the publication of his *Israel and Revelation* even though I did express some residual doubts concerning his understanding of the Christian metaphysics of being.[1] Some of us thought that the fierce and lonely transcendence of God emphasized in *Israel and Revelation* would be hard to stuff back into immanence in the volume that, we believed, would come to terms with the Christian experience. After all, Professor Voegelin had led us through Israel, the Greek *polis*, the philosophical breakthroughs of Plato and Aristotle, and, we anticipated, not without some justification, that he would culminate his great work with an apotheosis given over to Christianity and history. There were others, however, who thought that the preeminence given Plato in volume 3 would make the advent of Christ something of an afterthought in history. Nothing of the kind happened when Voegelin published *The Ecumenic Age*. Voegelin simply outfoxed his own critics, even his sympathetic critics. Volume 4 of his series is not about the Christian epoch and, in a very significant sense, the book turned out not to be about Christ.

The issue is important to Christian political thinkers because too many of them have looked to Voegelin as their man. The confusion was understandable because Professor Voegelin's most marked enemies are the enemies of the Christian thing: pragmatism; positivism; gnosticism; communism. Again, Dr. Voegelin brought to political philosophy in the United States an almost awesome erudition and a breadth of intellectual synthesis discouraged by the narrow specialization of the American graduate school system. I suspect that the very authority that the man justly commands has tended to overawe both friends and foes, but especially friends, with justice. After all, it was Professor Voegelin whose *New Science of Politics* exposed, with peculiar brilliance, the nature of gnosticism as the new very essence of the modern experience: modern man has tended to immanentize the transcendent and thus taste salvation within history.[2] And it was the same Voegelin who later turned the tables on conventional historiography by demonstrating that there is an equivalence between the history of order and the order of history, that history is a peculiarly Western experience in which man breaks out of cosmological civilizations which pattern his life on the cycles of nature.[3] We have all learned from this man and our gratitude to him must far outweigh any second thoughts on the deeper import of his work. But second thoughts I have and intellectual candor demands that they be expressed.

What, in a word, is Eric Voegelin's understanding of Christianity? He represents our common Western religion through the prism of the experience of Saint Paul and almost exclusively through that prism. The historical figure of Jesus is totally bypassed by Voegelin and the only Christ to emerge in Voegelin's pages is the resurrected Christ of Paul's experience, the Christ who appeared to Paul and who transfigured his life and the life of all mankind as well. The resurrected Lord is not the figure of Easter Sunday. The fact of the Resurrection does not interest Voegelin but the experience of that "fact" (if indeed it be a fact) interests him very much. The figure of the Apostle to the Gentiles follows, in the thought of Voegelin, on those of Plato and Aristotle and all three of them are understood by the professor as men who experienced the divine in the depths of their own consciousness and who thus are represented as discovering the very structure of historical existence. Nowhere in Voegelin's thought does the Church play any significant role whatsoever in this act of constituting man's life in history under God. This omission has certainly disturbed a number of Voegelin's Christian friends, both Protestant and Catholic. However, had these followers attended carefully to Voegelin's conviction that revelation comes to privileged individuals and tends to get distorted when pressed into the service of institutions, their disenchantment would be less than I judge it to be.

For Eric Voegelin, "the fact of revelation is its content." Revelation is one with its presentation. The key concept orchestrating Voegelin's thought is the concept of experience: Abraham had an experience of the divine; Parmenides had an experience of the divine; Heraclitus had one; Plato had a preeminently poignant experience of the divine and Aristotle had a somewhat lesser experience of the divine. So too did Saint Paul. Those experiences, so runs the Voegelinian thesis, have been derailed in time because of their conversion into propositional doctrines, because of their having been pressed into the service of gnostic movements, because of their debasement at the hands of politicians grubbing for naked power. Voegelin insists, quite rightly, that an experience cannot be reduced to any conventional subject-object polarity and hence escapes the probing of pragmatic historians and behaviorist psychologists. Putting the business in my own language, I think Voegelin's thesis can be expressed quite bluntly: nobody can quarrel with somebody's account of his own experience; by definition, the man is either telling the truth (or he thinks that he is telling the truth) or he is a liar. Unless a man who has had an experience, religious or otherwise, advances certain objective data which back his claims they can be evaluated only by looking at their content.

For Voegelin the privileged experiences referred to reveal the structure of human existence in space-time, a structure which aims at transcending itself in the very act of self-discovery. In *The Ecumenic Age*, Voegelin argues that the divine "Beyond" is discovered as a "Within" and this discovery is made by men existing in a natural space and time which are then swept into history, history being constituted by this discovery of the divine in man. Voegelin seems to have conceived of his own task as an educator as consisting in recreating in the reader the original experience. What matters, for Voegelin, as the late Willmoore Kendall once put it to me, is not whether Moses ever lived or not; what matters is the Mosaic experience and any new order in history depends upon the refashioning within the consciousness of men today of those crucial brushes with the divine which created history. Eric Voegelin is essentially an apostle with a mission. His very style has always aimed at working the reader into the vortex, into what Voegelin calls "the turbulence" in which the divine "erupts" in a "theophanic act," thus revealing to man who he is in history. For Voegelin, the divine stupefies those to whom it reveals its mysteries.

For Professor Voegelin there is a fundamental anxiety that is answered by the experience of the divine. He speaks in terms common to German existentialism: existence out of nothing underlies all anxiety. Underneath any surface equilibrium achieved by either an individual or a society there lurks the ultimate enemy, the absolute threat, Nothingness, Nonbeing. Voegelin on this point is almost as dramatic as is Heidegger and Simone de Beauvoir. Voegelin's dependence on the Philosophy of Dread of Martin Heidegger is evident but Heidegger is never cited by him in this connection. In any event, man seeks some ground to explain that whatever comes into being must perish. No reality is its own ground of existence. Voegelin insists, however, that there is no answer to this ultimate mystery of being. And this lack of an ultimate answer is the ultimate truth. Human conscious-

ness asks these questions and the questions are a constant;
the answers vary: "Platonic Father-God . . . Aristotelian
prote arche . . . an Israelite creator god; the pre-and-
transmundane God of the Christian dogma; a Neoplatonic
world-soul, improved by Hegel's dialectically immanent
Geist; a Bergsonian *élan vital*; the epigonic Being for whose
parousia Heidegger waited in vain; or the Amon-Re for whose
parousia Queen Hatshepsut did not wait in vain."⁴ This is
quite a smorgasbord laid before the human spirit for its delec-
tation—but there is no main course. Voegelinian history of
religion is a history of *hors d'oeuvres*.

Voegelin insists that his enumeration is not intended to
suggest that one answer is as good as another but is rather
illustrative of the truth that all are answers to the fundamental question about the groundlessness of existence, sensed as
anxiety over contingency in both early and later societies.
But Voegelin's "no answer" rubric violates his own discovery
as well as his method. The question about the absoluteness of
man's experience of the divine suggests that there is a true
answer: that the answer be true is part of the experience
which poses the question. In a word: Eric Voegelin could not
have the experience of the divine. He tells us that all experiences, most especially the breakthrough to the divine, must
be explored from inside its own context. But this very experience, man's brush with the divine, is imperiously an-
tirelativistic and anti-Voegelinian. Relativists don't have it;
only absolute dogmatists have it, fierce fellows—and they
insist on the uniqueness of the truth that they have grasped.
To withdraw from the insistence of the witness to his own
experience that there is a true answer is to withdraw from the
history that the experience presumably establishes. On Voegelin's own grounds one cannot look at these things from an
outside perspective—and yet that is what he does in *The
Ecumenic Age*: the work of a Ph.D. judging the truth of

historic Christianity. Voegelin's fastidiousness about wars of religion wars against his earlier discovery: that is, history cannot be studied outside of itself. To speak, as he does, of the "fallacy . . . entertained by doctrinaire theologians, metaphysicians, and ideologists" (p. 75) is a kind of precious washing of the hands by a latter-day Pilate who is too pure to enter the Golgotha of history. Voegelin also dismisses, as the ideologue that he is, two thousand years of Christian history. If "every last answer is a penultimate in relation to the next last one in time, the historical field of consciousness becomes of absorbing interest" (p. 75): if this sentence is read in terms of the understanding of conceptual intelligibility, it makes sense—sense is what intelligibility is supposed to be about— but if the sentence is read in terms of truth, it dissolves into gibberish. If "every last" true answer is penultimate in relation to the "next last one," let it be a false one, than Voegelin's sentence is bad Alice in Wonderland. The sentence does not even make any better sense when worked the other way: if every last false answer is penultimate in relation to the next to the last true answer, then—well—well—nothing follows! Voegelin is simply not saying anything about anything. Meaning is not truth any more than intelligibility is the ground of being.

Our author here, *in acto exercito*, gives away his game. Eric Voegelin is a Platonist and for Platonists there is no distinction between being and meaning. This error of the *Platonici* is rooted in a failure to distinguish between the way in which things exist in the mind and the way in which they exist in the real. Thomas Aquinas called this a failure to distinguish between *separatio* and *abstractio*.[5] Platonizing thinkers confuse the state of abstractness thanks to which the mind can understand meanings and essences with a state of separation: that is, because I can think X without thinking Y in which X actually exists, then it follows that X does in

[201]

fact exist as separated from Y. This permits Platonists to think
that the meaning of Christ is his being even though he never
proved his claims by rising from the dead in fact, in *being*
understood not as *meaning* but as *existence*. Platonists, thus,
and rationalists as well can construct castles in the air. In
Voegelin's case this error permits him to confuse the meaning of answers with their existence. Experienced meaning is
one noetic situation but the verification thereof in existence
is something else. But it is precisely this conformity of the
mind of man to things as they are which constitutes the truth
as known.[6] Voegelin thus drives a wedge between being
("meaning" for him) and existence. Existence is a kind of
degeneration of being. This is curious because Dr. Voegelin
has always been sensitive to the grandeur of the "I Am" passage of Exodus but he has never barreled this sensitivity
through to a metaphysics of being as existential act. Whereas
Platonic being is all the more real the less it exists, Aquinas's
"existence" is so much being that it does not even admit of a
contrary.

Voegelin tells us that he holds that "the fact of revelation is
its content."[7] This looks curiously like the same kind of reasoning that led Saint Anselm to conclude that God existed
because existence was included in the meaning of the concept of God. Years ago the late Hannah Arendt told us that
Voegelin had an unsophisticated notion of the relations between essence and existence because he tended to see factual
history as falling under certain paradigms or models understood by him to be somehow explanatory principles for grasp-
ing history.[8] Dr. Arendt was right: she spotted the Platonism.
(I confess that I did not see it at that time: *mea culpa*.) In any
event, if the "fact of revelation is its content," then it is highly
cavalier to hunt around for evidence of historicity. If the
meaning, once again, or the content of religious experience
is intellectually interesting to Voegelin then the question

about the meaning's historical verification existentially is irrelevant for him. The abstraction from existence of the experience is sufficient verification of separability from reality and hence contempt for reality. Reality does not count for Professor Voegelin. The very question, hence, of the historicity of Christ and of His resurrection, of the Easter we Christians celebrate as the central feast of our Faith, annoys Voegelin: he finds it vulgar. In fact only fundamentalists, for Voegelin, are worried about whether the empty tomb on the third day was really empty after all. Whether Christ arose in deed or arose from the dead only in Paul's experience of a deed that occured only in Paul is an irrelevant distinction for the German professor. Voegelin is a right-wing Bultmann but whereas Bultmann takes a properly Teutonic glee in proving that God would do nothing that a German Professor would not do, Voegelin considers the very subject to be trivial. The Platonizing metaphysics at play must find this kind of realistic questioning utterly vulgar because, for Voegelin, fact (read: being which equals, for Voegelin, meaning) equals content (read: meaning; experience, etc.).

But, Dr. Voegelin, "if Christ be not risen"—in the words of the same Paul—then I for one don't give a damn about Paul's experience of him.

This is not the place to develop an entire epistemology but just as Voegelin's political philosophy sails under a Platonic bottom so too does mine sail under a Thomistic bottom. The hulls have got to be looked at. Distinctions are in order. There are two completed acts of cognition discoverable in man: an understanding of essences, structures, meanings, deep thoughts, profound experiences, turbulent visions, etc.; and an act, traditionally called judgment, that affirms all of this business to exist in fact or not to exist in fact, to be checked out by the evidence of being or not. This can be awfully humbling but the humiliation is rendered bearable because the Christian God gave us as his name: Existence. The difference between the judgment "It is raining outside" when in fact it is raining and an understanding of the meaning of the same proposition when in fact the sun is shining and there is no rain at all is evident. It seems curious that this ineluctable evidence, pointed to by Thomas Aquinas very early in his career, is always missed by Platonists who insist on confounding being and meaning. Further, the distinction between these acts bespeaks the distinction between a religion based on being and one based on meaning. Christianity is a religion of being in the sense of existence as exercised act: He did not say, "I have the Truth"; He said: "I am the Truth."

Christ rose from the dead and thus established his claims. He did this or he was the most gigantic fraud in history. And if he was a fraud, then all of Paul's experiences serve us as nothing: "our faith is in vain." This entire drama is totally lacking in Professor Voegelin's clinically academic approach to the Person of the Incarnate God. The Professor who would establish the order of history from the history of order suddenly steps outside history and assumes the posture of a man who is above it all.

Long before Eric Voegelin, George Santayana insisted that there is no historical Christ behind, or distinct from, "the Christ of the Creeds." Santayana was justly irritated with the pedantry of prigs who kept talking, in his day, about some historical Jesus behind the Christ we all know about and have known about for some two thousand years. Santayana simply laid down a gauntlet and defied the "new critics," they were then called, to pick it up or shut up: there is only one Jesus Christ and that Jesus Christ is the Lord proclaimed by his Church in and through the creeds. Take him or leave him. There is no historical Jesus, a Germanic myth, behind the Christ of the Church. But this Christ, for Santayana, possessed only the reality of a poem.[9] Therefore Santayana chose "disillusion."[10] The old joke about Santayana not believing in God but insisting that Mary is his mother is consistent with the Catholic-Platonic atheism of the man. Voegelin's "Resurrected" who arises only in Paul's turbulent experience on the road to Damascus is consistent with his Protestant-Platonic atheism. Santayana was saddened by his loss of faith but Voegelin is cranky about folk who fuss over whether Easter is a fake or not. But unless the Resurrection happened, his entire speculation about history is worthless; but then everything else is equally worthless. *Ave Crux: Spes Unica.*

Voegelin is paralyzed in the face of Christian history and therefore he cannot write about it. Tons of erudition about folk in China and Egypt and other out of the way places but not one book about the adventure that has been Christendom.

The man does not like the creeds—and the creeds made Christendom and gave us all our dignity and liberties. And it is the Nicene Creed that tens of millions of us recite in dozens of languages around the world every day of the week. Without the creeds mankind would have sunk back into a simulacrum of the paganism from which Christianity liberated him. The old paganism was bad enough: the new paganism, a kind of disguised heresy under the mask of Arianism, would have been worse. And the creeds, the historic creeds—must we teach this professor?—are doctrinal statements. But the professor does not like doctrinal statements. "The historical field of consciousness becomes of absorbing interest" to pathologists of the human spirit, I suggest, if the subjective experience of the divine cannot be articulated doctrinally, and therefore truly. Otherwise these experiences of the divine melt without distinction into the babbling of fanatics who would impose themselves because they think they have seen something! When they seize the sword, they murder us. When we seize the sword, we put them in hospitals. The

West has been shaped by the great creeds of Christendom and for this Christian they are far more thrilling than the experience of even the greatest of the genuine mystics. Without an understanding of these creeds, especially in their political implications, the West is simply unintelligible as a potential subject for philosophical penetration. In the West we do not honor the fakir: we consider him a fake. We adjudicate claims to talk to the divine in terms of public standards: for example, canon law. We do all this because we take existence seriously and we live in the light and not in turbulence. Our God does not trick us with private breakthroughs. He was publically murdered on a cross.

The creeds of Christendom are made up of propositions. Dr. Voegelin sneers at propositions but he does his sneering as well as makes his living with propositions. I suspect that the distinguished German professor has a very modern notion of propositions: the logical linking together of bloodless propositions. Years ago Gilbert Keith Chesterton called this sort of thing "the Usual Article." We have all heard the weary story a thousand times from relativists and skeptics, and so too has Dr. Voegelin—but he ought to know better.

This celluloid and sophomoric complaint against abstract thinking astonishes when it comes forth from the erudite pen of Eric Voegelin. A proposition when affirmed is a word, a *verbum*, a conscious expression of what a man knows, an analogue—Augustine teaches us—to the eternal uttering of the Word, the Son of God, by His Father, the *arche* (in Athanasian terms) of the Trinity. Propositons do not derail or debase experience. On the contrary, there are no human experiences without propositions, words of the spirit—of the heart (again, Augustine's felicitous phrase)—that utter in a eureka point what man knows or believes. This has always been and shall be the role of the creeds. There is no role for the Church in the world view of Eric Voegelin. Therefore he cannot come to terms with the Middle Ages and the Renaissance. But thanks to the doctrinal articulation of the creeds we know more today about the risen Christ than did the early Christians, because the Spirit of God, the Third Person, has quickened the Church throughout all these centuries and what was always believed is now believed, but believed with greater luminosity than it was then. Voegelin does not like fundamentalists. In the conventional sense of the term I am not a fundamentalist, possibly because I think that, for example, Baroque Christianity is far more Christian than Patristic Christianity: the Spirit had a longer time to work. Time is on God's side. Today has the advantage of knowing yesterday but yesterday is denied that very advantage. But Voegelin gives a new twist to the term: for him a fundamentalist—fundamentally a "Devil Term," to use Richard Weaver's language—is any Christian who insists on anchoring his faith in things and deeds that happened in history, principally what happened on that first Easter Sunday. But once a man's faith or the faith of a society is so anchored, theological science can expand. I say it can expand because it did. Voegelin does not like the eighteenth century. That century is not my favorite either but I would bet my last dollar that a European peasant of that century—living his faith in festivals and in ritual; recalling the richness of centuries of Faith in his daily prayers and in his simple devotions, expressing, through that simplicity, a complexity of doctrine inherited from a thousand-year tradition and more—knew more than did a convert in Egypt of the second century. I set aside mystical experience which seems to be Voegelin's only avenue into Christian faith.

History is not mystical experience. A very wise Christian tradition has seen to it that men acting thanks to propositional creeds judge men presuming to have privileged experiences of the divine. Who is to judge Plato's experience of the divine (we must face it: this is laughable to a Christian) to be superior to, let us say, Oliver Cromwell's special pipeline to the Lord? And yet that very pipeline, because unjudged by any institution acting according to objective norms and disciplined theology, permitted him to murder—and murder with a good conscience—an anointed king. The gnosticism of the regicide, fingered with peculiar brilliance by Dr. Voegelin in *The New Science of Politics*[11] can only be distinguished from genuine mysticism by institutions and by men, such as Dr. Voegelin himself, who reason about these phenomena and who come to measured conclusions, hence propositions.

There is a last humiliation in bringing privileged experiences before a tribunal of reason as well as religious authority. Possibly here we can find the humility of Jesus Christ. Or, possibly, we can find the wisdom of our God, the only God, who, in making men reasonable, did not create ontological cripples but made creatures who could affirm, in faith, truths about him proposed by the Church his Son established on this earth. And for this we men of our time—and men of all seasons—do not need any experiences. Should these experiences pass our way, let us thank the Lord; should they not come, let us not be troubled. We have the faith. We need only the grace of God and the truth of the Church that goes back to a risen God-Man who walked with men and who established himself by cooking for them. Upon those fish I base my faith.

[8]

JAFFA, THE SCHOOL OF STRAUSS, AND THE CHRISTIAN TRADITION

✍ The newly quickened interest in political philosophy in recent years owes much to the pioneering work of the late Professor Leo Strauss of the University of Chicago and to the large band of followers who today occupy significant positions in American universities in all parts of the nation. The friends of political wisdom and sanity can only doff their hats in gratitude at the careful demolition of philosophical positivism undertaken at the hands of the school of Leo Strauss. But with so much said there nonetheless remains a curious lacuna in the thought and even in the interests of the Straussians that has puzzled outsiders for some years. Why do these men skirt Christian political philosophy as though it were a body of speculation unworthy of serious consideration? Their books and their articles, replete with references to classical antiquity, not only span Greece but they probe the modern mind from Machiavelli to Locke and beyond. We can note as well a fascination and peculiar reverence for the figure of Averroes.[1] But very little is taught us about the contribution, if any, of Christian thought to politics.[2]

The reader who has done me the courtesy of following the march of reasoning displayed in this book will have noted that each issue and philosopher have been focused within a series of questions that have grown out of the author's Christian faith. A Christian political philosopher must, therefore, be puzzled by the very existence of an ambitious body of political theory that largely ignores the very existence itself of the civilization of the West. By this civilization I mean, of course, the world that was produced by the religion of Christ, even as it was deeply influenced by the inheritance of pagan antiquity. It seems fitting, thus, that these meditations conclude with a meditation on the political philosophy of men who ignore the very soil out of which they were born. If the Straussians are right in their emphasis and presuppositions then the kind of reasoning that has engaged my attention in this book must be dismissed as nonphilosophy or as an exercise in political theology. Since I am a philosopher and in no *ex professo* sense a theologian, Straussianism presents itself as a kind of objection which intellectual integrity demands be answered. Men of philosophical sophistication, regardless of their convictions, possess the tools to distinguish opponents who are frauds from opponents who are serious men. Straussians are serious men and my words here are a testimony to my admiration for their integrity and sobriety.

It may be accidental that most Straussians are Hellenized Jews, but it is by no means accidental that a Hellenized Jew must find the Christian mind and sensibility something foreign and distant to his mind and heart. This proposition follows from the principle of noncontradiction: had these men found Christianity a doctrine which attracted them in some fashion, even without eliciting assent, they would be neither Hellenizers nor Jews; classicism and Jewry have little in common outside of their mutual rejection of the Incarnation. No thinker has probed this issue with greater delicacy than has Professor Harry V. Jaffa in his tribute to Leo Strauss republished in Jaffa's *The Conditions of Freedom*.[3] Jaffa's perspicacity is sharpened because he shares the religious and philosophical presuppositions of his teacher, Leo Strauss.

A Hellenized Jew retains his Jewish awe before the might and majesty of the God of Israel but, because he is Hellenized, he cannot cope with this God, his own God. His mind has been fashioned in the wisdom of pagan Greece and a gulf separates the two dimensions of his being: his heart is Jewish but his head is Athenian. The Hellenized Jew, therefore, opts for the position of a man who was thoroughly Hellenized in his philosophy but who was no Jew: the Moslem, Averroes, a figure utterly sinister and dangerous to the Latin Christendom of the high Middle Ages. Averroes taught the following, granted that his Latin followers tended to heighten and thus slightly distort his own formulations: there exist two truths which cannot be reconciled or synthesized with one another, a truth of philosophy and a truth of faith; what a man does with his believing right hand is undone by his philosophizing left hand. Faith moves us in a mysterious world which is irrational, but moved we are by this faith. Reason guides us away from this call to faith. Given that we are men of both reason and faith, we are torn to pieces by two conflicting authorities. We therefore give a pious obeisance to the God of Moses even though we spend our lives disengaging the texts of Plato and Aristotle, knowing all the while that those texts tell us something completely contradicted by the Scriptures which are, we hold as Jews, the word of the Lord. Such men walk as did Cicero, internally denying the gods but professing them publicly. Straussians are very pious men externally and they are serious about this external piety. An esoteric and exoteric contradiction dominates their thinking.

The Strauss and Jaffa position on this point reiterates and even heightens, as would a distorted mirror, the dilemma in which the Christian West finds itself today.Enjoying a culture and a liberty, a largeness of spirit, which themselves are the products of the historic creeds of orthodox Christianity, our world, on the whole, rejects the faith that made it free. This rejection is occasionally formal and explicit; more often, the rejection is implicit and marked by a subtle bad will, even truculence towards open manifestations of the Christian thing in the public forum. We borrow money from a bank that we secretly think is bankrupt, but borrow we do. We need only think of Christmas which is kept alive by commercialism. From a political point of view thoughtful men must judge it incredible that an entire society should continue to live within a moral atmosphere and a dignity which are little more than the epiphenomena of a faith which is receding into the backwaters of the civilization that the religion in question threw absentmindedly into existence: that is, unless Christ be a Divine Person, personal dignity is a sham—nobody ever heard of the very concept itself of person before the Christological disputes of the Patristic Age; unless we are all brothers under a common Father, the pretensions of a universal liberty for all men are ridiculous; unless we have been called into existence by a Providential Creator who fingers each one of us uniquely with life and being, then slavery is perfectly sensible: Aristotle showed how sensible it was in the *Politics*. Our entire legal and ethical world is sustained by a faith in the Christian God and in the consequences of his incarnation. Every product of the West down to the flowering of a free and independent peasantry have been deductions from the religion of Christ. Cancel the religion and you ought to cancel the ethics and the politics, and subsequently sink back into the faceless quagmire of paganism: the conclusion is perfectly logical. But men do not operate by logic.

The new Averroism, not for Hellenizing Jews but for backsliding Christians, preaches Christ on Sunday but strictly inside the church building and secularism rampant without. Psychologically this new Averroism is not surprising. Averroism, in all its forms, works because it is a shift of attention. This shift of concentration by the mind and will permits men to violate the principle of noncontradiction with ease. Sin is a kind of principled stupidity and failure to bring to bear upon issues a knowledge which is tucked away in the recesses of the mind. Averroism is a political sin. The tension between politics and religion or politics and philosophy, when such a tension is truly entertained as existent, breaks down only when somebody tries to take both poles of the tension seriously in one and the same act of thinking. But the West today, both European and American West, does not consider the consequences of this tension in one and the same act of thinking. A secularized political order exists side by side with a population that is still basically, if tepidly, Christian. The old complaint about doing one thing on Sunday and something else the rest of the week finds here a justification. Advanced in the past by puritans who were impatient with the human condition, the Averroistic split today is held by men who want Christian consequences in the social order without Christianity in their public orthodoxy.

Psychologically and morally the tension between politics and religion breaks down only in a man who takes both poles of the opposition seriously. We have noted this in the case of Cicero. What is truly surprising, however, is the long survival in a lived or exercised belief of a religion that promises nothing secure here below to those who follow its often harsh demands. That man immanentizes as do the pagans is consubstantial with the very human desire to get our pie here and not in the sky. The Vergilian religion of this world is not a scandal: it is a permanent possibility. The Straussian posture which accentuates an opposition between the demands of revelation and those of philosophy symbolizes a perennially human tension between what man can believe and what he can know. The thirteenth century faced this issue when Averroism gripped the mind of the University of Paris and threatened to destroy a Christendom only recently born out of the forests of Frankish barbarism. When Thomas Aquinas hurried to Paris on a mule in 1269 to meet that challenge, he insisted on a basic harmony between faith and philosophy, between the truths of God and the truths known by unassisted reason. His stunning synthesis was a magnificent work of reason in the service of revelation. The synthesis was bold because it was by no means easy. Expressed abstractly, Aquinas's contention that something cannot be true in philosophy and false in religion seems almost banal, a platitude. How can truth contradict itself? But when lived to the hilt, the Thomistic marriage of faith and reason requires an almost heroic energy. That energy, because heightened, inevitably tends to wind down and wear out at the edges. Man's capacity for compromising is limitless. It is not easy for us to live in the hope of things unseen. As insisted earlier, Augustine's voice is always with us to warn against a Christianity which guarantees the fulfillment of every wish of the human heart here below. The Averroistic divorce of faith and mind is psychologically a way out and that way out is the path upon which the Western world today has set its tired and blistered feet. God became man: was crucified: rose from the dead—well, maybe and maybe not! Well, yes, inside the walls of some church building on Sunday for an hour or so, but certainly not in the real world as the central fact of human existence! We Europeans and Americans do not live this creed centrally nor do we dare draw its awesome consequences, not any more. Christianity has been too much of a cross for us. But a crossing of reason and revelation was never demanded of the Hellenized Jew reading his Plato or Philo one day and his Bible the next. What he embraces openly and willingly, a split between faith and reason, we Christians have begun to live uneasily but steadily in a secularized society that still admits the faith in Christ but that shoves it into a corner of the psyche. Public and political

Christianity was just too much for us! Too many thousands of men in the past tore their enemies and themselves to pieces in its name. But the failure of Christian civilization to be itself in no sense suggests any theoretical inferiority to either Athens or pre-Christian Jerusalem to say nothing of Rome. This proposition, however, is precisely the one advanced by Professor Harry Jaffa.

For Jaffa, glossing the text of Leo Strauss in *The Conditions of Freedom*, "the Jews [possessed] a heritage which made them the highest symbols of the demand of God himself that men live on the highest level" (p. 6). The proposition can be entertained rationally; it is not a contradiction. But the proposition is by no means self-evident. It must be, always has been, challenged by Christianity which finds in the demands of Christ the highest call to which man has been chosen. But the god of philosophy is not the God of revelation, according to Jaffa. The God of Abraham and Isaac is not the same god who, in the words of Harry Jaffa, "The Signers [of the Declaration of Independence] assume to exist" (p. 153). This latter-day god of the Enlightenment might exist, Jaffa tells us, but then again he might not. Even his trinitarian nature is nothing other than the unity in an idea of the three divided functions of government: the legislative, the judicial, and the executive. Jaffa strongly gives the impression that the philosopher's god is some kind of a perfect nature, an essence "of a certain sort" (p. 153). Once given that essence or nature, politics has all it needs, in the opinion of Jaffa. We purge limited perfections such as justice and mercy of their human limitations; we project them into an idea of absolute perfection; we then call that idea God. One wonders whether Jaffa got this theory from Feuerbach. The blatant anthropomorphism demands the surgery of the Negative Theology of the eastern Christian tradition as well as the analogy of the metaphysics of Aquinas. Be that as it

[215]

may, such a divine essence, however, can hardly be the "I Am Who AM" of Exodus who imperiously told Moses that the only truth Moses could know about him is the inexorability of his existence—because that is what he is: Existence.[4] A perfect nature stripped of existence or entertained as some kind of quintessence whose being is irrelevant to political life is not the God in whose name Europe and subsequently America came to be, to exist. But it is this God of revelation, not the bloodless abstraction of the Declaration (on Jaffa's reading of that god and document) who lifted his own people to demands never exceeded in subsequent history. Read in another way, Jaffa's proposition comes out as follows: the God of Israel before the advent of Christianity demanded of his people more than did that same God after the advent of His Son. The statement bears analyzing. Jaffa is not a Christian and therefore quite properly denies that the man Jesus is the Son of God. But Jaffa advances a religious proposition as though it were a philosophical observation. The philosophical observation, of course, turns into a religious proposition made by a Hellenized Jew when he wears his Jewish hat rather than his Greek one. Jaffa's assertion can be made consistently only by someone who has rejected the transcendent claims of Christianity or who ignores them through ignorance or lack of interest.

Jaffa insists that Strauss maintained that revelation at its highest, God's to Israel, stands in a kind of polarized opposition to philosophical reason as enshrined in the wisdom of Greece. The reader will note that Jewish revelation is revelation at its highest for Jaffa and that Greek philosophy is reason at its highest: that is, Jewish religion is superior to Christian religion and Greek philosophy is superior to Christian philosophy. We Christians lose both ways! But again there lurks an undemonstrated premise. When spelled out that premise reads: reason is only reason at its best when unaided by revelation, and revelation is only revelation at its purest when unmixed with reason. Again, I must point out to Dr. Jaffa for whom I have the highest professional and personal regard: the assertion is not self-evident; it is no more self-evident than the proposition that a woman is more a woman without a man and a man more a man without a woman.

Theology, in Christian terms, is neither philosophy nor faith but a body of doctrine produced by men reasoning about the content of God's revelation. Men theologize in a Christian context because Christianity releases men to be fully themselves, men who think about and puzzle over what they believe. But Jaffa prefers that revelations not be thought about. His argument in favor of his position is drawn from the structure of synthesis. In a word, his argument is philosophical and must be treated as such. "Nor did he [Strauss] believe in the possibility of a synthesis [between faith and reason], since any synthesis would require a higher principle than either, a principle which regulated the combination."[5]

Dr. Jaffa's contention here reflects a delicacy of metaphysical and epistemological thinking which the author of this book can only commend in the highest of terms. Instead of merely talking about the philosopher as so many of his colleagues do, Jaffa has philosophized. And the professor has philosophized well. No synthesizing principle can form part of any synthesis. The conclusion lies at the nerve center of Aquinas's theory of being as existential act which synthesizes or "togethers" the principles of nature but which constitutes no one of these principles in isolation nor all of them in conjunction; being, in the sense of existing (*esse*), is reality's "being-composed" but is not the composed reality.[6] In the context of Thomistic existential metaphysics this means that existence is absolutely prior to essence. In the context of Kant's philosophy this means that synthesis always precedes analysis.[7] No analysis is reducible to any synthetic principle composing the analysis itself. Every analysis moves away from the original synthesizing activity which knits into unity that which is subsequently analyzed by the mind. We need only think of what happens when a literary critic analyzes a poem or when a connoisseur of wines attempts to dilate on why this wine is a great wine. Were analysis the same as synthesis, critical acts would be creative. We need only think of the comic situation encountered when a man in love tries to explain to a friend just why he is. "We murder to dissect," according to Wordsworth. Harry Jaffa is absolutely right in insisting that "a principle which regulated the combination" of faith and reason would have to transcend both.

Professor Jaffa is no mean logician. He knows his Aristotle. But in this case he has failed to define his terms. What does he mean exactly by faith and reason? By *faith*, he seems to mean God's revelation to man, be that revelation Jewish or otherwise. Such a revelation is believed even though it is not self-evident to reason, nor evident to experience, nor deducible from either. But to believe is certainly not to understand the objects of belief, God and the things of God. To believe is to assent intellectually, moved by a will primed by the grace of God, in propositions, to the truth of what is believed. More accurately, to believe involves knowing at the very least—and this very least turns out upon inspection to be the very most—that such and such a predicate is truly affirmed of such and such a subject. Apes cannot receive the gift of faith because they cannot think: therefore apes cannot take anybody's word for it. To assent to testimony, to anyone's testimony, is to make an act of faith in the truth of the content of what is proposed to the mind for assent. A man can assent reasonably to testimony: he has solid grounds for believing in the word of the witness; or he can assent blindly and thus irrationally to testimony advanced by a known liar or an untested witness or a lunatic. But to assent to the word of God is reasonable and to understand what God proposes for belief requires the use of reason. (As a Christian I believe that Mongolian idiots can be baptized but they can never exercise in propositions the content of the faith that they have. To proclaim a faith, a creed, any creed, is to use reason well or to use reason poorly.) Jaffa cannot counterpoint revelation and reason as though they were contraries. I use *contraries*, of course, in the context of Aristotelian—hence, Greek—logic.

The issue concerns the use of reason before the acceptance of faith and the use of reason after that acceptance. In the Catholic tradition, faith is reasonable even though faith is not reason. The *praeambula fidei* constitute the science of apologetics, a science much neglected nowadays but a science which forms one dimension of the Christian apostolate. That God exists and that he is one and good and just are religious truths that can be known in faith but they are also philosophical truths that can be known without faith but as a preparation for its acceptance. Jaffa is a free man and is under no constraint to adhere to this tradition but he cannot, in all fairness, ignore it when he addresses his attention to the complex issue of faith and reason. But even beyond this lacuna in the professor's tribute to his teacher, Leo Strauss, there remains, as indicated, his striking failure to account for the use of reason within the context of faith. No adult can believe the word of God unless he expresses in some creed, no matter how minimal it might be, the content of the revelation proffered. This expression is propositional and hence requires that we talk and think about it, that we reason. Jaffa and his fellow Straussians at large use the term *reason* as a kind of shorthand for philosophy. This is acceptable as long as we are aware of what we are doing. Philosophical reasoning, however, is only one kind and exercise of a rationality that extends to every facet of human existence. I must reason in order to get out of bed and across town to my place of work every day of the year and yet it would be an abuse of English usage to equate my rationality with philosophical speculation. Too often we are tripped into hardening into generic opposition differences which, under inspection, turn out to belong to the same genus. The valid polarity does not run from revelation to reason; the polarity is somewhat different: it runs from revelation to philosophy. And the synthesizing principle, reducible to neither—thus fulfilling Professor Jaffa's requirement for a genuine synthesis—is reason itself as an act.

The teaching is Aquinas's. The doctrine seems to have had no antecedents and it certainly has not been emphasized by the Thomistic tradition until recently and then by only a few Thomists.[13] Analagous to the way in which being (Aquinas's *esse*) synthesizes the manifold of nature into unities, the existing of reasoning is a synthetic activity which unites hitherto unrelated propositions. In so doing, the mind concludes. Aristotle's earlier insistence that all reasoning produces new knowledge is swept into Aquinas's existential metaphysics. The proposition that "a Platonist holds that self-subsistent essences are prior to empirical existents" tells me nothing about Henry of Ghent; knowing that "Henry of Ghent held to a priority of self-subsistent essences prior to empirical existents" tells me nothing about Platonism. Synthesizing the two statements, however, yields the conclusion that Henry of Ghent, on this point, was a Platonist. This is reasoning. In the example, the reasoning is historical. Knowing that John Doe was found shot in his living room one night with a slug from a forty-five tells me nothing about the killer. Knowing that Jake Doe was in the same room, and that Jake was discovered with a smoking forty-five in the hand tells me nothing about the murder. Maybe Jake was firing into a pillow. Matching the bullet with Jake's gun, united with other circumstances excluding other far-fetched possibilities, permits me to conclude that Jake killed John. This is reasoning and the example is taken from police detection. This is not philosophy. Nor is it theology.

Jaffa has taken a reasoned conclusion, a content, namely philosophical content, but he has forgotten about reasoning as an *act*. Theological content as well as philosophical content are concluded to by the mind reasoning. Theology is a synthesis of faith and philosophy. It seems amusing that Professor Jaffa looks for and cannot find a synthetic principle to unite reason and reasoned conclusions about revelation when one of the terms of his polarity is a synthetic act of the mind. On his own showing, in the light of this necessarily brief discussion on the synthetic structure of reasoning, reasoning simply cannot be a component of anything reasonably synthesized. Reason does not synthesize itself. The difference, as suggested, is one between content concluded to and concluding. Every synthesis achieved by an individual or by a civilization presupposes reasoning; in no case is reason as an act a component of the synthesis. The great synthesis of faith and philosophy of Aquinas was itself a magnificent work of a human mind, of an intelligence reasoning. In a word: I accept Jaffa's major premise that no synthesizing principle can be part of a synthesized combination. I deny his minor premise according to which the components are reason and revelation in the sense in which he understands one of the terms, namely, reason. Hence I deny his conclusion.

In denying Jaffa's conclusion, I refuse to grant the validity of the putative opposition between the Christian tradition and reasoning promoted by the school of Leo Strauss. If reason is not exclusively philosophical reasoning nor philosophical content, if the exercise of faith itself requires reasoning, then the Straussians simply are not talking about anything real at all, unless, of course, they are expressing a deep preference for Athens over Jerusalem, B.C., but especially over Jerusalem, A.D. This preference is, of course, their own to make, but they ought to be reminded that it is a preference made in terms of historical sympathies. Their choice looks to civilizations and ways of life. Straussians like Athens better than they do Christian Jerusalem, or Rome. The issue is only peripherally concerned with philosophy. We are talking about something far deeper, about where a man feels at home. To mask an uncomfortableness in Christian culture under the guise of a presumed superiority of Greek pagan thought to Christian thought is principled ignorance because nowhere do the Straussians demonstrate their assertion point for point. To think that Socrates, a Straussian hero, was a better philosopher than Suárez or John or Saint Thomas or Leibniz, on the grounds that Socrates asked questions and the gentlemen mentioned did not, is pure fanaticism. This posture has nothing to do with serious philosophy and even less to do with any epistemological penetration of the structure of reasoning.

Einstein put it very well once when he said that the "only thing in the entire universe which is unreasonable is reason itself." I would amend him slightly and substitute "trans-reasonable" for "unreasonable." When we synthesize we are already reasoning and by then it is utterly too late to make reason itself a component of the synthesis. If anyone were to ask me for a reason for reasoning, I would answer as I think Professor Jaffa might answer, as Aristotle did answer: I do not quarrel with givens; reasoning, the mark of man as man, is a given, not as an intelligible content, but as the act which produces intelligible contents as conclusions.[8]

All kinds of strange people reason. The act is exercised by men of faith and by men without faith, by theologians and by philosophers, by Christians and by pagans and by Jews. To assert an a priori opposition between philosophy and revelation on the grounds that the former is equivalently reason and the latter is antithetic to reason is to propound a prejudice, not to advance an analytically self-evident proposition.

A prejudice prevents the school of Leo Strauss from seriously giving its attention to the claims of Christian philosophy. Christian philosophy, as Etienne Gilson has taken pains to demonstrate, is not a theory; Christian philosophy is an historical reality.⁹ Ab esse ad posse valet illatio. This reality can be bracketed as Hüsserl bracketed existence; but, like existence, when confronted, it presents problems and puzzles to the inquiring intelligence. These problems themselves bend back upon the origins of philosophy. As indicated earlier in this book, all philosophical questioning grows out of some prephilosophical horizon within which a man simply finds himself as given in a world. But the world itself Christians do not take as some kind of comfortable given. Christians and Jews (non-Hellenized Jews) know that all reality is a kind of suspended earthquake. Existence is disturbing only when it is no longer taken for granted. And if a Christian begins to think rationally and honestly on the structure of being, he will not take existence for granted. On testimony he has already been told that all things are created by God. He may be a believing Christian or he may have lost his faith. In both cases, however, the man has heard of the doctrine and he cannot pretend, as he signs up for a philosophy course in a secularist university, that he never heard of it. This man already believes, or he was told to believe, that existence is a gift. If he can subsequently prove that existence is a gift, he has become a Christian philosopher, not, obviously, because his faith substitutes for thinking but because his thinking has been guided by his faith, or, in the case of an unbeliever, by an ambient of faith. Even Socrates, the Straussian hero, was guided by an oracle. Christians do not have oracles but they do have God's word and that is oracle enough. The hidden presuppositions behind Professor Jaffa's divorce of reason and revelation is the old presumption that philosophy must have no presuppositions lest it spoil its pristine purity. This study has already indicated the self-contradictory status of the judgment: that, philosophy with no presuppositions has at least one, namely, that there be none. But Jaffa's presupposition is not merely logically motivated; it is primed by an historicist prejudice. Because philosophy began in classical Greece, philosophy must remain there. The world of Leo Strauss seems to have very little in common with the world of Eric Voegelin but both men, however, are motivated at bottom by a similar act of faith in pagan Greece and by the subsequent sorrowful conviction that everything has been going downhill ever since.

Professor Jaffa, in *The Conditions of Freedom*, expressed his conviction that "in the final analysis, not only American politics, but all modern politics, must be clarified on the basis of classical political philosophy" (p. 8). The proposition is true but not exclusive. Political philosophy began in the classical world and Harry Jaffa is right, in my judgment, in insisting that classical models must be used "to clarify" (his term) the American regime. But we must ask the professor why only classical pagan Greeks are useful to us in our attempt to understand a political history that grew out of the English common law, a tradition so thoroughly medieval and Germanic and Christian that there is nothing at all in distant Athens even remotely related to it? A good case can be made for a more Roman than Greek inspiration in the American political tradition and this case has been made by Professor Melvin Bradford.[10] Jaffa seems never to have gone to Washington where Rome, not Greece, stares us in the face on Capital Hill. And an equally good case can be made that

America did not turn its back totally on the Christian European heritage despite the Enlightenment overtones of the times. Any principled refusal to read and assess the meaning of America that ignores Christianity is at the very best a game of ideological partisanship; at the worst, this game dooms political theory to antiquarianism.

Dr. Jaffa, despite his splendid analysis of Aristotle's *Politics* in his *The Conditions of Freedom*, falls back on Socratic agnosticism as the term of the calculus of knowledge. "Socrates confessed that he knew nothing, and that knowledge of ignorance is, or should be, moderating, if not humbling" (p. 7). Shakespeare is revered by the professor because he "was the great vehicle within the Anglo-American world for the transmission of an essentially Socratic understanding of the civilization of the West" (p. 7). Now it is highly doubtful whether Shakespeare spent a half hour in his entire life thinking about Socrates and his message. This message, intelligible and noble in the context of the Athens of antiquity, is nothing more than ultimate agnosticism for men of the late twentieth century. To literally know that I know nothing and that I am simultaneously a learned man, *docta ignorantia*, is by no means humbling. Such a confession of ignorance damns two thousand years of Christian history for being so very ignorant indeed that it did not know, as I know, that it knew nothing. The village atheist like the village idiot can be forgiven. The one could not learn anything anyhow and the other never ran into anybody to teach him anything. But the American professor in the winter of our dying world who tells us that we must return to Socrates and confess that we know nothing presumes to an arrogance that is stunning in its boldness. I am moved to ask Professor Jaffa: was it all for nothing?

NOTES

INTRODUCTION

1. Frederick D. Wilhelmsen, *The Metaphysics of Love* (New York: Sheed and Ward, 1962), pp. 43–80.

2. Emilion Novack, "Hungary and the Problem of Providence," (Ph.D. diss., Univ. of Dallas, 1973). The author is indebted to Dr. Novack for his insights on the ontology of East and West.

3. Etienne Gilson, *Reason and Revelation in the Middle Ages* (New York: Charles Scribner's Sons, 1938).

CHAPTER ONE

1. *Summa Theologiae* 1–2, qq. 90–98; *Sentences*, Lib. 3, dist. 37, a. 2; *Ethics*, Lib. 5, lect. 2; *De Veritate*, q. 17, a. 3; *Quodlibetales* 1, q. 9, a. 2.

2. This judgment in the moral order corresponds to the principle of noncontradiction in the metaphysical order.

3. The literature on this issue is vast. The reader might well consult G. B. Phelan, *Selected Papers* (Toronto: Pontifical Institute of Mediaeval Studies, 1967), pp. 95–123.

4. Etienne Gilson, *Being and Some Philosophers* (Toronto: Pontifical Institute of Mediaeval Studies, 1952), passim.

5. Eric Voegelin, *Order in History*, vol. 1: *Plato and Aristotle* (Baton Rouge: Louisiana State University Press, 1957), 331–336.

6. Bad law, in the Thomist tradition, is still law unless it violates the natural law; e.g., *ST* 1–2, q. 85, a. 2.

7. Willmoore Kendall, *Contra Mundum* (New Rochelle: Arlington House, 1971), pp. 149–167.

CHAPTER TWO

1. Leo Strauss, *Natural Right and History* (Chicago: Univ. of Chicago Press, 1953), p. 137.

2. Hilaire Belloc, *The Nature of Contemporary England* (London and New York: Constable and Co., 1937), passim.

3. *The Works of the Late Right Honorable Henry St. John, Lord Viscount Bolingbroke* (London: 1809), 1:8–11.

4. Strauss, *Natural Right*, pp. 136–137.

5. T. S. Eliot, *Notes Towards a Definition of Culture* (London and New York: Faber and Faber, 1949), p. 30.

6. For further treatment of this point, see Frederick D. Wilhelmsen, *Man's Knowledge of Reality* (New York: Prentice-Hall, 1956), pp. 101–157.

7. St. Thomas's most celebrated passage dealing with existence is to be found in *De potentia Dei*, q. 7, a. 2, ad. 9. The *hoc quod dico esse* clearly shows the importance that he attaches to it and insinuates his awareness that what he is saying about being is brand new in the history of philosophy.

8. Etienne Gilson, *Le Realisme Methodique* (Paris: Vrin, 1935). This, Gilson's *vade mecum* for any youth aspiring to philosophical realism, lays down the following as a cardinal principle: Never speak of values, speak always of goods or of the Good.

9. Paul Tillich has brilliantly demonstrated the Stoic identification of the ontological and the ethical in *The Courage to Be* (New Haven: Yale Univ. Press, 1952), especially pp. 9–20, 23–26. In Stoicism, he argues, the ethical imperative is one with being itself. To neglect or deny such an imperative would be to fall into nonbeing, into Nothing, the ultimate enemy both of the human spirit and of reality at large.

10. On the role of *gravitas* in Cicero's thought, see Antonio Fontán, *Artes ad Humanitatem* (Pamplona: O Crece O Muere, 1957), passim.

11. For a profound and beautiful meditation on the Roman sense of *place* and its economy in the religious life of Western man, see Hilaire Belloc, *Hills and the Sea* (London: Methuen and Co., Ltd., 1906), the essay entitled "The Men of the Desert."

12. Cf. Romano Guardini, *The End of the Modern World* (New York and London: Sheed and Ward, 1956); Etienne Gilson, *God and Philosophy* (New Haven: Yale Univ. Press, 1939).

13. Eric Voegelin, *New Science*, pp. 87–91. In the following paragraphs of our text we have drawn heavily from Professor Voegelin's analysis.

14. *New Science*, p. 90.

15. Charles Norris Cochrane, *Christianity and Classical Culture* (New York and London: Oxford Univ. Press, 1947), p. 242.

16. *New Science*, p. 90.

CHAPTER THREE

1. Paul Tillich, *The Courage to Be* (New Haven: Yale Univ. Press, 1954), passim.

2. Xavier Zubiri, *Naturaleza, Historia, Dios* (Madrid: Editora Nacional, 1959), pp. 341–371.

3. John Wild, *Plato's Modern Enemies and the Theory of Natural Law* (Chicago: Univ. of Chicago Press, 1953), p. 151.

4. Charles Norris Cochrane, *Christianity and Classical Culture* (New York and London: Oxford Univ. Press, 1957). Cochrane's work is indispensable for the entire question of Rome's collapse into superstition following on the failure of virtue. The author wishes to acknowledge his debt to Cochrane.

5. Frederick D. Wilhelmsen, "Toynbee and the Betrayal of the West," *Modern Age* 1 (1957), 33–47. Polybius's theory is discussed in some detail in this essay of the author.

6. Antonio Fontán, *Gravitas en Ciceron* (Madrid: O Crece O Muere, 1964).

7. Eric Voegelin, *The New Science of Politics* (Chicago: Univ. of Chicago Press, 1952), pp. 161–191.

8. *Christianity and Classical Culture*, p. 158.

9. Charles Lamb, *Constantinople: Birth of an Empire* (New York: Charles Scribner's Sons, 1938), p. 183.

10. Eusebius, *Vita constantini*, 1.26., A. Heikel, Grieschischen Cristlichen Schriftsteller, Eus. 1, 1902; translation by the author.

11. For example, Alfred Berthold-Stuiber Altanar, *Patrologie*, (Freiburg: Herder, 1966), pp. 220–222.

12. *Classical Culture*, p. 262.

13. *Patrologie*, p. 262.

14. Altanar, ibid., p. 263.

15. Cochrane, *Classical Culture*. The most important texts of Lactantius are quoted by the author, pp. 192f.

16. Altanar, *Patrologie*, p. 210.

CHAPTER FOUR

1. Alvaro D'Ors, *Forma de Gobierno y Legitimidad Familiar* (Madrid: Ateneo, O Crece O Muere, 1960), pp. 7–12.

2. Sir John Fortescue, *De Laudibus Legum Anglie*, ed. and trans. with introduction and notes by S. B. Chrimes (Cambridge; rpt. ed., London, 1949), p. 15. All references to the *De Laudibus* throughout are made from this critical edition.

3. *In Librum Boethii de Trinitate, Quaestiones Quinta et Sexta*, Nach dem Autograph Cod. Vat. lat. 9850 mit Einleitung herausgegeben von Paul Wyster, O.P. (Fribourg: Société Philosophique, 1948), q. 1, a. 1.

4. Sir R. W. Caryle and A. J. Caryle, *A History of Medieval Political Theory in the West* (Edinburgh and London: William Blackwood and Sons, Ltd., 1922), 6:142. St. Thomas Aquinas, *On Kingship to the King of Cyprus*, trans. Gerald B. Phelan, rev. ed., I. Th. Eschmann, O.P. (Toronto, Pontifical Institute of Mediaeval Studies, 1949, pp. xxii–xxxix.

5. Thomas Aquinas, *Commentary on the Politics*, (2, 1. 5, n. 212), tr. by Ernest L. Fortin and Peter D. O'Neill, in *Medieval Political Philosophy: A Sourcebook*, ed. by Ralph Lerner and Muhsin Mahdi, (The Free Press of Glencoe, Collier-Macmillan Limited, Canada, 1963).

6. E.g., Raymond Di Lorenzo, "The Collection Form and the Art of Memory in the *Libbellus Super Ludo Schachrum* of Jacobus de Cessolis," *Mediaeval Studies* 35 (1973): 217. "(Image): The king is seated on a throne dressed in purple robes, (Mnemonic Significance). Purple robes are royal vestments. The king ought to excell all others; for as his body is clad with beautiful robes, so are his inner thoughts and soul to be clad with the moral virtues."

7. St. Thomas Aquinas, ibid., lect. 3, n. 376; cf. *Summa Theologiae*, 1–2, q. 58, a. 4; 1–2, q. 92, a. 1, c et ad. 4.

8. *De Veritate*, q. 1, a. 1.

9. *In I Sent.*, d. 38, q. 1, a. 3 Sol.

10. Cf. chap. 2, pp. 35–83.

11. Cited by Chrimes, pp. 153–155.

12. In terms of Thomistic metaphysics, this proposition could be stated in the form of an analogy: essence is related to existence as is specification to the specified, as is exercise to its own determination; power is exercise, being; the laws are its specification, essence.

13. Hilaire Belloc, *The Nature of Contemporary England* (London: George Allen and Unwin, Ltd., 1932).

14. *De Laudibus*, p. 31. Fortescue's position in his *Governance of England* is not quite what we find in the *De Laudibus*. In the former book he suggests that initially all regimes were of a purely royal nature and that later, "in England at least, men grew in virtue and agreed to be ruled by suche lawes as that all wolde assent unto: which laws therefore is called 'Politicum.'" (Cited by Caryle, vol. vi, p. 143, n. 3). Chrimes places *The Governance of England*, known in Latin as *De Domino Regale et Politico*, as having possibly been written after *De Laudibus* (Chrimes, p. lxxvi). If this teaching represents Fortescue's mature mind on the issue it would have him suggesting that the historical origin of all governments, if we trace them back far enough, originate in some act of violence: that is, somebody takes over from somebody else. This transfer of power, itself violent in nature, can subsequently be converted into the royal and political regime. However, we must not make the mistake of converting Fortescue's purely royal government into a tyranny. The royal regime is both legal and just but the legality and the justice are exclusively the king's, not the people's. The royal regime is more open to degenerating into tyranny than is the *dominium regale et politicum*. Also, the simply royal regime with its "civil law" is more tolerant of sin in both king *and subject*. This was a disadvantage for Fortescue but it might have appeared an advantage to sinners, be they royal or common, in the Germanies. In a word: you could get away with more mischief under the purely royal regime than you could under the English medieval system (at least in theory). The severity of the latter is attributed throughout by Fortescue to the superior virtue of Englishmen. The subsequent titling of the *Governance of England* with the subtitle, "The Difference Between an Absolute and Limited Monarchy," dates from the eighteenth century. The language and the concepts are totally modern. The *dominium regale* is not the modern absolute monarchy of the French Bourbon tradition nor is the *dominium regale et politicum* the so-called limited monarchy of the nineteenth- and twentieth-

century liberal tradition or the even earlier English monarchy dominated by Parliament that emerged in the seventeenth century. The limited monarchy—as that term is used in comparative government rhetoric—is not a monarchy at all in the classical or medieval, hence Fortescue's, sense of the term. A king who only reigns and does not govern does not possess a limited power but no power at all; called "monarchy" because the crowned symbol remains in office, the government in question is not a monarchy but some form of crowned republic. The medieval *dominium regale* itself was far more *politicum* than the French or, let us say, Prussian kingdoms of the eighteenth century. McIlwain erred on this in his *The Growth of Political Thought in the West* (New York: Macmillan, 1932), pp. 331–332.

15. Cf. the Pauline background: Saint Paul, *Col.* 1:18; *Eph.* 5: 31–32.

16. Fortescue, *Opusculum de Natura Legis Nature et de eius censura in successione regnorum suprema.* "*Rex regaliter et rex politice imperans equalis potentiae et libertatis est cum rege regaliter dominante*"; c. xxvi. (Cited by Chrimes, pp. 153–155). Given that Fortescue in the *De Laudibus* assumes his argument on an equality between the two powers to have been already demonstrated in the earlier *De Natura*; given that he simply reports conclusions he achieved in the first book, it is imperative that contemporary scholarship procure an edition (and translation) of this seminal work by the English lord chancellor. Lord Claremon's edition of Fortescue's works (1869) is practically unavailable.

17. Hilaire Belloc, *The House of Commons and Monarchy* (London: George Allan and Unwin, Ltd., 1920), esp. pp. 173–188.

18. Juan Donoso Cortés, *Obras Completas*, ed. de Carlos Valverde, S.J. (Madrid: Biblioteca de Autores Cristianos, 1970), esp. 2 "Carta al director de la *Revue des deux mondes*," pp. 762–781; cf. Raúl Sánchez Abelenda, *La teoría del poder en el pensamiento político de Juan Donoso Cortés* (Buenos Aires: Universitaria de Buenos Aires, 1967). Cf. chap. 5.

CHAPTER FIVE

1. Cf. Alvaro D'Ors, *Una introducción al estudio del derecho* (Madrid: Ediciónes Rialp, S.A., 1963) pp. 78–84.

2. The classic statements are found in *The Statesman* and *The*

Republic; the irony of the philosopher-king against society is explored in the Socratic dialogues.

3. The Thomistic treatise on law forms part of Aquinas' basic theological work: St. Thomas Aquinas, *Summa Theologiae*, 1–2, qq. 91–95. After locating the natural law within the divine law, St. Thomas discusses its structure and meaning.

4. Aristotle, *Nicomachean Ethics*, 6, esp. chaps. 12–13; St. Thomas Aquinas, *Expositio in decem libros Ethicorum Aristotelis ad Nichomachum*, 6; *Summa Theologiae*, 1–2, q. 57.

5. Relevant medieval testimony is marshalled in Ewart Lewis, *Medieval Political Ideas* (New York: Alfred A. Knopf, 1954), esp. chaps. 2, 3, and 8.

6. Jean Bodin, *Six Books of the Commonwealth*, abgd. trans. by M. J. Tooley (New York: Macmillan, 1955).

7. As typical of the medieval treatment of power, we might consult the order followed by Aquinas. First he treats of the meaning of power; then he demonstrates that power belongs to God; finally, he removes any limits to that power: see, *Summa Theologiae*, 1, q. 25, a. 1–6.

8. E.g., *Summa Theologiae*, 1, q. 75, a. 6, ad. 2.

9. "All the princes of the earth are subject to them [i.e. divine and natural laws] and cannot contravene them without treason and rebellion against God. The absolute power of princes and sovereign lords does not extend to the laws of God and nature" (Bodin, op. cit., p. 28). But let us note that the subject has no legal recourse should the sovereign prince act against divine and natural law. The prince himself is not even bound by the laws of his predecessors nor is he bound to oaths he takes freely.

10. From this conviction there was deduced what medieval theologians called "The Royal Sovereignty of Christ": i.e. only Christ was king of creation by virtue of his divine nature; all earthly kings held their kingdoms from him by participation. Cf. George de Lagarde, *La Naissance de l'esprit laïque au déclin du moyen age* (Louvain: Editions E. Nauwelaerts, 1962), 4, esp. chap. 8.

11. "Rey serás si hicieses derecho y si no lo hicieres, no serás Rey." The formula read the king of Aragon was even more blunt: "Each one of us is as good as you are and all of us are greater than you are."

12. Eric Voegelin, *The New Science of Politics* (Chicago: Univ. of Chicago Press, 1952), pp. 42–46.

13. Sir John Fortescue, *De laudibus legum Anglie,* ed. S. B. Chrimes (Cambridge: Cambridge Univ. Press, 1942), chap. 13; cf. chap. 4.

14. Baron de Montesquieu, *The Spirit of the Laws,* trans. Thomas Nugent (New York: Hafner Publishing Co., 1959), bk. 9, pp. 151–162.

15. "Whereas early medieval law had been the declaration of custom, discovered perhaps by itinerant justices or settled by consultation with the magnates, and the purpose of legislation had been to expand and reinforce what had been implicitly present from of old, after the thirteenth century a sovereign body began to emerge slowly as the master, not the creature of law. New law was made, the force of which did not lie in its moral cogency or conformity with ancient usage, but in fact and threat of enactment and enforcement. Here law came to mean statute, and custom sank to an inferior condition. . . . [It] existed on sufferance according to the goodwill of the prince." Thomas Gilby, *The Political Thought of Thomas Aquinas* (Chicago: Univ. of Chicago Press, 1958), p. 173.

16. Montesquieu, *Spirit,* pp. 151–152.

17. Polybius, *The Histories,* trans. W. R. Paton (Cambridge, Mass.: Harvard Univ. Press, 1927), 6:11–12.

18. The fact that the theory in question had become the common doctrine of European liberalism by the time Donoso Cortés began to write is evidenced by his *never* (to my knowledge) referring the teaching to its source in Montesquieu. For Donoso, the doctrine of the three powers and their separation is simply a common liberal position of his times, easily identifiable as a stock in trade of liberal rhetoric and theory.

19 The complete works of Donoso Cortés are found in the *Biblioteca de Autores Cristianos: "Obras completas de Donoso Cortés, con la aportación de nuevos escritos, por el Dr. Juan Jeretschke"* (Madrid: BAC, 1946). Unless otherwise specified, quotations are taken from the more readily available *Textos políticos* (Madrid: Ediciones Rialp, S.A., 1954). Also helpful is the edition of the *Ensayo sobre el catolicisismo, el liberalismo y el socialismo* (Argentina: Colección Austral, 1949). Translations are my own. Cf. Gabriel de Arnos, *Donoso Cortés, su sentido trascendente de la vida* (Madrid: Colección Cálamo, 1953); Raúl Sanchez Abelenda, *La teoria del poder en el pensamiento político de Juan Donoso Cortés* (Buenos Aires: Editorial Universitaria de Buenos Aires, 1969); John T.

Graham, *Donoso Cortés: Utopian Romanticist and Political Realist* (Columbia: Univ. of Missouri Press, 1974).

20. We must distinguish political traditionalism, itself largely Catholic, from theological traditionalism in the context of the European use of those terms. Theological traditionalism, denying any value to the individual reason, insisted that all truth was reducible to a primitive revelation. Maintained by Bonald (although not, as often claimed, by de Maistre), this position was condemned formally by the Catholic Church. *Tradicionalismo* in Spanish political language means Carlism. Donoso never became a Carlist although it is thought that he was about to do so when his life was cut short at the age of forty-two.

21. Carl Schmitt, *Interpretacion a Donoso Cortés* (Madrid: Rialp, S.A., 1964), p. 266.

22. Federico Suarez, *Introducción a Donoso Cortés* (Madrid: Rialp, S.A., 1964), p. 266.

23. *Textos políticos*, p. 461.

24. I have already pointed to a pervasive tradition in Spanish thought, as old as Ramón Lull, which seeks to find within the specifically Christian doctrine of the Trinity a clue to the metaphysical structure of being. Frederick D. Wilhelmsen, *Metaphysics of Love* (New York: Sheed and Ward, 1962), pp. 93–95. There is some possibility that Donoso's fascination with the trinitarian structure of the real may have been influenced by Hegel. In one place at least Donoso refers to God as "thesis, antithesis, synthesis" but he does not develop the idea. The decisive difference lies in Donoso's paradoxical refusal to dissolve the tensions found within existential oppositions, whereas Hegel, in common with all gnostics, is constrained to dissolve every existential tension. Technically, he does so by reducing the opposition between thesis and antithesis in a synthesis which transcends both poles of the opposition.

25. This is not an argument against their ultimate identity in the metaphysical order.

26. *Textos políticos*, p. 210.

27. Cf. Charles Norris Cochrane, *Christianity and Classical Culture* (New York: Oxford University Press Galaxy Books, 1957), pp. 234–249.

28. *Textos políticos*, p. 462.

29. Raimundo Aldea Eguilaz, *Los Derechos de Navarra* (Pamplona: Prontuario de Divulgacíon Foral, 1957).

30. See chaps. 2 and 3.
31. *Textos políticos.*
32. Ibid.
33. Donoso wrote immediately after the new electoral laws and he insisted that his remarks referred principally to England before the radical reforms which had, in his opinion, altered profoundly the British Constitution by shifting the center of power. On the earlier shift of power in England, see: Hilaire Belloc, *The Nature of Contemporary England* (New York: Scribners, 1937), passim; *Charles II: The Last Rally* (New York and London: Harper and Brothers, 1939).
34. Fortescue, *De laudibus*, pp. 31–33; cf. chap. 4.
35. *Textos políticos*, p. 472.
36. Alvaro D'Ors, *Estudio del derecho*, p. 19.
37. Ibid.
38. E.g., Harvey Cox, *The Secular City* (New York: Macmillan, 1965).

CHAPTER SIX

1. Francisco Elias de Tejada, "La cuestíon de la vigencia del derecho natural," *El Derecho Natural Hispánico, Actas de las Primeras Jornadas Hispánicas de Derecho Natural,"* (Madrid: Biblioteca Hispánica de Filosofia del Derecho Natural), pp. 17–40.
2. *Didache*, Rouet De Journal, ed., *Enchiridion Patristicum*, 8th and 9th ed. (Friburgi: Brisgoviae, 1932), pp. 1–4.
3. The teaching is standard Thomistic epistemology; cf. Armand Maurer, "St. Thomas and Eternal Truths," *Mediaeval Studies* 32 (1970): 91–107.
4. Sir R. W. Caryle and A. J. Caryle, *A History of Mediaeval Political Theory in the West* (Edinburgh and London: Blackwood, 1922), vol. 2, esp. pp. 91–142.
5. Hilaire Belloc, *The House of Commons and Monarchy* (London: Allen and Unwin Ltd., 1920), pp. 173–188.
6. Martin Diamond, "Democracy and *The Federalist*: A Reconsideration of the Framer's Intent," *American Political Science Review* 53 (March 1959): 53–68.

7. L. Brent Bozell, *The Warren Revolution* (New Rochelle, N.Y.: Arlington House, 1966), pp. 328–340.

8. Russell Kirk, *The Roots of American Order* (La Salle, Ind.: Open Court, 1974), pp. 228, 390. Peter Stanlis, *Edmund Burke and the Natural Law* (Ann Arbor: Univ. of Michigan Press, 1958).

9. Cf. Rawley Smith, *Richard Hooker and the Defense of Public Orthodoxy*, (Ph.D. diss., Univ. of Dallas, 1971).

10. Bozell, *Warren Revolution*, passim and esp. pp. 300–340.

CHAPTER SEVEN

1. Frederick D. Wilhelmsen, "The Achievement of Eric Voegelin: *Israel and Revelation*," *Modern Age* (Spring, 1959): pp. 184–185.

2. Eric Voegelin, *The New Science of Politics* (Chicago: Univ. of Chicago Press, 1952), pp. 128–131.

3. Eric Voegelin, *Order in History*, vol. 1: *Israel and Revelation* (Baton Rouge: Louisiana State Univ. Press, 1956), esp. pp. x–ix, 1–13.

4. Eric Voegelin, *Order in History*, vol. 4: *The Ecumenic Age* (Baton Rouge: Louisiana State Univ. Press, 1974), p. 75.

5. Thomas von Aquin, *In Librum Boethii de Trinitate Quaestiones Quinta et Sexta*, ed. Paul Wyser, O.P., Nach dem Autograph Cod. Vat. lat 9850 (Fribourg: Société Philosophique, 1948). The English translation of this work was done by Armand Maurer, *The Division and Methods of the Sciences* (Toronto: Pontifical Institute of Mediaeval Studies, 1963).

6. Frederick D. Wilhalmsen, *Man's Knowledge of Reality* (Englewood Cliffs, N.J.: Prentice-Hall, 1956), pp. 134–165.

7. Voegelin, *Order in History: The Ecumenic Age*, p. 233. Essentially the same criticism as advanced by the author against Professor Voegelin on the historical figure of Jesus Christ is lodged in an otherwise highly sympathetic essay by Gerhard Niemeyer, "Eric Voegelin, Philosopher, and the Drama of Mankind," *Modern Age*, 20 (Winter 1976): 28–39.

8. Hannah Arendt, "Ideology and Terror: A Novel Form of Government", *The Review of Politics* (July, 1953): pp. 303–327.

9. George Santayana, *The Idea of Christ in the Gospels* (New York: Charles Scribner's Sons, 1946).

10. Ibid.

11. Voegelin, *The New Science*, pp. 150–152. The fraud of religion by "experience" is splendidly articulated by Melvin Bradford, "A Writ of Fire and Sword: The Politics of Oliver Cromwell," *The Occasional Review* (Summer 1975): pp. 61–80.

CHAPTER EIGHT

1. Averroes did not specifically teach the famous "double truth" doctrine in those terms. He did, however, insist that theological thinking is a kind of bastardization in which dialectics unite with faith and produce a misbegotten child which is neither philosophy nor faith.

2. Leo Strauss and Joseph Cropsey, *History of Political Philosophy* (Chicago: Rand McNally and Co., 1972). Thirty-four political theories as represented by thirty-four thinkers are discussed; only five could be specifically identified as Christian. This indicates a poverty in Christian thinking, by omission, in the political order according to the Straussians. The Straussians may, of course, be absolutely right if political philosophy must be purged of considerations prompted by religion. Once purged of these considerations, very few Christians could be called philosophers. The presuppositions guiding this thinking have been evaluated in the text.

3. Harry V. Jaffa, *The Conditions of Freedom* (Baltimore and London: Johns Hopkins Univ. Press, 1975), esp. pp. 3–9. The original appeared in *National Review* 25 (December 1973): 1353–1355. For Jaffa's political philosophy see also *Equality and Liberty: Theory and Practice in American Politics* (New York: 1965); "Equality as a Conscious Principle," *Loyola of Los Angeles Law Review*, 8 (June 1975): 471–505; *Crisis of the House Divided: An Interpretation of the Issues in the Lincoln-Douglas Debates* (Seattle: Univ. of Washington Press, 1959).

4. *Exodus*, III, 14. This text has been the inspiration of the school of "existential" Thomism. The literature is vast and fairly recent because the school is contemporary. Possibly the seminal work is: Etienne Gilson, *Being and Some Philosophers* (Toronto: Pontifical Institute of Mediaeval Studies, 1952).

5. *Conditions of Freedom*, p. 6.

6. St. Thomas Aquinas, e.g.: *In I Sent.*, d. 38, q. 1, a.3; *In I Sent.*, d. 19, q. 5, a. 2, sol.; *In I Periherm.*, lect. 5, n. 22; *In Boethii de Trin.*, q. 5, a. 3.

7. Emmanuel Kant, *Critique of Pure Reason*, trans. Norman Kemp Smith (New York: St. Martin's Press, 1965), pp. 134, 151–152, 154.

8. E.g. Joseph Owens, *An Elementary Christian Metaphysics* (Milwaukee: Bruce Publishing Co., 1963), pp. 49, 52, 74; *An Interpretation of Existence* (Milwaukee: Bruce Publishing Co., 1968), pp. 55–57; Frederick D. Wilhelmsen, *The Paradoxical Structure of Existence*, 2nd. ed., (Dallas: Univ. of Dallas Press, 1975), pp. 47–57; Leonardo Polo, *El Acceso al Ser* (Pamplona: Universidad de Navarra, 1964), passim and esp. pp. 203–222.

9. Etienne Gilson, "Le Probleme de la Philosophie Chretienne," *La Vie Intellectuelle* 12: 214–232; "La Nation de Philosophie Cretienne," *Bulletin de la Societé Française de Philosophie* 31: 37–93; *Christianisme et Philosophie* (Paris: Vrin, 1936).

10. Melvin Bradford, "The Heresy of Equality: Bradford Replies to Jaffa," *Modern Age* 20 (Winter 1976): 62–77.

INDEX

INDEX